Visual

CORELDRAW 2

Carrie Webster
Paul Webster

Peachpit Press

CORELDRAW 2: Visual QuickStart Guide
Carrie Webster and Paul Webster

Peachpit Press, Inc.
2414 Sixth St.
Berkeley, CA 94710
(510) 548-4393
(510) 548-5991 (fax)

Copyright © 1991 by Webster & Associates Pty Ltd

All rights reserved. No part of this book may be reproduced or transmitted in any form or by any means, electronic or mechanical, including photocopying, recording, or by any information storage and retrieval system, without prior written permission from the Publisher. For information, contact Peachpit Press.

Notice of Liability:
The information in this book is distributed on an "As Is" basis, without warranty. While every precaution has been taken in the preparation of this book, neither the author nor Peachpit Press, Inc., shall have any liability to any person or entity with respect to any liability, loss, or damage caused or alleged to be caused directly or indirectly by the instructions contained in this book or by the computer software and hardware products described therein.

Trademarks:
Throughout this book, trademarked names are used. Rather than put a trademark symbol in every occurrence of a trademarked name, we are using the names only in an editorial fashion and to the benefit of the trademark owner, with no intention of infringement of the trademark. Where those designations appear in this book, the designations have been printed in initial caps.

First Edition published 1991

ISBN 0-938151-70-3

0 9 8 7 6 5 4 3 2 1

Printed and bound United States of America

Why a Visual QuickStart?

Virtually no one actually reads computer books; rather, people typically refer to them. This series of **Visual QuickStart Guides** has made that reference easier thanks to a new approach to learning computer applications.

While conventional computer books lean towards providing extensive textual explanations, a **Visual QuickStart Guide** takes a far more visual approach—pictures literally show you what to do, and text is limited to clear, concise commentary. Learning becomes easier, because a **Visual QuickStart** familiarizes you with the look and feel of your software. Learning also becomes faster, since there are no long-winded passages to comb through.

It's a new approach to computer learning, but it's also solidly based on experience: Webster & Associates have logged thousands of hours of classroom computer training, and have authored several books on desktop publishing topics.

Chapter 1 provides a general introduction to CorelDRAW 2 and discusses its screen components.

Chapter 2 describes the functions of the Toolbox.

Chapters 3 to **9** provide a summary of each CorelDRAW menu.

Chapters 10 and **11** concern the two extra programs that come with CorelDRAW—CorelTRACE and MOSAIC.

Appendix A provides a roadmap through all major dialog boxes and shows how they're accessed.

Acknowledgments

The authors wish to acknowledge the assistance of Tony Webster and Wayne Clarke for editing and technical accuracy checking.

Contents

Chapter 1: Introducing CorelDRAW 1
Installation guide 1
    Summary of installation steps 1
Starting CorelDRAW 2.0 2
The screen 4
    Screen components 5
        Menu bar 5
        Title bar 5
        Maximize and minimize buttons 5
        Windows system menu 5
        Status line 6
        Rulers 6
        Working page 6
        Pasteboard area 6
        Mouse cursor 6
        Toolbox 7
        Scroll bars 7
        The Color Palette 8

Chapter 2: The Tools 9
Using the Tools 9
    The Pick Tool 10
        Selecting objects 10
        Moving objects 10
        Rotating and skewing objects 10
        Multiple selection 11
        Deleting objects 11
    The Shape Tool 11
        Modifying rectangles 12
        Modifying ellipses 12
        Converting to curves 12
        Moving nodes 13
        Selecting multiple nodes 13
        Changing the properties of nodes 13
        Moving individual letters 18

- Modifying kerning and leading 18
- Changing single character attributes 19
- Cropping bitmaps 19

The Zoom Tool 20
The Pencil Tool 23
- Freehand mode 24
- Straight lines 24
- Closed objects 24
- Bezier mode 25
- Drawing curves 25
- Autotrace 25

The Rectangle Tool 26
- Drawing squares 26

The Ellipse Tool 27
- Drawing circles 27

The Text Tool 27
- Placement of text 28
- Changing type style 29
- Changing size 29
- Text alignment 29
- Spacing 29
- Paragraph Text 30
- Columns 30
- Importing text 30
- Paste 31
- Symbols 31

The Outline Tool 33
The Outline Pen 33
- Dashing 34
- Arrows 34
- Editing Arrows 35
- Corners 35
- Line Caps 35
- Pen Shape 36

Outline Color 36
- Color dialog boxes 37
- Spot color selection 37
- Adding a Spot color 38
- Process color selection 38
- CMYK 39
- RGB 39
- HSB 40
- Named 40

  Palette button 40
  Converting Spot to Process 41
  PostScript 42
 The Fill Tool 42
  Uniform Fill 43
  Bitmap Fill 43
  Importing Bitmap Fills 44
  Deleting a Bitmap Fill 45
  Creating a Bitmap Fill 45
  Offsets 45
  Bitmap Color 46
  Vector Patterns 46
  Editing a Vector Pattern 47
  Fountain Fills 47
  Linear Fill 48
  Radial Fill 48
  PostScript Fill 49
 Setting up Outline and Fill Defaults 49
 The Fill Indicator 50

Chapter 3: The File Menu 51
The File menu commands 51
 New 51
 Open 52
 Save 52
 Save As 53
 Import 53
 Export 54
 Print 55
 Print Merge 57
 Page Setup 57
 Control Panel 58
 Exit 58

Chapter 4: The Edit Menu 59
The Edit menu commands 59
 Undo 59
 Redo 59
 Repeat 60
 Cut 60
 Copy 60
 Paste 61

    Clear 61
    Duplicate 61
    Copy Style From 62
    Edit Text 62
    Character Attributes 63
    Select All 63

Chapter 5: The Transform Menu 65
The Transform menu commands 65
    Move 65
    Rotate & Skew 66
    Stretch & Mirror 66
    Clear Transformations 67

Chapter 6: The Effects Menu 69
The Effects menu commands 69
    Edit Envelope 69
        Control and Shift keys 70
    Clear Envelope 70
    Copy Envelope From 71
    Add New Envelope 71
    Edit Perspective 72
    Clear Perspective 72
    Copy Perspective from 73
    Add New Perspective 73
    Blend 74
        Creating highlights 75
    Extrude 76

Chapter 7: The Arrange Menu 79
The Arrange menu commands 79
    To Front 79
    To Back 80
    Forward One 80
    Back One 80
    Reverse Order 80
    Group 81
    Ungroup 82
    Combine 82
    Break Apart 84

    Convert To Curves 85
    Align 86
    Fit Text To Path 87
    Align To Baseline 88
    Straighten Text 89

Chapter 8: The Display Menu 91

The Display menu commands 91
    Snap To Grid 91
    Grid Setup 92
    Snap To Guidelines 93
    Guidelines Setup 93
    Show Rulers 94
    Show Status Line 94
    Show Color Palette 95
    Show Preview 95
    Full Screen Preview 95
    Show Preview Toolbox 96
    Preview Selected Only 97
    Auto Update 97
    Show Bitmaps 98
    Refresh Wire Screen 98

Chapter 9: The Special Menu 99

The Special menu commands 99
    Extract 99
    Merge Back 100
    Create Pattern 100
    Create Arrow 101
    Preferences 102

Chapter 10: CorelTRACE 109

Using CorelTRACE 109
    The Tracing Options menu 111
    The View Image menu 112
    The Preferences menu 113
        Importing CorelTRACE images into CorelDRAW 116

Chapter 11: MOSAIC 117

Using MOSAIC 117
    The File menu 119

The Open/Import menu 122
The CorelDraw menu 123
The Preferences menu 124

Appendix A: Dialog Boxes 127

Locating Dialog Boxes 127
    The File menu 127
    The Edit menu 128
    The Transform menu 129
    The Effects menu 130
    The Arrange menu 131
    The Display menu 131
    The Special menu 132
    The Text Tool 134
    The Outline Tool fly-out 134
    The Fill Tool fly-out 136

Index 139

Introducing CorelDRAW

Installation Guide

Installing CorelDRAW 2.0 is a relatively simple operation, with additional instructions found in the CorelDRAW Installation Guide.

SUMMARY OF INSTALLATION STEPS

1. Insert the CorelDRAW number one disk into the A drive and type INSTALL at the A:\> prompt.

Press ENTER.

The on-screen instructions will now take you through the entire procedure of installing CorelDRAW.

CHAPTER 1: INTRODUCING CORELDRAW

STARTING CORELDRAW 2.0

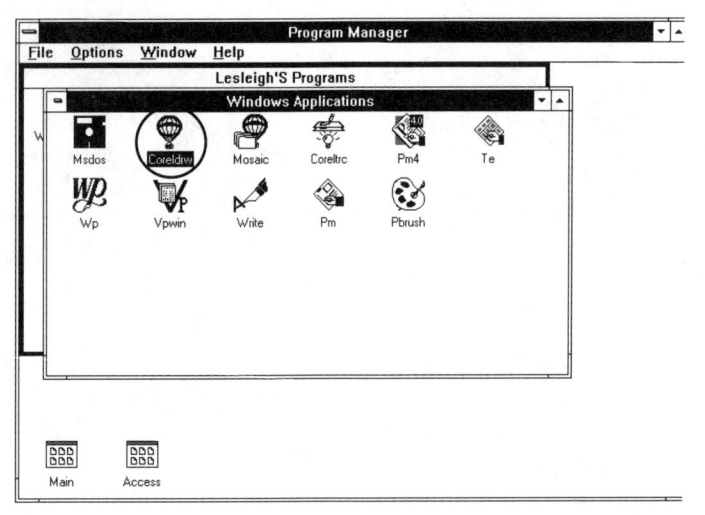

Figure 2. To activate CorelDRAW, you may be able to select it from a menu, if not, you must be in Windows. Locate the CorelDRAW icon in the Windows Program Manager and double-click on it.

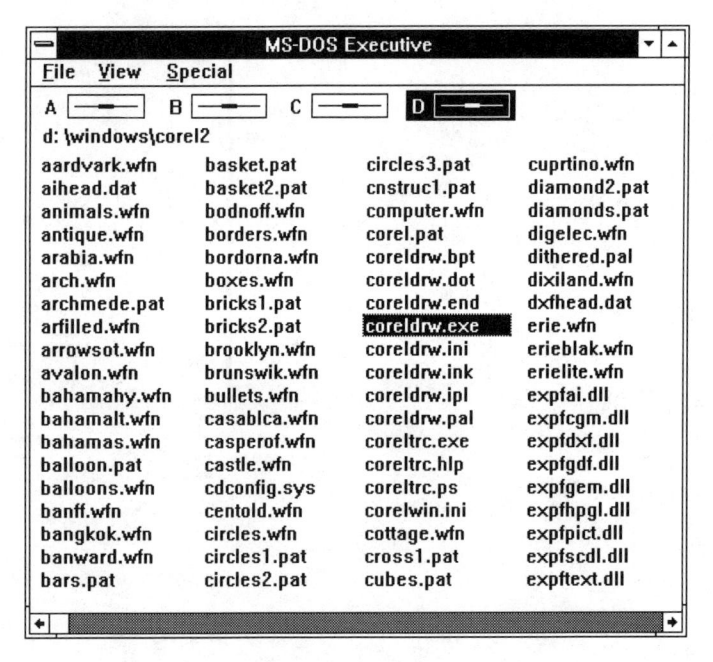

Figure 3. You can also start CorelDRAW by double-clicking on the coreldrw.exe file from within the MS-DOS Executive utility or the Windows File Manager.

Figure 4. After starting CorelDRAW, your screen will look like this. You are in a new, UNTITLED CorelDRAW file.

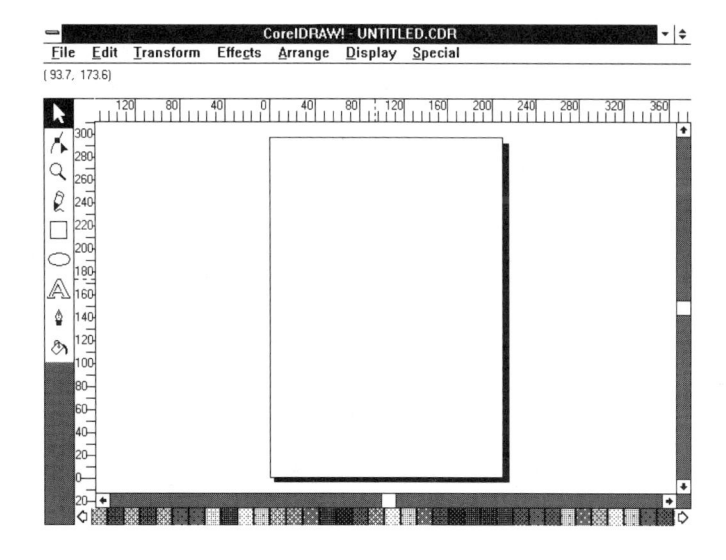

Figure 5. If you wish to open a file that has already been saved to the hard disk, select *Open* from the **File** menu. The *Open Drawing* dialog box gives you access to the computer's drives and directories. Here you locate the desired file, select it and click on *Open*.

Alternatively, you can double-click on the file name in the list of files in the *Open Drawing* dialog box to open the file.

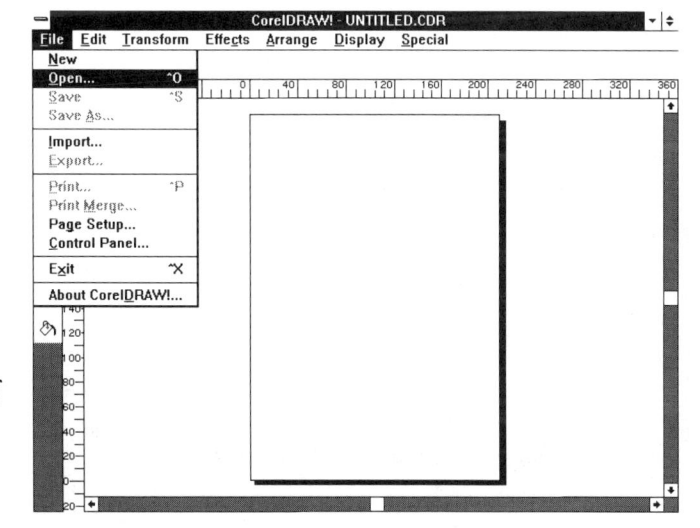

The Screen

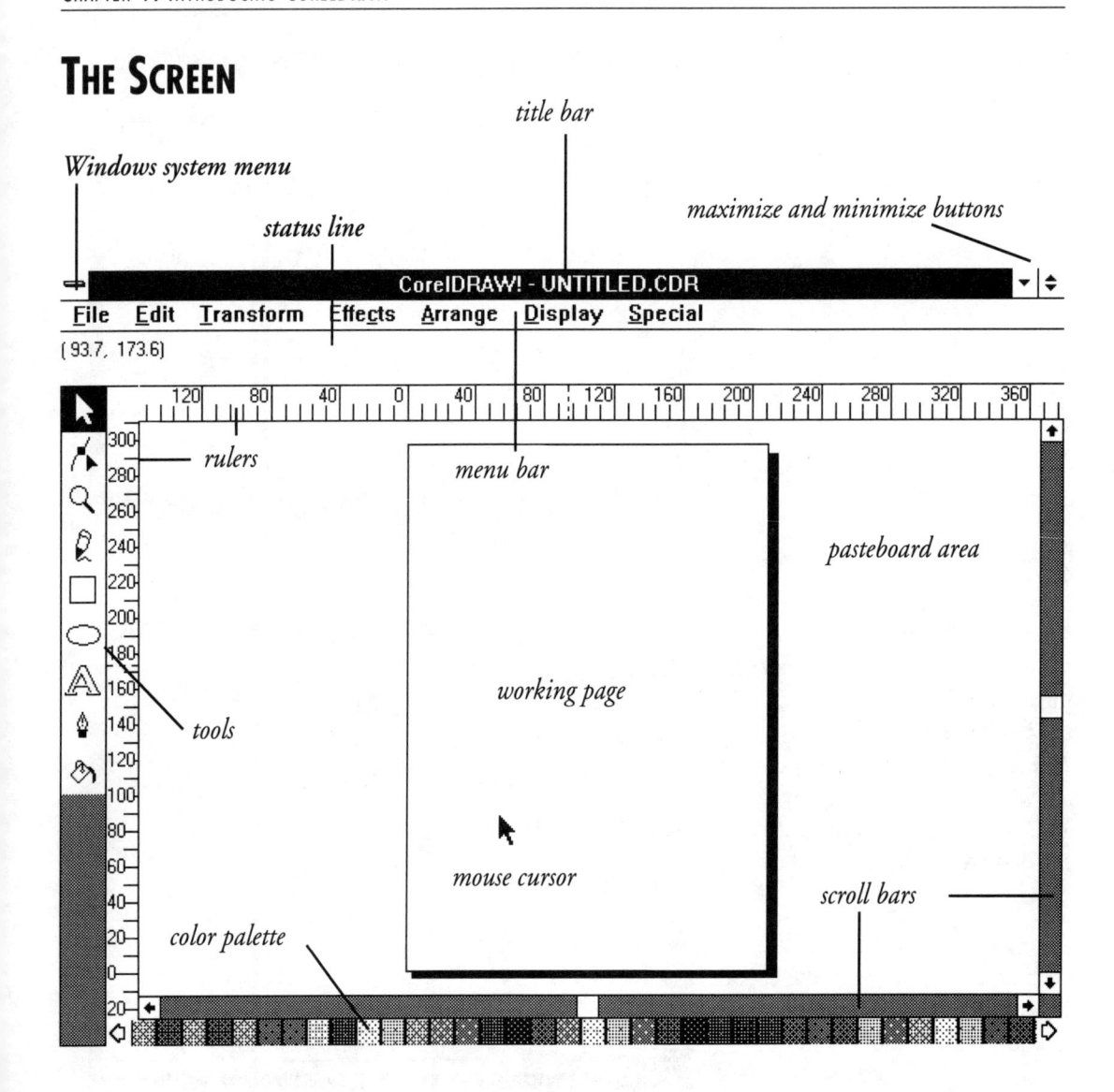

Figure 6. The CorelDRAW screen and its components.

SCREEN COMPONENTS

Menu bar

Figure 7. The **menu bar** contains a series of commands which produce a menu of options if clicked on with the mouse. Menus are common to most Windows programs.

menu bar *title bar*

Title bar

The **title bar** contains the name of the CorelDRAW publication. If it has not yet been given a name, it will read UNTITLED.CDR.

Maximize and minimize buttons

Figure 8. The single down arrow will minimize the window to an icon in the bottom left of the screen. This icon can be double-clicked on to activate the window. The up and down arrow button will reduce the size of the window to its custom size.

Windows system menu

maximize/ minimize buttons

Windows system menu

This tiny box, when clicked on, activates a menu of options which are contained in every Windows application. From it, you can maximize, minimize or close the current application.

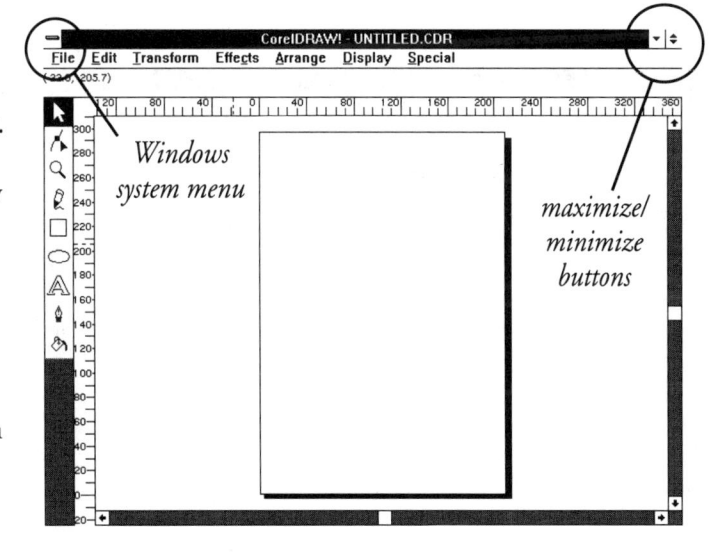

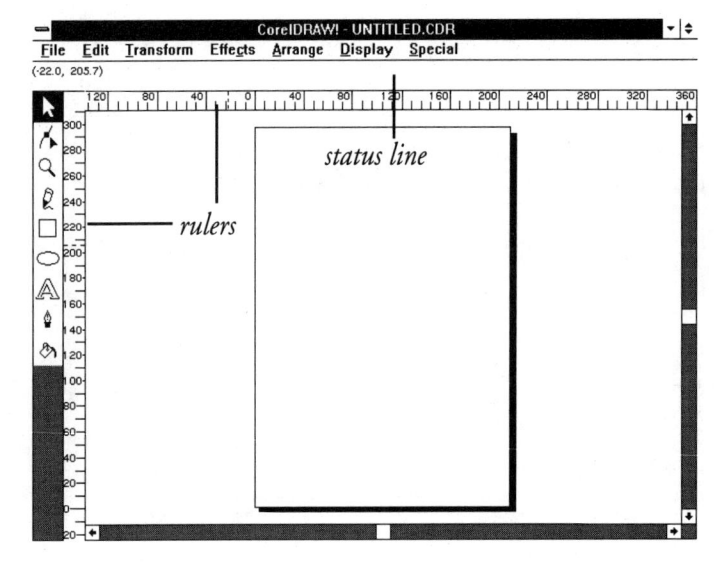

Status line

Figure 9. This is a bar of information that will indicate what object is selected, as well as its dimensions; the font and point size of selected text; outline and color of selected objects; the angle of rotation; as well as other vital pieces of information. It also tells the position of the mouse on the page in relation to the rulers.

Rulers

The rulers are used to measure distance and placement of objects on the page.

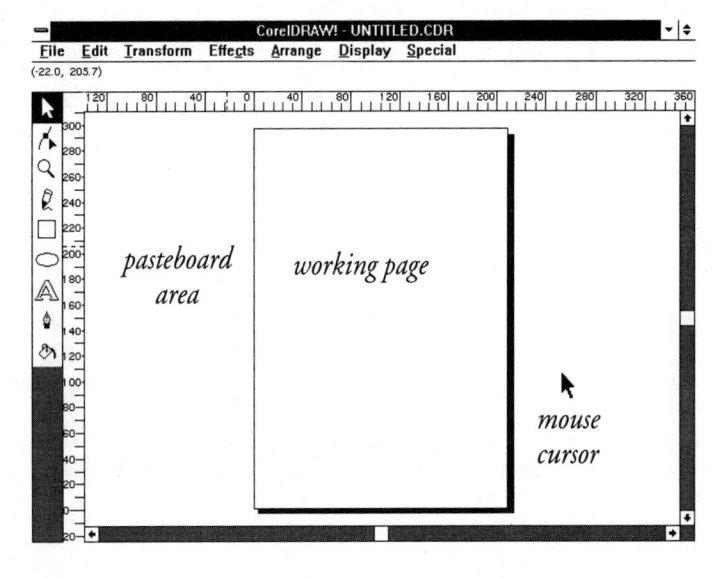

Working page

Figure 10. The working page represents the area of the page that will print.

Pasteboard area

This is like a desk around your page that can be used to place any object. Objects on the pasteboard area will not print unless you select the *Fit To Page* option in the *PRINT OPTIONS* dialog box.

Mouse cursor

The mouse cursor is the icon that moves around the screen, corresponding to where you move your mouse.

Toolbox

Figure 11. The tool icons within the toolbox can be selected with the mouse. They have a wide range of functions and uses which are explained in detail in Chapter 2, **The Tools**.

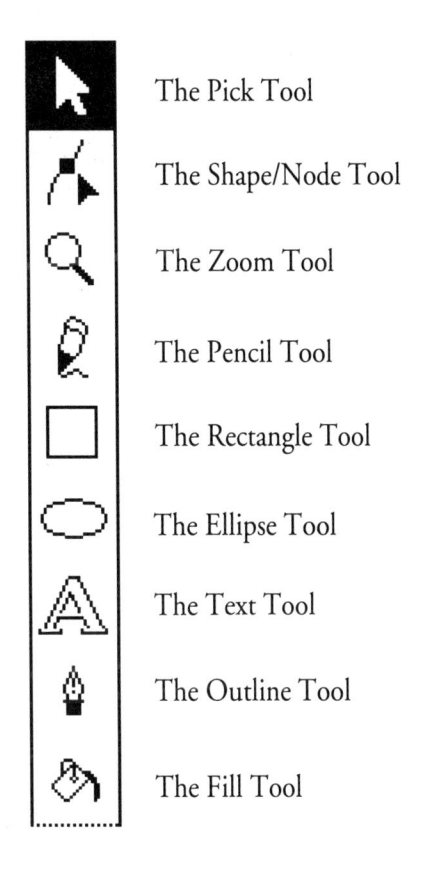

The Pick Tool

The Shape/Node Tool

The Zoom Tool

The Pencil Tool

The Rectangle Tool

The Ellipse Tool

The Text Tool

The Outline Tool

The Fill Tool

Scroll bars

Figure 12. The scroll bars are used, in conjunction with the mouse, to move different parts of the screen into view. Scroll bars are common to most Windows applications.

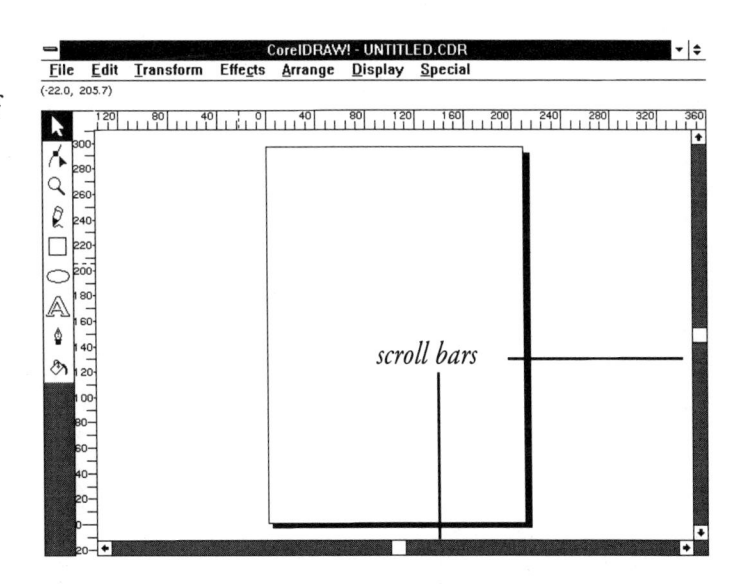

scroll bars

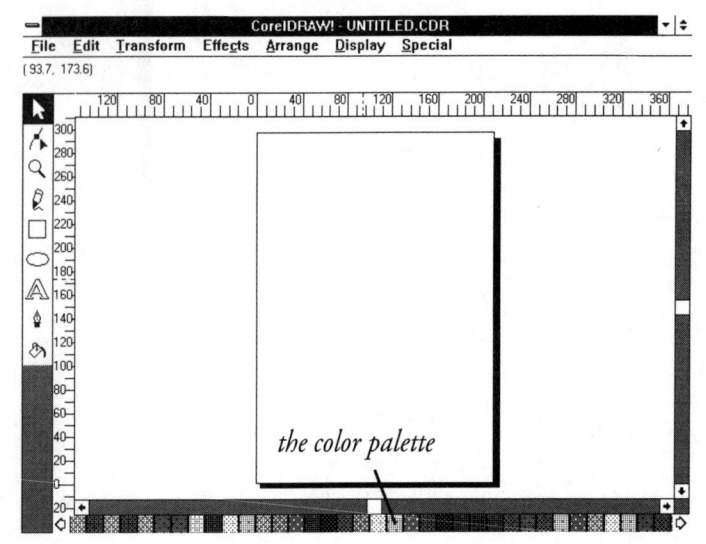

The Color Palette

Figure 13. The Color Palette is a bar that runs along the bottom of the screen that lets you quickly apply colors to a selected object(s). For more information see Chapter 8: **The Display Menu**

The Tools   2

Using the Tools

The Tools contained in the CorelDRAW toolbox will always be in use. Some of the most common and numerous functions are achieved by using one of these Tools. In this chapter you will learn the various functions of each Tool, and learn how to use them in conjunction with each other, and with the menu commands.

Figure 1. The Tools are contained in a window called the Toolbox. Once selected, a tool will remain selected until another tool is clicked on from this Toolbox.

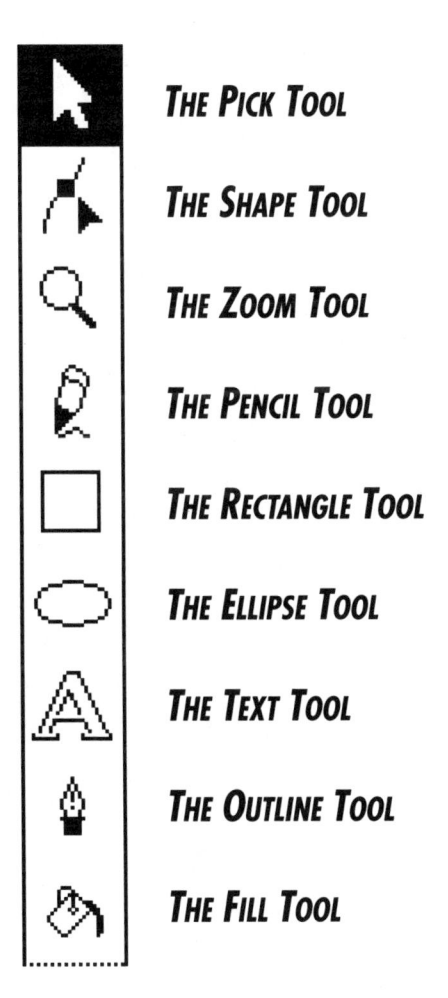

- The Pick Tool
- The Shape Tool
- The Zoom Tool
- The Pencil Tool
- The Rectangle Tool
- The Ellipse Tool
- The Text Tool
- The Outline Tool
- The Fill Tool

THE PICK TOOL

Figure 2. The Pick Tool is used mainly to select, resize, move, rotate and skew objects. This is the tool that you will be using most of the time.

Selecting objects

Figure 3. To select any object with the Pick Tool, click once, directly on its perimeter with the mouse. Once selected, handles will become apparent around the edge of the graphic.

selection handles

Moving objects

Figure 4. With the Pick Tool selected, hold the mouse button down directly on any part of the object's perimeter, move it to its new position, and release the mouse.

Rotating and skewing objects

Figure 5. (**a**) Double-click on any object (or once on an object already selected), with the Pick Tool to invoke the *Rotate* & *Skew* handles. (**b**) To rotate an object, hold the mouse button down on any corner handle, and move the object in the direction you wish it to rotate. (**c**) After releasing the mouse the object is rotated. (**d**) To skew an object, hold the mouse down on any middle handle and move it in the direction you wish to skew the object. (**e**) The result of skewing the square.

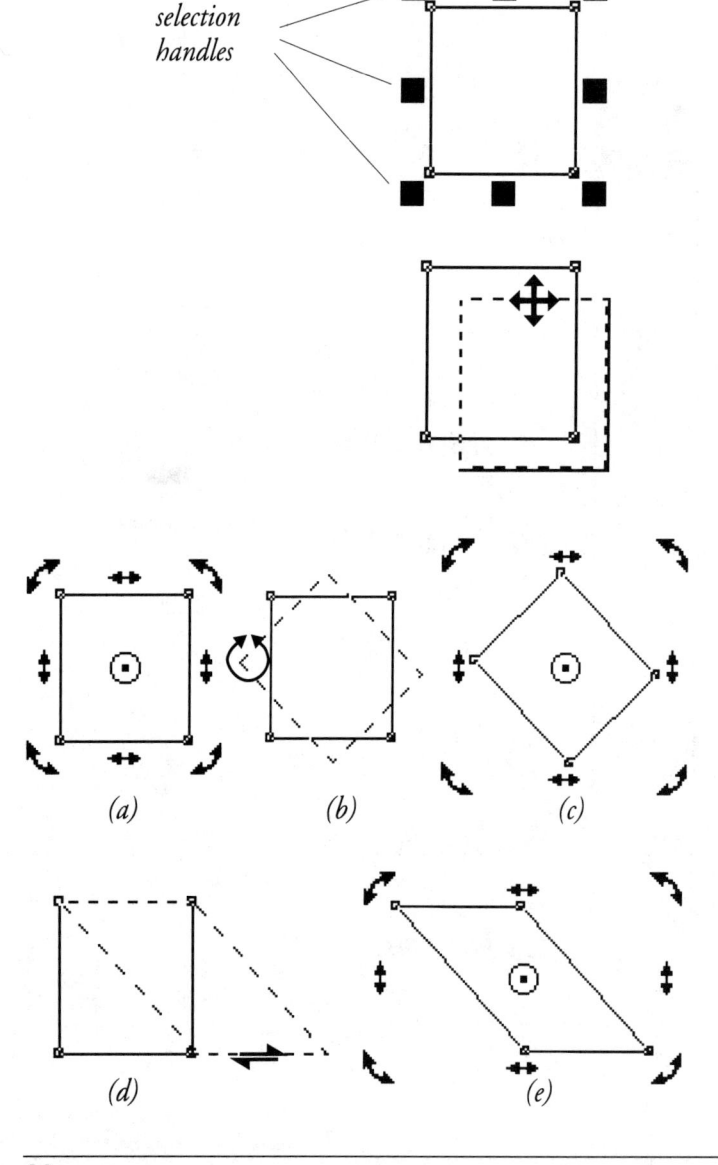

(a) (b) (c)

(d) (e)

See Chapter 5, **The Transform Menu** on how to rotate and skew using the menu commands.

Multiple selection

Figure 6. To select more than one object at a time, hold down the Shift key and click on the objects, in turn, you intend to select with the Pick Tool. Alternatively, draw a square, with the Pick Tool, around the objects you wish to select. This latter method is called Marquee selection. Figures (**a**) and (**b**) illustrate this.

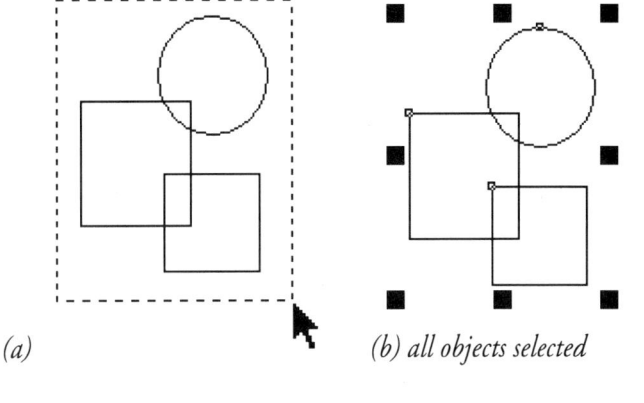

(a)

(b) all objects selected

Deleting objects

Figure 7. To delete an object, first select it with the Pick Tool, then press the Delete key on the keyboard; alternatively select the *Clear* command from the **Edit** menu.

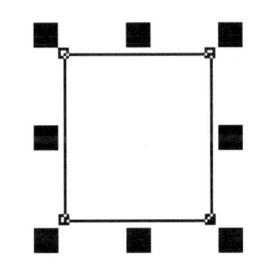

THE SHAPE TOOL

Figure 8. The Shape Tool (**a**) (sometimes called the Node Tool) is used to manipulate objects that have already been placed or drawn on the page. Once you select an object with this tool (**b**), a series of nodes become apparent. These nodes can be moved and manipulated, and also have their properties changed. Other features of the Shape Tool include cropping of Bitmaps, and modifying rectangles, ellipses and text.

(a)

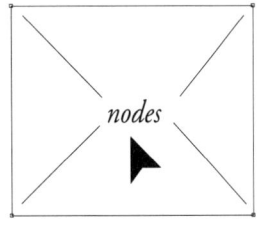

(b) selected object with nodes showing

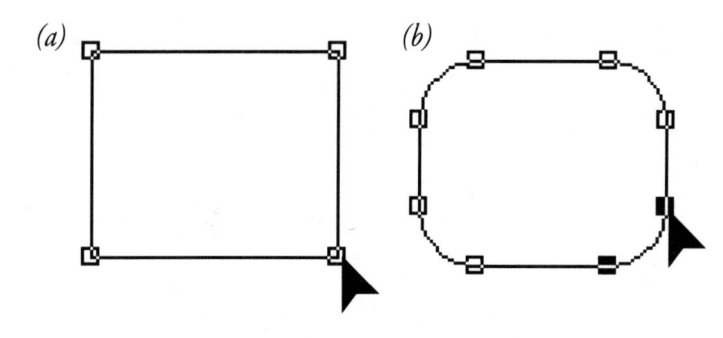

Modifying rectangles

(a) (b)

Figure 9. (a) To modify a rectangle with the Shape Tool, select one of its four corners and move it towards the center slightly to create the effect of Figure (b).

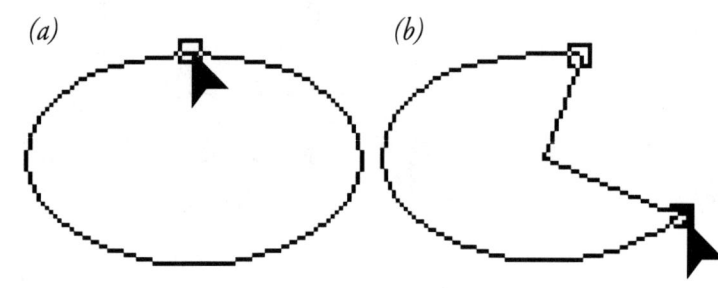

Modifying ellipses

(a) (b)

Figure 10. To modify an ellipse with the Shape Tool, move the node on the circumference of the ellipse (a) to make an arc or a wedge (b).

Note: The modifications shown in Figures 9 and 10 can only be done before using the Convert To Curves command.

Converting to curves

Text, rectangles and ellipses cannot be manipulated with the Shape Tool the same way as objects that have been created with the Pencil Tool. They must be converted to curves first. This is done by selecting the object with the Pick Tool and choosing the *Convert To Curves* command from the **Arrange** menu. Once this is done, you will see a series of nodes appear along the object which allows you to change the shape of the object. For more information, see the *Convert To Curves* command in Chapter 7, **The Arrange Menu.**

Moving nodes

Figure 11. To move a node with the Shape Tool, hold the mouse down on a node and reposition it. You will notice that some nodes have control points coming from the node, which you can also select and move when manipulating curves. This shape was created with the Ellipse Tool and was converted to curves before we could move its nodes.

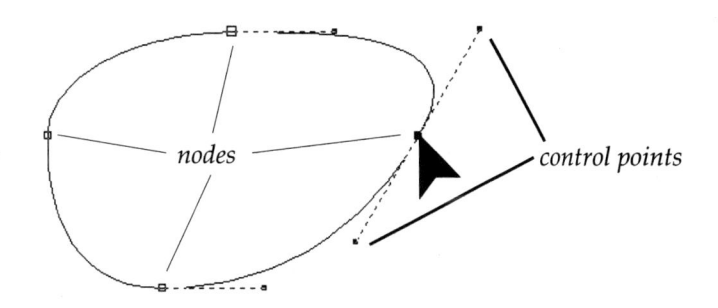

nodes

control points

Selecting multiple nodes

Figure 12. To select more than one node, hold down the Shift key and click inside each node in turn. Alternatively, draw a square to encompass the nodes you wish to select with the Shape Tool. The nodes that fall inside this square will become selected and highlighted.

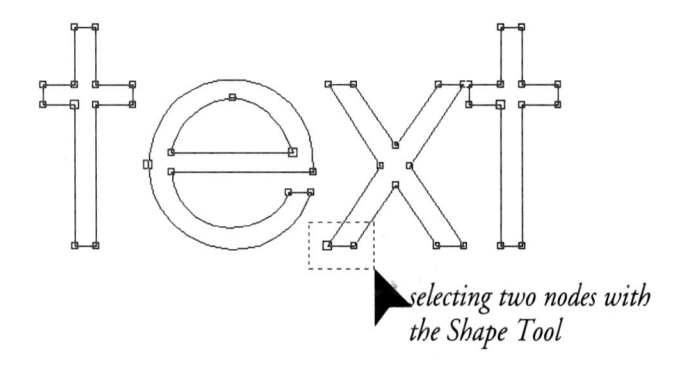

selecting two nodes with the Shape Tool

Changing the properties of nodes

Figure 13. If you wish to change the properties of any node or nodes, double-click on an object or one of its nodes with the Shape Tool, to activate the *Node Edit* dialog box of Figure 14.

Note: This text was converted to curves before we could change its node properties.

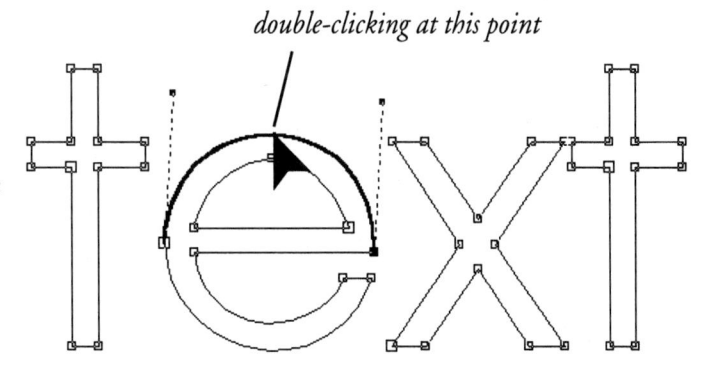

double-clicking at this point

Figure 14. The *Node Edit* dialog box has several options available that will change the properties of a node. This dialog box can be moved by holding the mouse inside the title bar and dragging it to a new position.

Figure 15. (a) To add a node, double-click on the line segment with the Shape Tool where you wish to add a node. Then click on *Add* in the *Node Edit* dialog box. (b) To delete a node, double-click on that node and select the *Delete* option when the *Node Edit* dialog box appears.

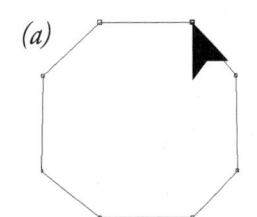

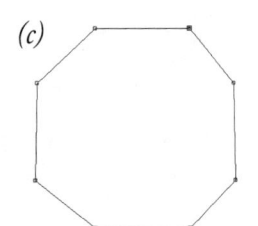

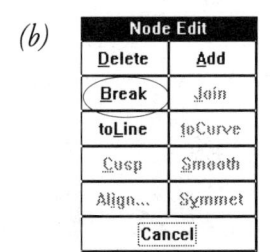

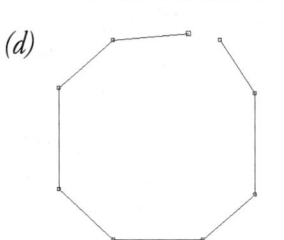

Figure 16. The *Break* option is used to make a break in a line or a closed object.
(**a**) Double-click on the node where you want to make a break in the object.
(**b**) Select the *Break* option from the *Node Edit* dialog box.
(**c**) There will now be two nodes where you selected the first one.
(**d**) These nodes can then be moved separately with the Shape Tool.

Figure 17. The *Join* option is used to join two nodes together to create a closed object or to join two separate paths.
(**a**) Two nodes must be selected with the Shape Tool, and they must be the last or first nodes of a path. Double-click on one of them to activate the *Node Edit* dialog box and then click on *Join*.
(**b**) The two nodes are now one.

Figure 18. To join two separate paths, first select them both with the Pick Tool. Then follow (a) and (b).
(**a**) Select the *Combine* command from the **Arrange** menu. (**b**) Select the end two nodes you wish to join with the Node Tool. Double-click on a selected node and choose the *Join* command from the *Node Edit* dialog box.

two separate paths selected with the Pick tool.

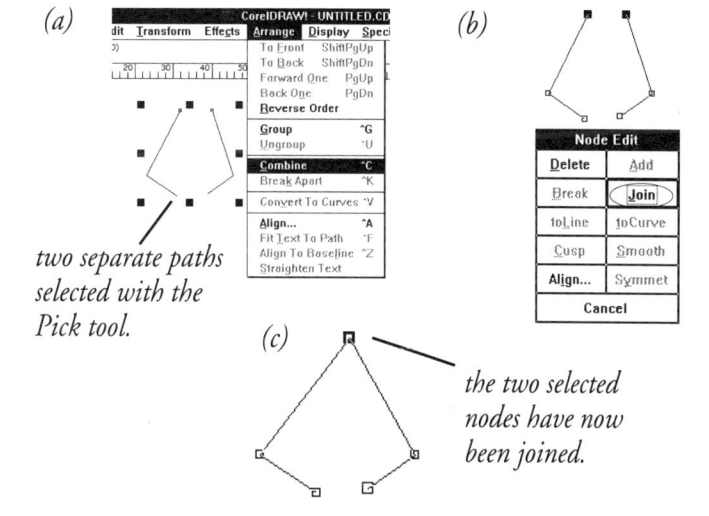

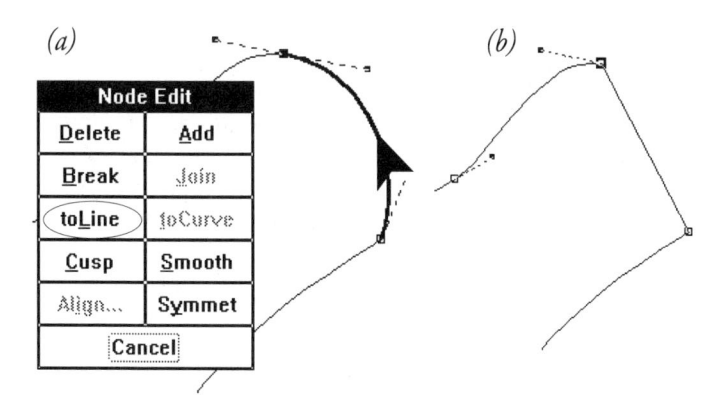

the two selected nodes have now been joined.

Figure 19. The *toLine* option converts the distance between two nodes from a curve to a straight line.
(**a**) Double-click on a line between two nodes to activate the *Node Edit* dialog box and click on the *toLine* option. This option is only available if the selected segment is a curve.
(**b**) The curved line is now straight.
(**c**) The final result.

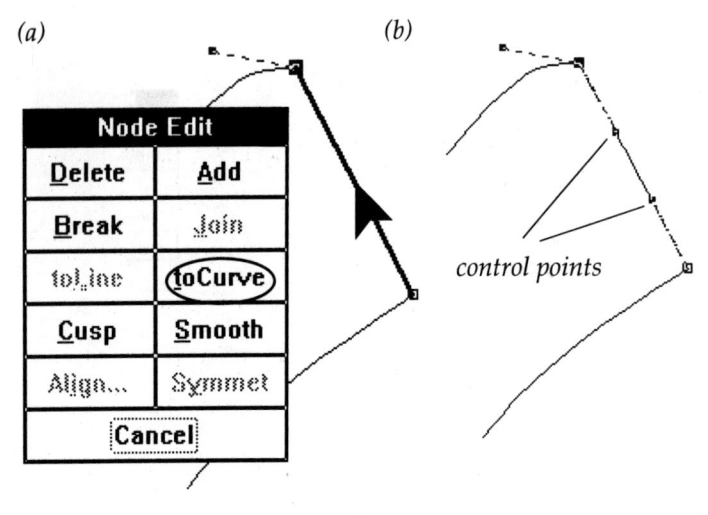

Figure 20. The *toCurve* option changes the distance between two nodes from a straight line to a curve. When you select either node of a curve, control points will become available for manipulation with the Shape Tool
(a) The straight line is double-clicked on to activate the *Node Edit* dialog box and the *toCurve* option is selected.
(b) The line can now be manipulated as a curve. Notice the control points coming out of the nodes on either side of the line.

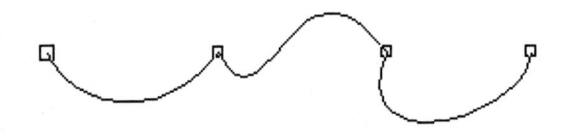

Figure 21. The *Cusp* option changes the selected node's attributes so that the control points on either side of the nodes can be moved independently, without affecting another part of the line.

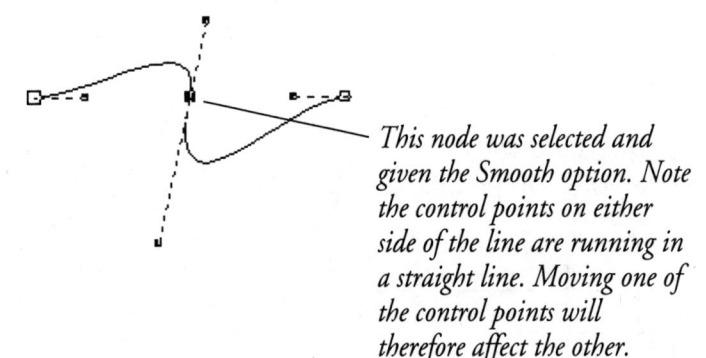

Figure 22. The *Smooth* option will convert a sharp point to a smooth point. Unlike the *Cusp* option, the control points of a node that has been converted to *Smooth*, when moved, will affect the lines on both sides of the node. The control points on either side of the node will also run along a straight line in the opposite direction.

This node was selected and given the Smooth option. Note the control points on either side of the line are running in a straight line. Moving one of the control points will therefore affect the other.

Figure 23. To make use of the *Align* command in the *Node Edit* dialog box, you must first have two or more nodes selected with the Node tool. After double-clicking on one of the selected nodes, you then click on the *Align* option.

We selected these two nodes with the Node tool and activated the Node Edit dialog box. The Node Align dialog box of Figure 24 was then accessed by clicking on the Align option.

Figure 24. The *Align* option will activate the *Node Align* dialog box. Here you can align nodes horizontally, vertically, or by their control points. This is useful for technical drawings where accuracy is required. For this example we have selected the *Align Vertical* option for the two nodes selected.

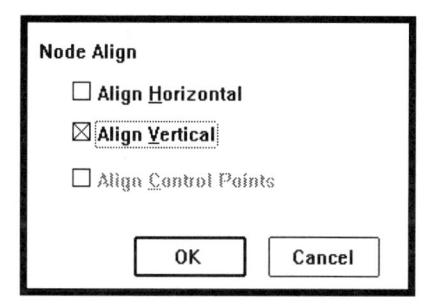

Figure 25. The two nodes are now vertically aligned.

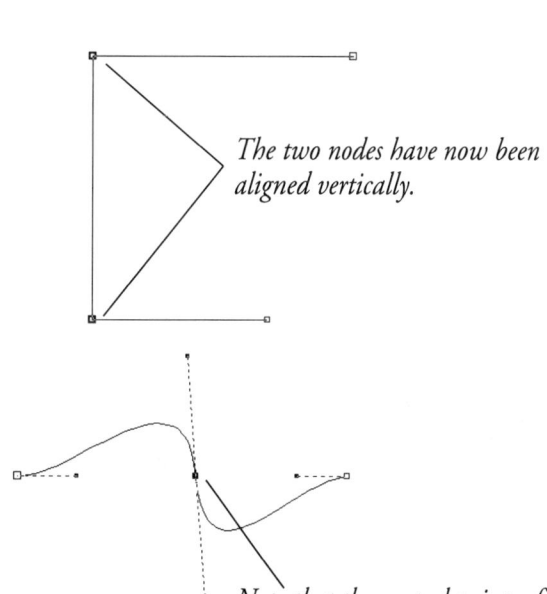

The two nodes have now been aligned vertically.

Figure 26. The *Symmet* option is similar to the *Smooth* option, but the control points will move the line in opposite directions of equal distance.

Note that the control points of a node, that has been given the Symmet option, will move in opposite but equal directions and so will the line on either side of the node.

The *Cancel* option in the *Node Edit* dialog box brings you straight back onto the working page without making any changes.

Moving individual letters

Figure 27. (**a**) If you select a text block with the Shape Tool, you will notice that to the left of each letter is a node. (**b**) You are able to move each letter independently simply by holding down the mouse on a specific node and repositioning the letter. (**c**) Some examples of moving multiple characters away from the original text block with the Shape Tool.

Modifying kerning and leading

Figure 28. (**a**) To modify the kerning or inter-letter spacing of a text string, hold the mouse down on the right arrow marker and drag it to the right or the left.

(**b**) The spacing between the letters is increased when dragging to the right.

Note if you hold down the Control key as you drag the right arrow marker, you will increase only the inter-word spacing.

(**c**) The arrow marker to the left of the selected text block can be moved up or down. This will modify the leading (line spacing) of the text, but only if there is more than one line of text.

Dragging this marker to the right will increase inter-letter spacing.

Dragging this marker down will increase inter-line spacing.

Changing single character attributes

Figure 29. (a) If you double-click on any node to the left of a letter with the Shape Tool, the *Character attributes* dialog box will be invoked.

(b) Here you can change font, point size, position and angle of any letter or letters.

(c) The result of the changes made in the (b) dialog box. We changed the size, font and character angle of the letter o from the previous figure.

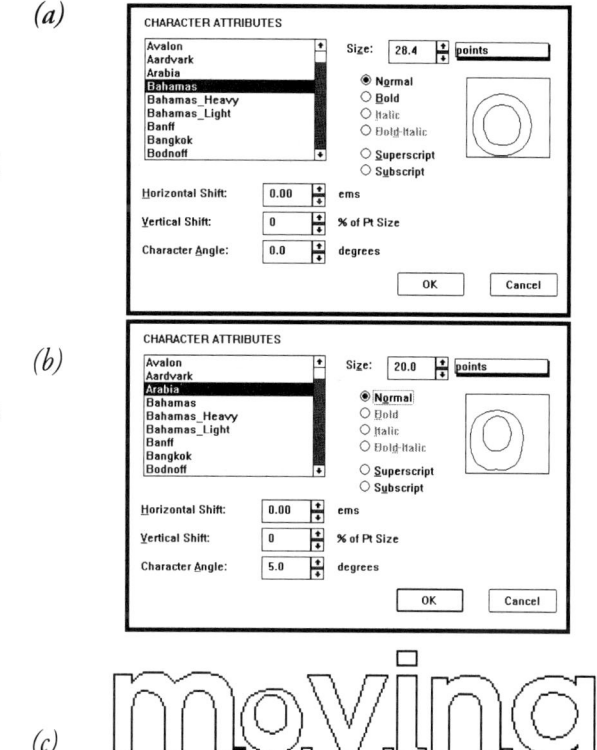

Cropping bitmaps

Figure 30. (a) To crop a bitmap, select it with the Shape Tool. Selection handles will appear around its edge.

(b) Hold the mouse down on any handle and drag it towards the centre of the bitmap. You may reverse this procedure to reveal any part which has been covered.

(c) The bitmap has been cropped from the bottom.

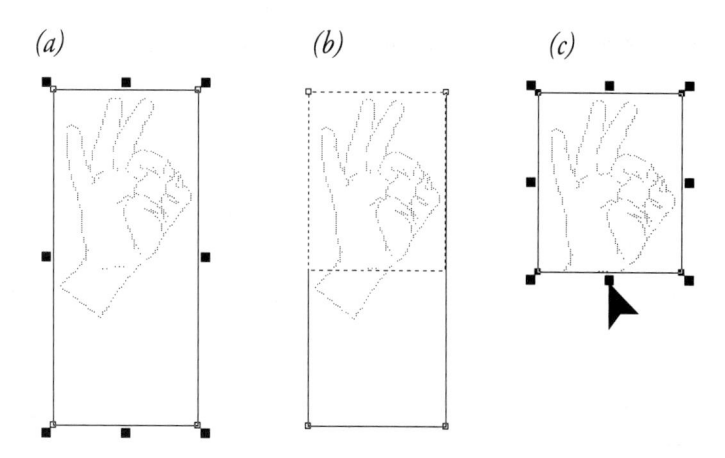

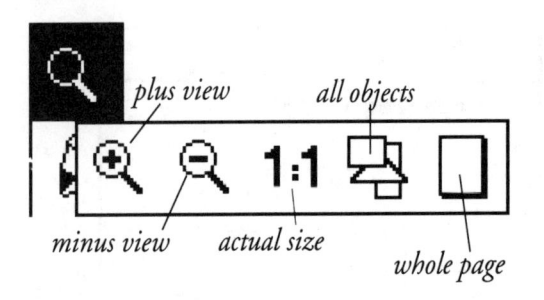

THE ZOOM TOOL

Figure 31. The Zoom Tool is used to change the viewing size and position of the screen. Once selected, the Zoom Tool flyout is activated.

plus view — all objects — minus view — actual size — whole page

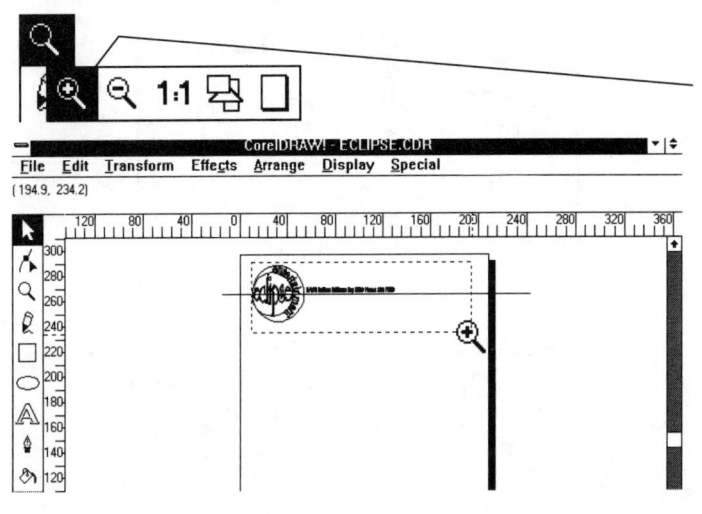

Figure 32. With the first option selected from the Zoom Tool flyout, draw a square over the section you wish to enlarge, and release the mouse. Figure 33 shows the result.

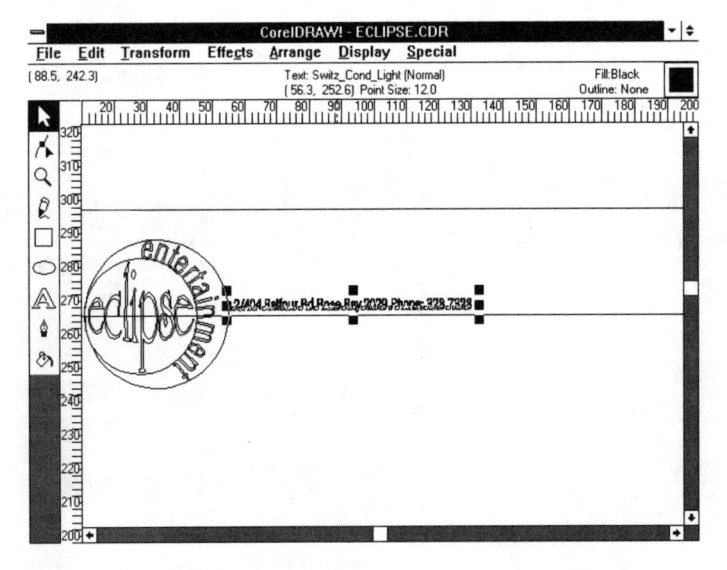

Figure 33. The section defined in Figure 32 will now fill the entire working screen. You may use this tool consecutively in order to re-enlarge the area you are working with.

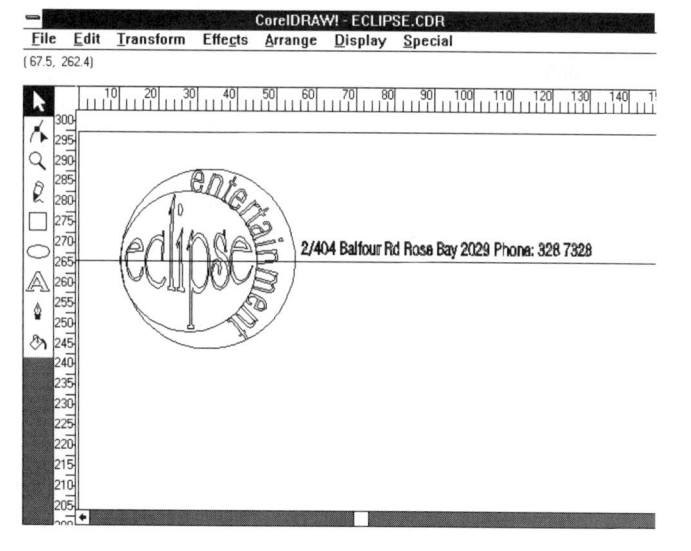

Figure 34. The second option in the Zoom Tool fly-out will take the page view back to the size it was before it was magnified.

Figure 35. The third option, when selected, will display your page in actual size view (see Figure 36).

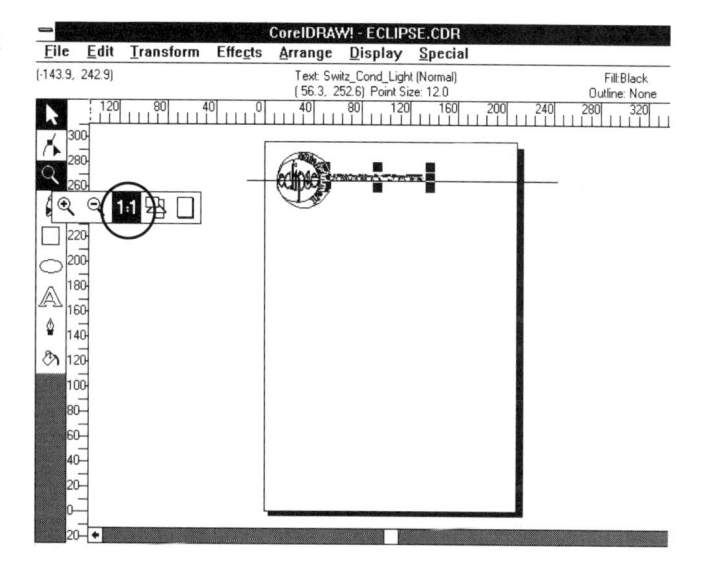

Figure 36. The page is now being displayed in actual size view.

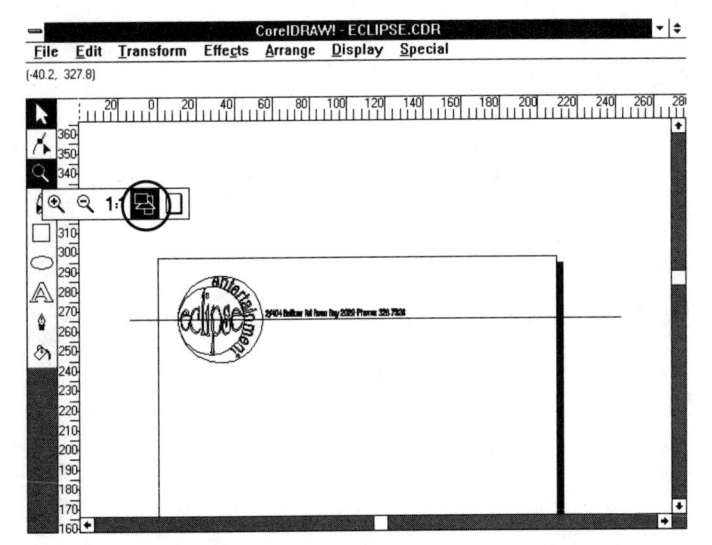

Figure 37. The fourth option in the Zoom Tool fly-out will display the page with every object in view, including any objects in the pasteboard area.

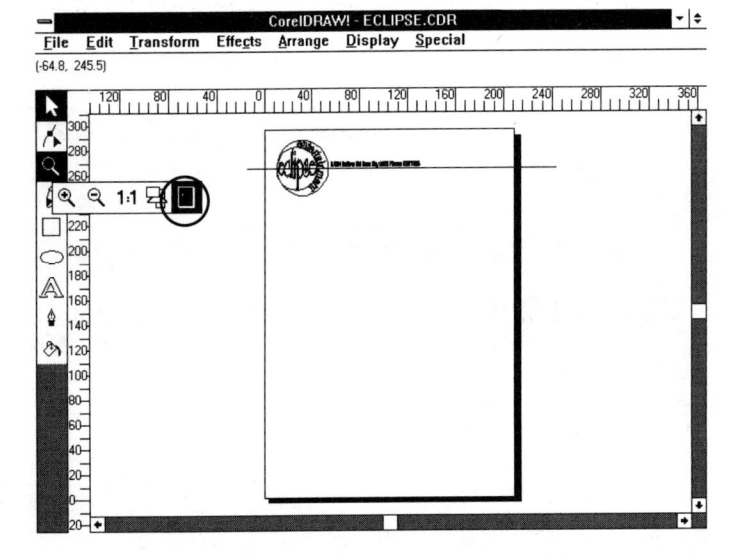

Figure 38. The last option in the Zoom Tool fly-out will bring the whole page into view.

THE PENCIL TOOL

Figure 39. This tool is the freehand drawing tool. After selecting this option from the Toolbox, move out onto the page, hold the mouse down and begin to draw as you would with a normal pencil. Release the mouse to stop drawing.

Figure 40. There are two different drawing modes you can swap between when drawing with the Pencil Tool. These are *Freehand* and *Bezier*. To swap between the two modes, select the *Preferences* command in the **Special** menu. From this dialog box, click on the *Lines & Curves* button, to activate the associated dialog box of Figure 41.

Figure 41. In the *Lines & Curves* dialog box select either *Bezier* or *Freehand,* and click on OK here and in the *Preferences* dialog box of the previous figure.

See Figures 42 through 45 to understand the differences between *Freehand* and *Bezier* drawing.

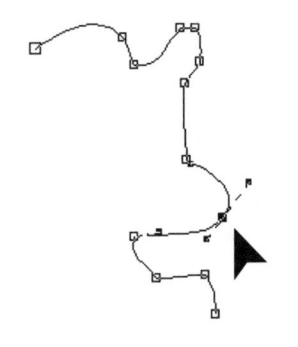

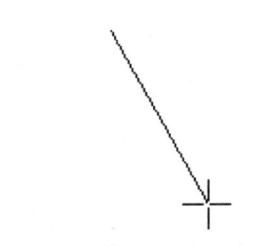

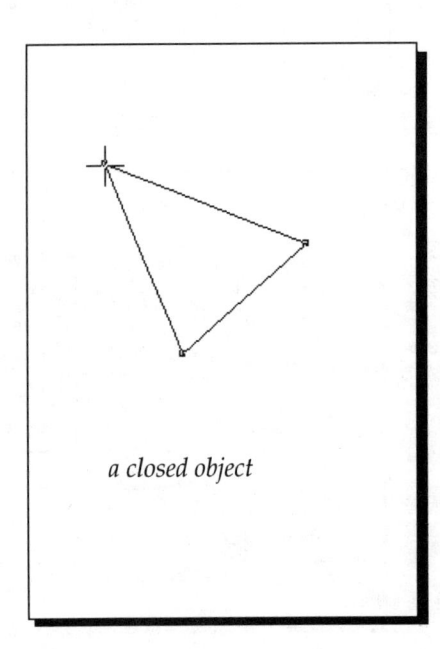

Freehand mode

Figure 42. To draw in this mode, follow the description in Figure 39. A series of nodes will be visible after you have drawn the line, which you can then manipulate with the Shape Tool.

Straight lines

Figure 43. To draw a straight line in *Freehand* mode, click the mouse once on the page, move it to where the end point of the line will be, and click the mouse once more to end the line.

Closed objects

Figure 44. To create a closed object in *Freehand* mode, begin drawing as if you were creating a straight line, but double-click in the second position, which will allow you to continue on with the line in a different direction.
(a) Repeat this procedure to create as many edit points as required for the shape of the object.
(b) To close off the object, click the mouse once on top of the starting point. If you weren't successful in closing the object, the right side of the Status Line will read *Open Path* once the object is selected with the Shape Tool.

a closed object

Bezier mode

Drawing in *Bezier* mode gives the nodes slightly different qualities, and also allows you to draw curves.

Drawing curves

(a) *(b)*

Figure 45. (a) Hold the mouse down and begin to draw. You will notice that you are able to manipulate control points that become visible in order to define the direction and angle of the curve. (b) Click once in a different position to continue this curve. Repeat this process to draw any shape you like.

Note: *To close off an object, and to draw a straight line in Bezier mode, follow the Freehand mode descriptions for these procedures. With Bezier mode you only have to click the mouse once at each change of direction, and for drawing a closed object.*

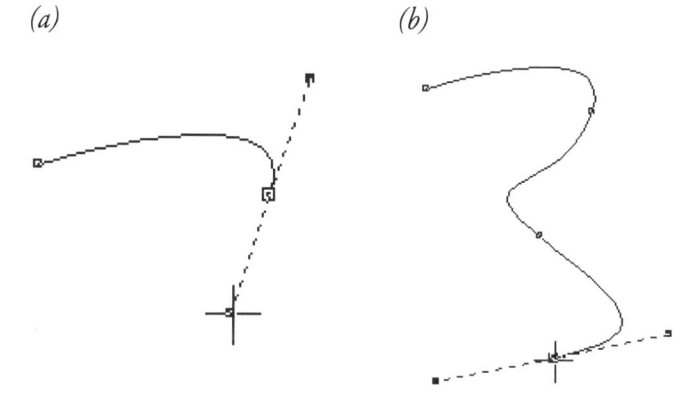

Autotrace

Figure 46. It is possible to trace imported bitmaps with the Pencil Tool. Only TIFF, PCX and BMP images can be traced, and the bitmap must be imported with the *For Tracing* option selected. A bitmap will always come into CorelDRAW inside a frame.

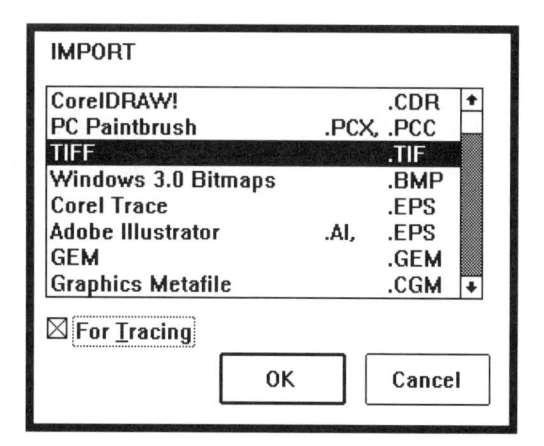

CHAPTER 2: THE TOOLS

This bitmap was traced using the Pencil tool.

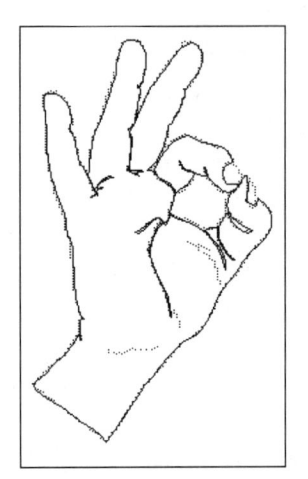

Figure 47. Once the Bitmap is on the page, select it with the Pick Tool, and then select the Pencil Tool. Note that the Pencil Tool icon will now look like a t on its side. Click the mouse on a point on the graphic that you would like traced. After a few seconds, there will be an outline around the selected area. Repeat this procedure until you are satisfied with the results. Once you have finished, the Bitmap may be moved or deleted, and the traced image can be edited and colored as any other drawing in CorelDRAW.

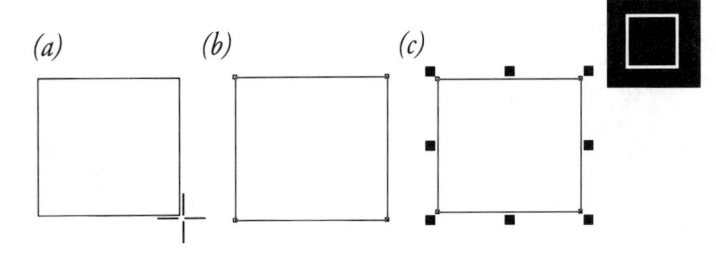

THE RECTANGLE TOOL

Figure 48. This tool is used to create rectangles and squares. To draw a rectangle, select the tool, hold the mouse down on the page, drag it diagonally in any direction (**a**), and release the mouse. Once released, the rectangle will look like (**b**). If the Pick Tool is then selected, it will look like (**c**).

(a)   (b)   (c)

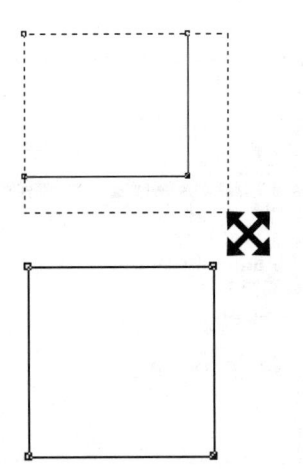

Figure 49. Resizing and moving a rectangle is done with the Pick Tool active. Note that the Status Line will always reflect the width and height of the object.

Drawing squares

Figure 50. To draw a perfect square, hold down the Control key while drawing the square, and do not release it until you release the mouse.

This square is currently being resized by holding the mouse down on the bottom right selection handle of Figure 48(c) and dragging it to a new position.

26

CHAPTER 2: THE TOOLS

THE ELLIPSE TOOL

Figure 51. This tool is used to create circles and ellipses.
To draw an ellipse, select the tool, hold the mouse down on the page, drag it diagonally to a new position, and release.

Figure 52. Resizing and moving an ellipse is done with the Pick Tool. Note that the Status Line will always reflect the width and height of the object.

Drawing circles

Figure 53. To draw a perfect circle, hold down the Control key while drawing the circle, and do not release it until you release the mouse.

THE TEXT TOOL

Figure 54. The Text Tool is used to place text on the page. Here the Text Tool is the currently active tool in CorelDRAW.

Text Tool selected and cursor moved onto the page.

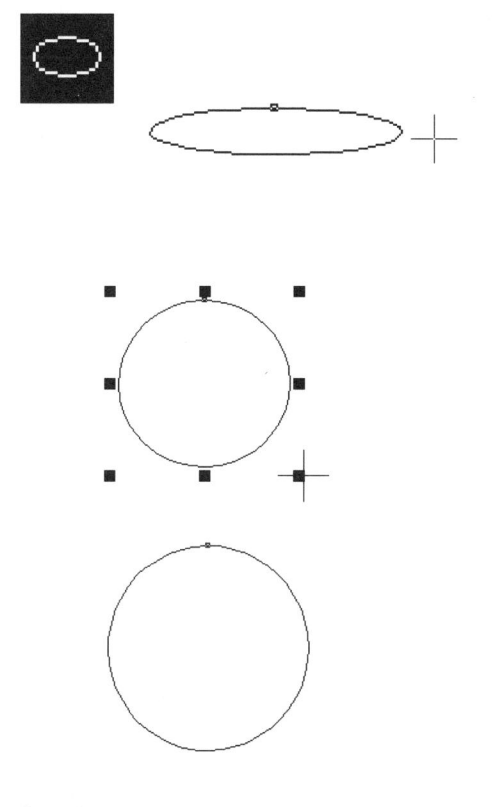

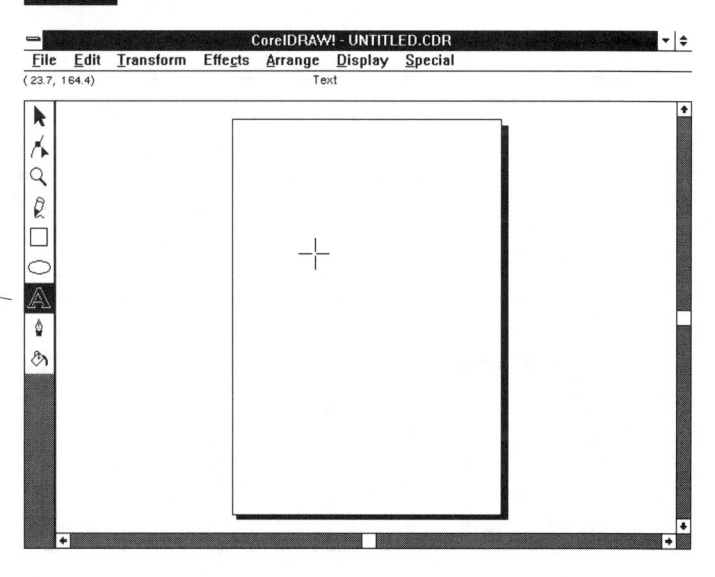

27

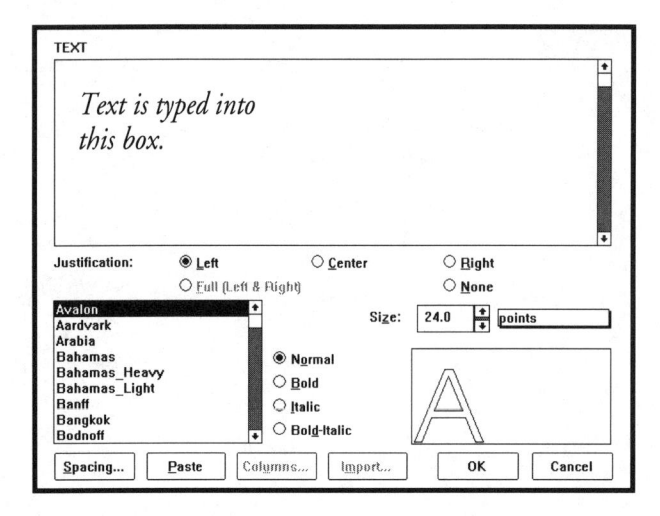

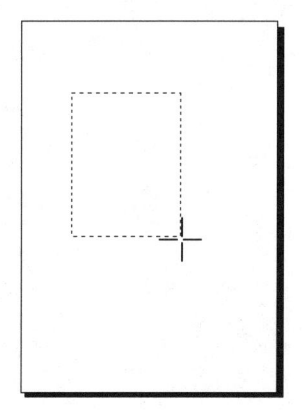

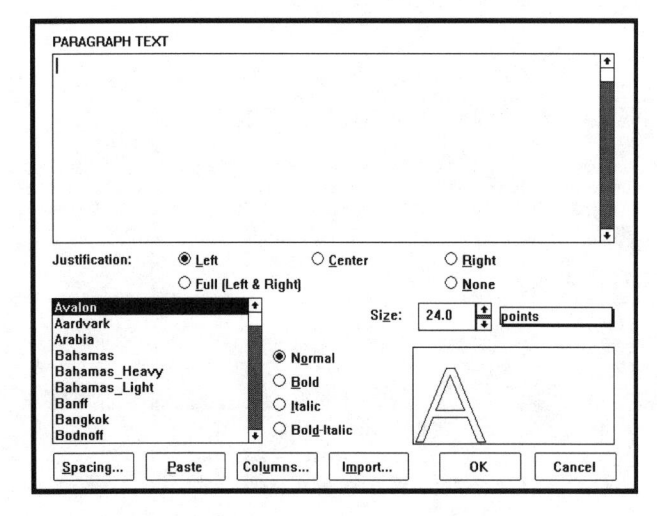

Placement of text

Figure 55. The first method of placing text is to select the Text Tool and click it once on the page as shown in Figure 54. This will activate the *TEXT* dialog box.

Text is keyed into the rectangular box as indicated, and a wide range of font types and other attributes may be selected.

Figure 56. The second text placement method is to draw a square on the page with the Text Tool. This will activate the *PARAGRAPH TEXT* dialog box of Figure 57, and the final placement of text will be inside the defined area that was drawn with the mouse. This method is used when a long string of text is required to be typed, or if you are planning on importing text into CorelDRAW. The *Full (Left & Right)* justification option and the *Columns* dialog box can only be used within the *PARAGRAPH TEXT* dialog box.

Figure 57. Once you have activated the *PARAGRAPH TEXT* or *TEXT* dialog box, you can type the required text straight into the empty text box. The maximum number of characters you can type into the *TEXT* dialog box is 250, and in the *PARAGRAPH TEXT* dialog box it is 4000.

Changing type style

Figure 58. To change type style, click on the desired font name from the list of fonts. Each font, once selected, is displayed in the box to the right for easy recognition.

Changing size

To change the point size of text, double-click on the *Size* box and retype in the new size, or click on the up and down arrows to the right of this figure.

Text alignment

Figure 59. These options effect the alignment of the text in relation to where the Text Tool was clicked on the page. The choices are: *Left, Center, Right, Full (Left & Right)* or *None*. The second last option is only available in the *PARAGRAPH TEXT* dialog box.

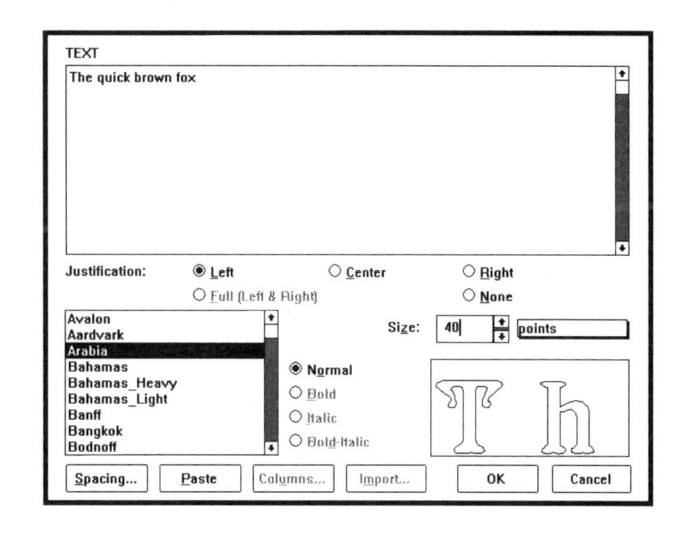

Spacing

Figure 60. The *TEXT SPACING* dialog box is activated by clicking on the word *Spacing* in the bottom left of the *TEXT* or *PARAGRAPH TEXT* dialog boxes. By adjusting the values in this dialog box, you will be modifying the corresponding spacing of the text on the page.

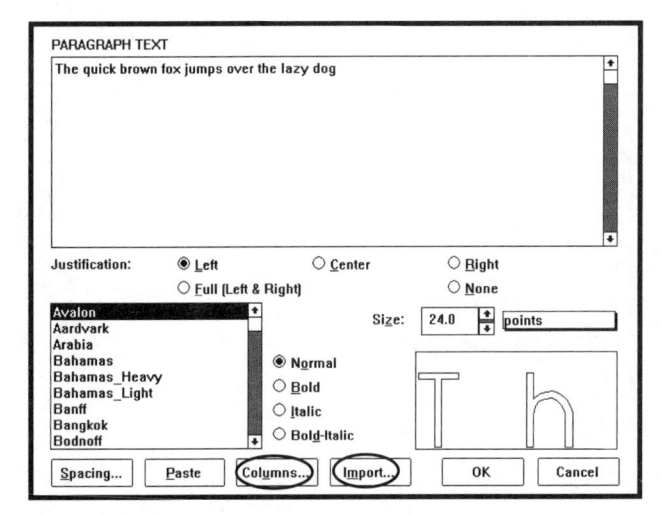

Paragraph Text

Figure 61. The *PARAGRAPH TEXT* dialog box is activated by drawing a square on the page with the Text Tool as explained in Figure 56. The *PARAGRAPH TEXT* dialog box allows you to choose the *Columns* and *Import* options as well as the *Full (Left & Right)* justification option.

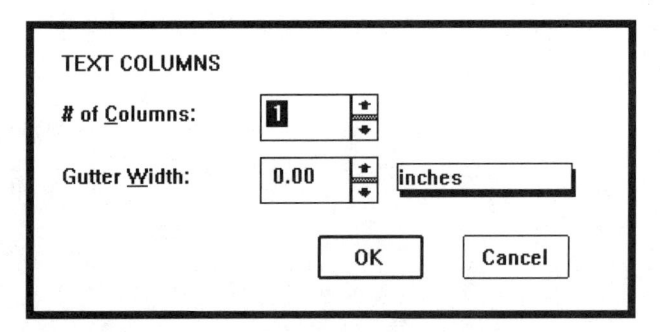

Columns

Figure 62. The *Columns* option activates this dialog box. The maximum number of columns is eight. The *Gutter Width* is the space between the columns.

Importing text

Figure 63. The *Import* command of Figure 61 activates the *Import Text* dialog box. From here, you can locate any text file on your hard disk to import into CorelDRAW. These text files can come from any word processor, as long as they have been saved in ASCII format. Text files in ASCII format generally have a .TXT extension. The selected text file will be visible in the *PARAGRAPH TEXT* dialog box after clicking on *Import* from the *Import Text* dialog box.

Paste

Figure 64. The *Paste* command is available in both the *TEXT* and *PARAGRAPH TEXT* dialog boxes. It lets you paste any text that has been copied to the Windows clipboard. This must first be copied from any program that generates text and uses the Windows clipboard.

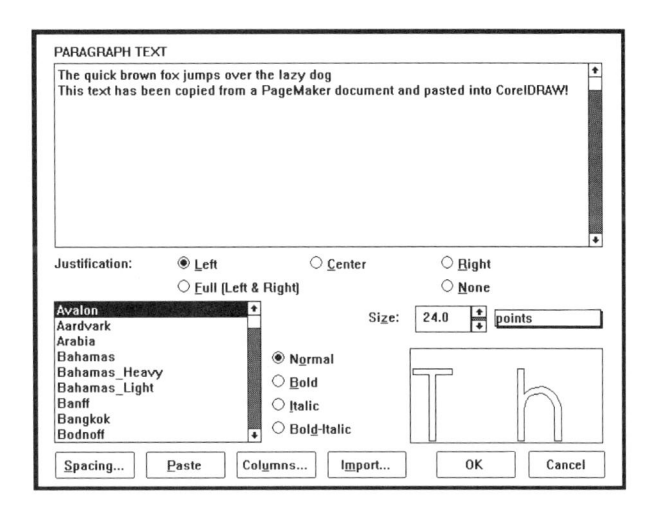

Symbols

Figure 65. If you fully installed CorelDRAW on your machine the Text Tool can also be used to place symbols on the page. To activate the *SYMBOLS* dialog box, hold down the Shift key while clicking the Text Tool on the page.

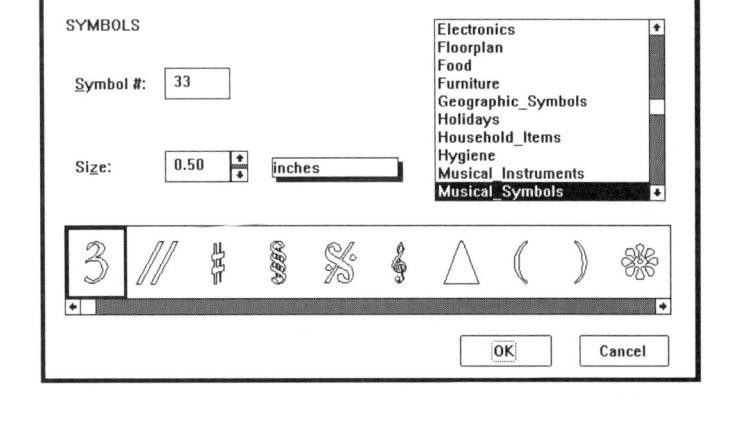

Figure 66. To select a symbol, first select a category from the symbols listing on the right. Scroll through the symbols displayed in the horizontal window, and make your selection by clicking on the symbol with the mouse.

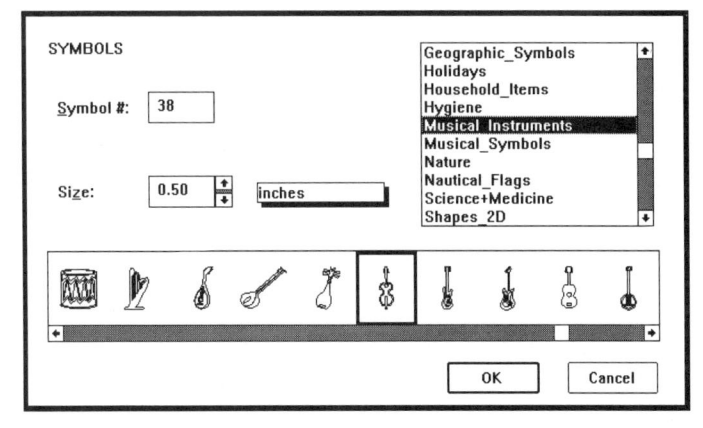

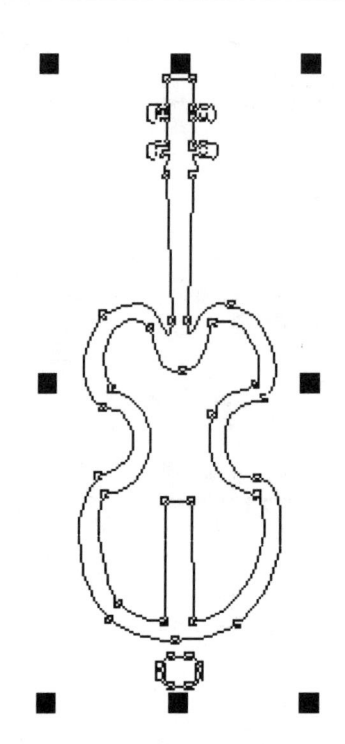

Figure 67. After selecting OK, this is how a symbol will appear on your page. Symbols appear on the page as combined objects. To be able to edit the symbol with the Pick Tool and the Shape Tool, in the same way as any object, you must first select it with the Pick Tool and apply the *Break Apart* command from the **Arrange** menu.

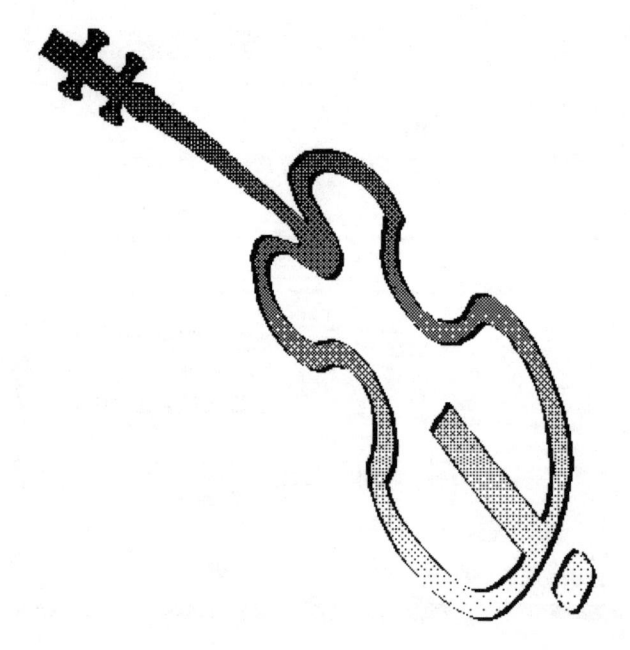

Figure 68. Here the same symbol as in Figure 67 has been given a *Fountain Fill* and a calligraphic outline. It was also rotated and was manipulated using the *Envelope* command. To perform these changes to the symbol we did not have to break it apart.

outline pen
outline color
thickness options
None Hairline .2 pt .5 pt 1 pt 2 pt 4 pt 8 pt 12 pt 16 pt 24 pt
White 100% 10% 20% 30% 40% 50% 60% 70% 80% 90%
shading options

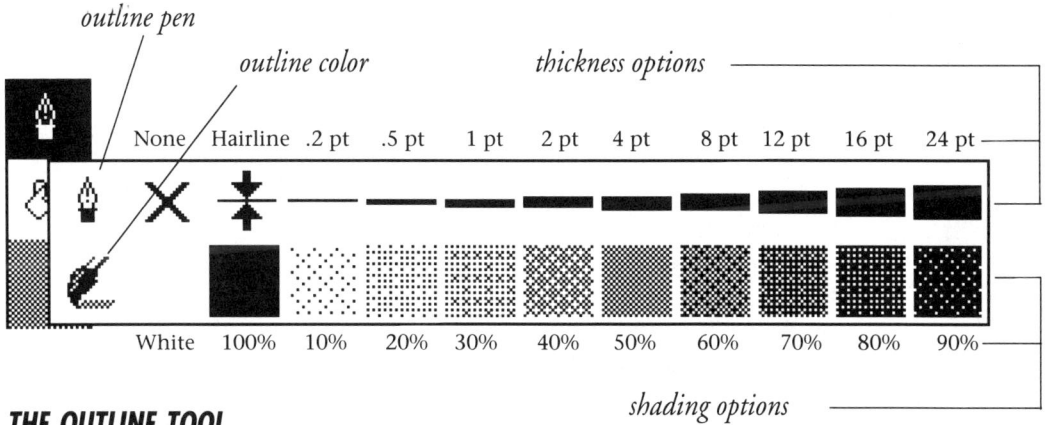

THE OUTLINE TOOL

Figure 69. The Outline Tool is used in conjunction with the Pick Tool to determine the outline color and thickness of an object. The Outline Tool fly-out (above) is activated when you click on the Outline Tool with the mouse. To apply a predetermined thickness to a selected object, click on one of the thickness options in the top row. To apply a shade of black, or white, to this outline, click on one of the shades displaying in the bottom row.

THE OUTLINE PEN

Figure 70. If you click on this option in Figure 69, the *OUTLINE PEN* dialog box appears. This dialog box gives you options allowing you to customize an object's outline thickness, and also create calligraphic and other effects.

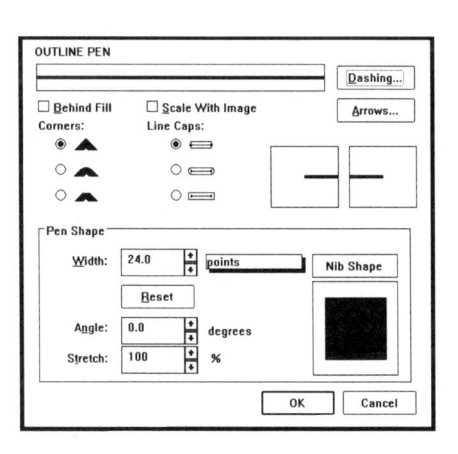

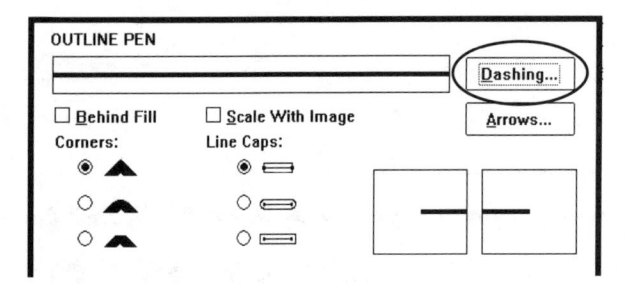

Dashing

Figure 71. The *Dashing* option allows you to apply different dash and dot patterns to a selected outline. By clicking on the *Dashing* option in the *OUTLINE PEN* dialog box, the dialog box of Figure 72 is activated.

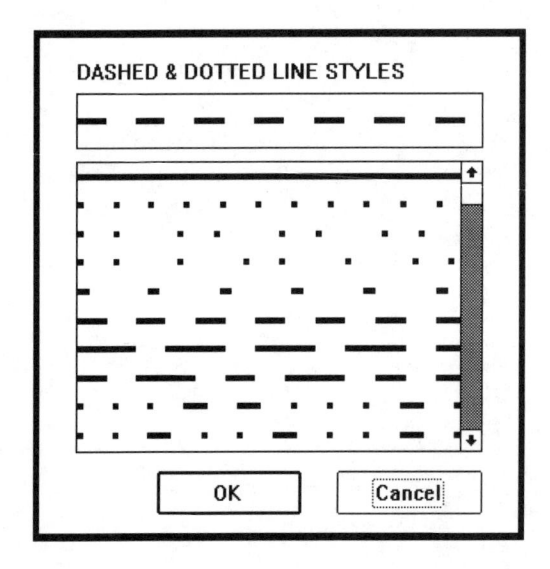

Figure 72. In this dialog box, select the dashes of your choice and then select OK, bringing you back to the *OUTLINE PEN* dialog box. To create additional line styles refer to page 79 of the *Technical Reference Guide* that comes with CorelDRAW

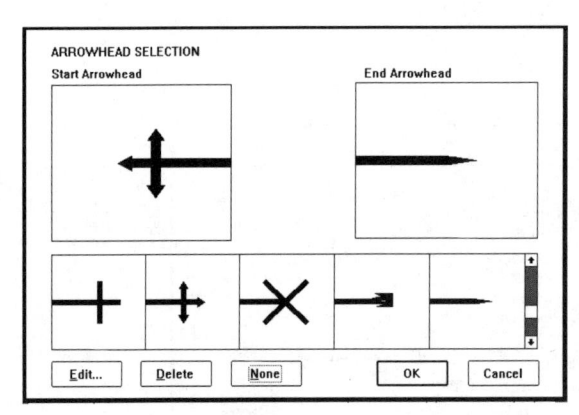

Arrows

Figure 73. Clicking on the *Arrows* option in the Figure 71 dialog box will invoke the *ARROWHEAD SELECTION* dialog box. Using the scroll bars to display available arrowheads, click on the arrow head of your choice. The left mouse button applies arrowheads to the *Start Arrowhead* option, and the right mouse button applies to the *End Arrowhead* option.

Editing Arrows

Figure 74. Select the arrow head you wish to edit and click on the *Edit* button of Figure 73. The *ARROW HEAD EDITOR* dialog box is activated. You may resize, move and change the direction of the arrowhead from within this dialog box.

Note: The size of the arrow head is determined by the thickness of the line, which can only be viewed on the Preview screen.

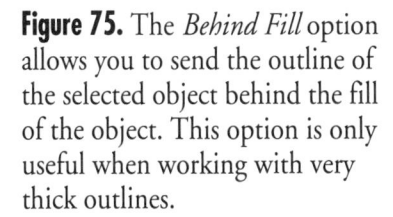

Figure 75. The *Behind Fill* option allows you to send the outline of the selected object behind the fill of the object. This option is only useful when working with very thick outlines.

The *Scale With Image* option will scale the outline thickness of an object as you resize it.

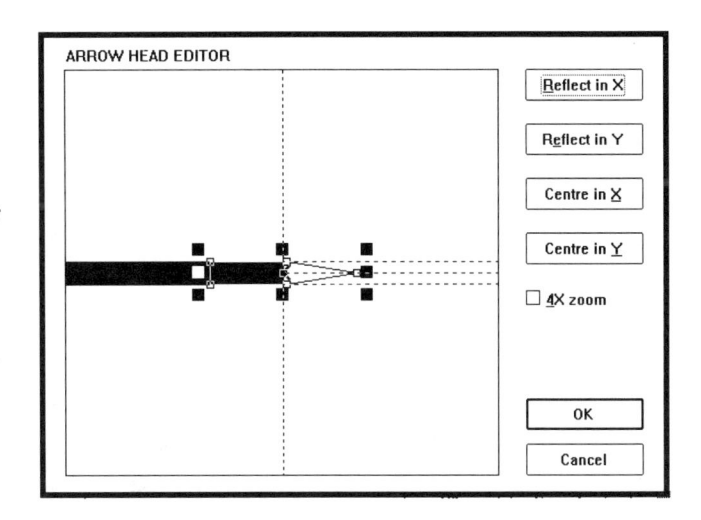

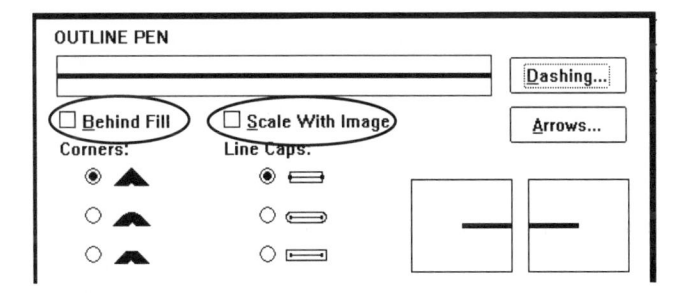

Corners

Figure 76. These three corner options can be used to modify the corners of an object, or where two lines meet.

Line Caps

These three options effect the ends of a line drawn with the Pencil Tool.

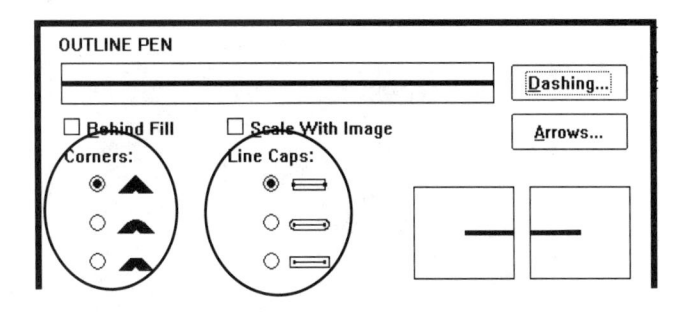

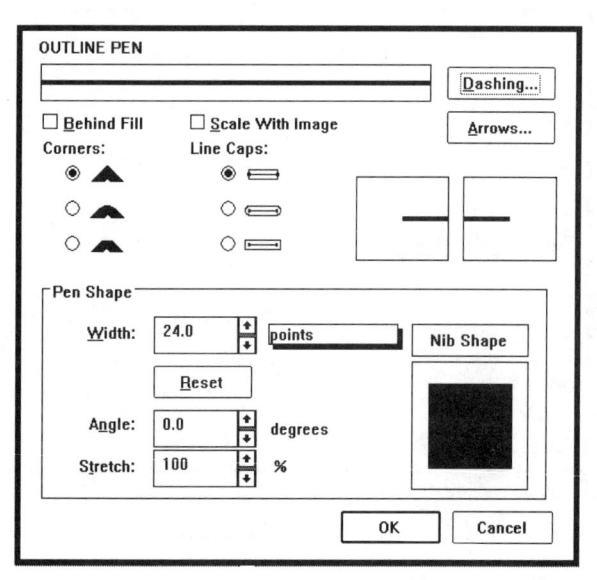

Pen Shape

Figure 77. The *Pen Shape* options are located in the lower section of the *OUTLINE PEN* dialog box. The *Width* box reflects the current thickness of the outline, which can be changed, as can the measurement system.
The *Reset* button will change any settings you have changed in this section back to the default settings.
The *Angle* and *Stretch* options effect the *Nib shape* box on the right. Changing these percentages can create calligraphic effects with an outline.

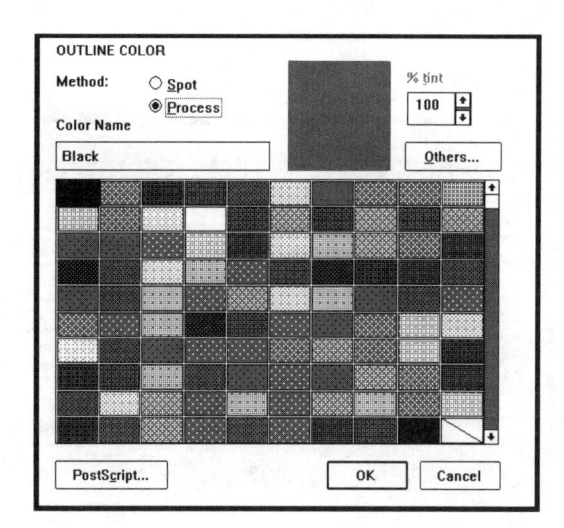

Figure 78. These examples were created by varying the *Width*, *Angle* and *Stretch* figures of the *OUTLINE PEN* dialog box.

OUTLINE COLOR

Figure 79. If you click on the Outline Color option (refer to figure 69), the *OUTLINE COLOR* dialog box appears. In this dialog box you may apply any outline color to a selected object.

Note: Bitmaps can have a color applied to them by either using the shades of gray in the second row of the Outline Tool flyout, or through the OUTLINE COLOR dialog box.

Color dialog boxes

Figure 80. At this point you may choose either *Spot* or *Process* color. Using the palette for either selection is the same. Click on the desired color, which will then be displayed in the square in the top right, and the name or number of the color will be displayed in the *Color Name* box. You may change the percentage of the tint for Spot colors only.

Spot colors give you a range of Pantone colors which are a predetermined choice of colors with numbers given to each one. These are recognized worldwide by commercial printers.

Process colors are a range of colors that have been made up of percentages of four colors, Cyan, Magenta, Yellow and Black. The color combinations are almost infinite.

Spot color selection

Figure 81. Once you have the *Spot* option selected, if you click on the *Others* option in Figure 79, the *INK COLORS* dialog box will be activated. It is recommended to select this option if you know the name and/or number of the Pantone color you wish to use. Select the color in the list on the left, and it will be displayed in the box to the right.

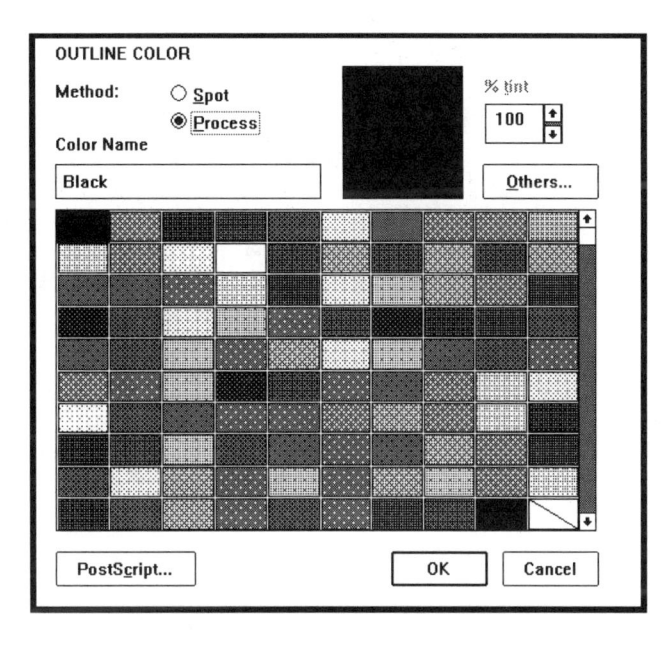

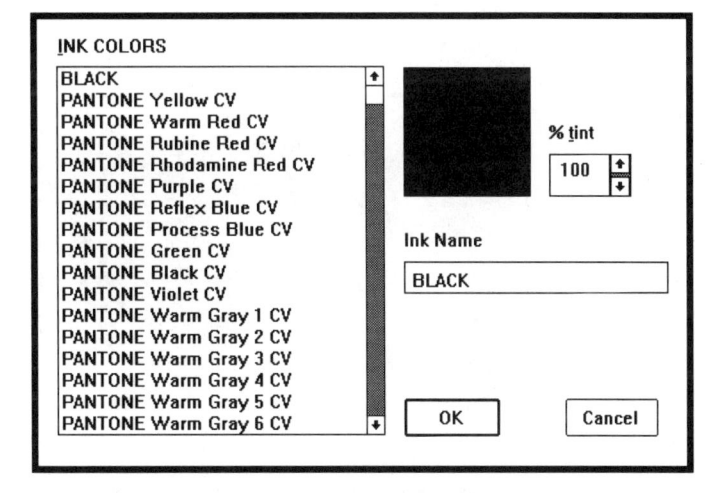

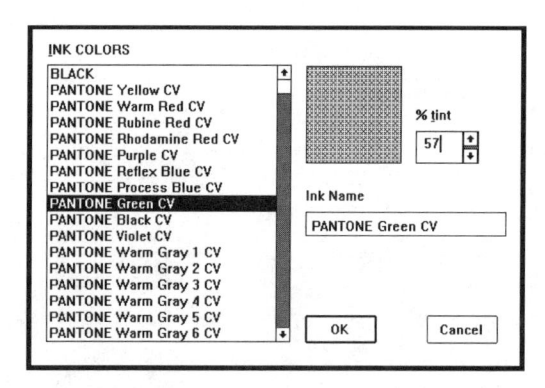

Adding a Spot color

Figure 82. If you scroll down to the end of the palette in Figure 79 with *Spot* selected, there will be a number of empty squares. To add a color to the palette for later use, double-click on an empty square in the *OUTLINE COLOR* dialog box. This will activate the *INK COLORS* dialog box. Select the color you wish to change, alter the tint percentage and select OK.

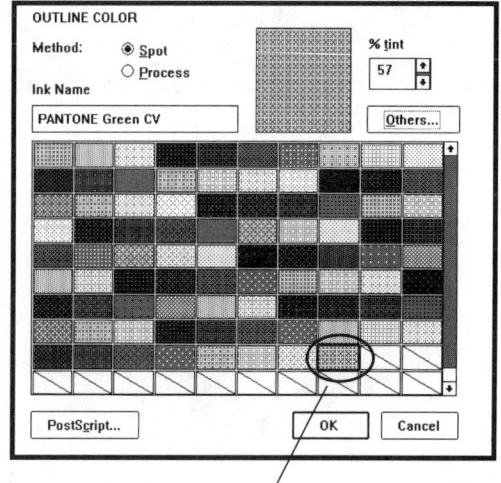

Figure 83. The new version of the color will now be displayed in the square double-clicked on originally. All the Pantone colors in the *INK COLORS* dialog box list are the same colors in the Spot color palette. If you alter a Pantone color, the new tint can then be saved in the Spot palette.

Process color selection

To create your own Process color, select *Others* when the Process palette is active in the *OUTLINE COLOR* dialog box of Figure 79, to activate the *OUTLINE* dialog box.

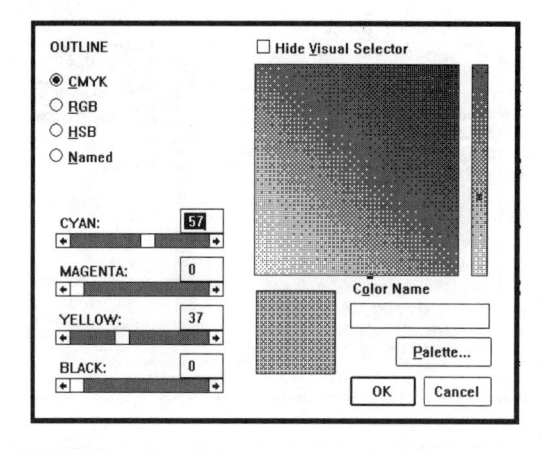

Figure 84. There are four different methods to choose from in creating or applying colors. Once you have created a color with any of the Process methods (see following figures), you may name your color by typing a title in the *Color Name* box and selecting OK. The new color will then appear in the *OUTLINE COLOR* dialog box.

The altered Pantone color is now part of the Spot palette.

CMYK

Figure 85. To define colors with this option, you may use the scroll bars and/or the percentage boxes. Alternatively, hold the mouse down on the *Visual Selector* and move it around to the color or hue of your choice. The large box adjusts the color settings for Cyan and Magenta, and the long thin box is for the Yellow setting. This will then be displayed in the box below.

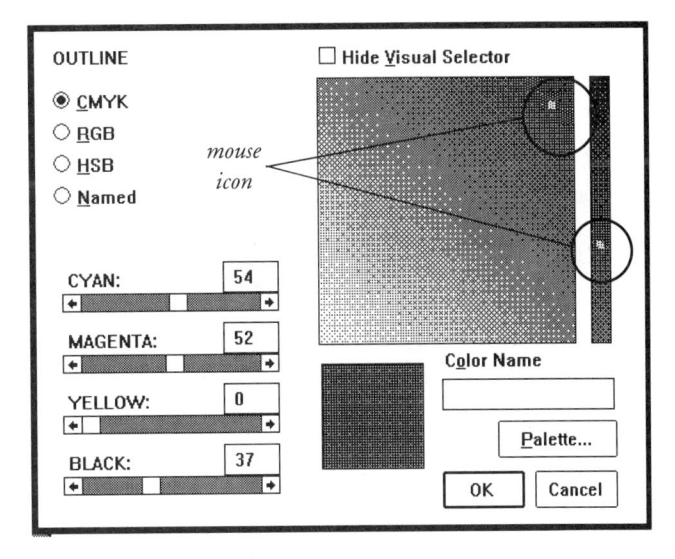

RGB

Figure 86. To define colors with this option, you may use the scroll bars and/or the percentage boxes. Alternatively, hold the mouse down on the *Visual Selector* and move it around to the color or hue of your choice. The large box determines the amount of red and green, while the long thin box is for blue. This will then be displayed in the box below.

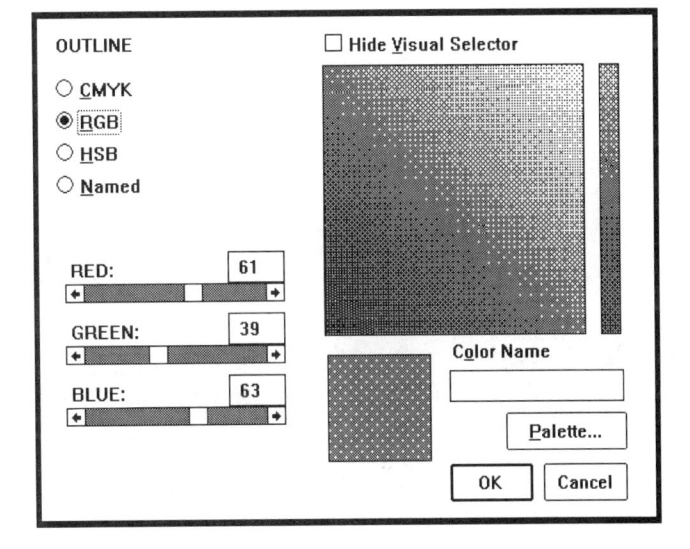

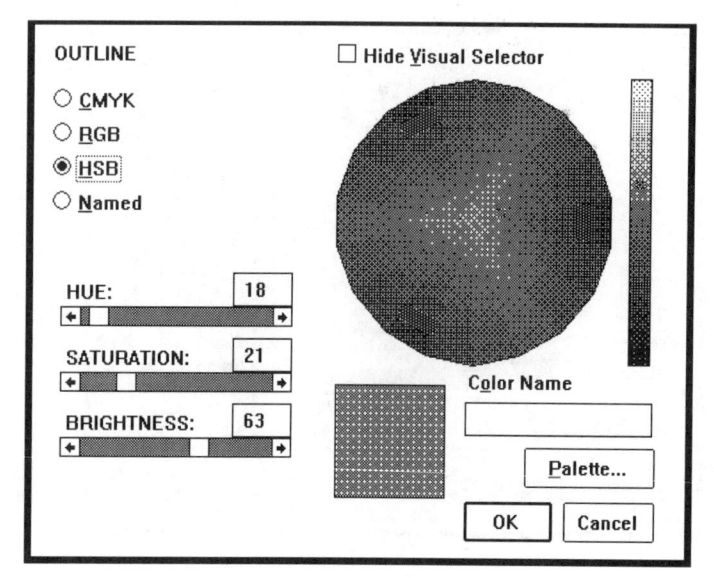

HSB

Figure 87. To define colors with this option, you may use the scroll bars and/or the percentage boxes. Alternatively, hold the mouse down on the *Visual Selector* and move it around to the position of your choice. The color wheel determines the hue, with the center of the wheel being the lightest and the outer perimeters the purest in hue. The long thin rectangle will lighten or darken the color . This will be displayed in the box below.

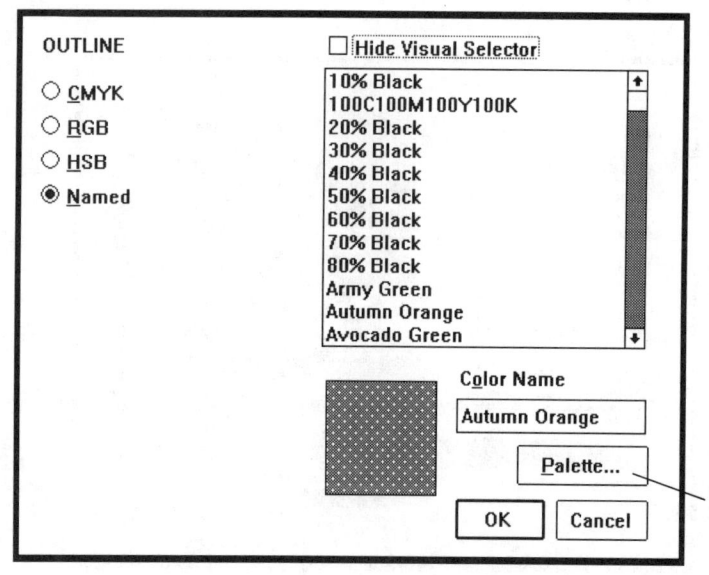

Named

Figure 88. With this option selected, CorelDRAW will display a list of predefined colors in a box to the right. Any color that is selected will be displayed in the box below. These are the same colors that are displayed in the palette of the *OUTLINE COLOR* dialog box of Figure 79.

Palette button

When the *Palette* button is displayed in any color dialog box (except for the Palette dialog box itself), selecting it will take you back to the *OUTLINE COLOR* dialog box.

Converting Spot to Process

Figure 89. If you have a specific color you wish to convert from Spot color to Process, follow these steps. First select the Pantone color you want to change from the palette. Then Select *Process* in the *Method* option of the *OUTLINE COLOR* dialog box, and then the *Others* button.

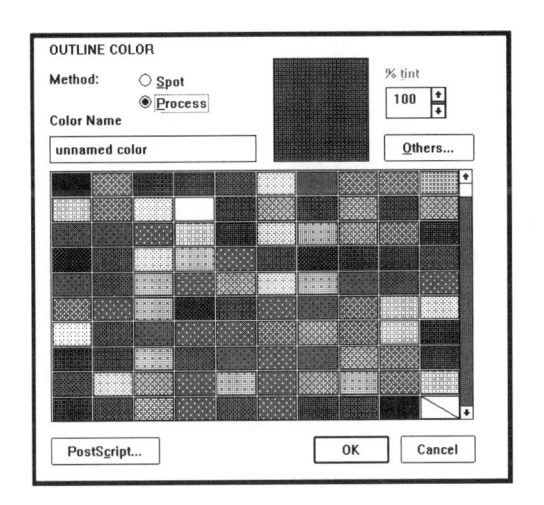

Figure 90. Here the CMYK option will display the Pantone color as a process color, as closely as it can. Give the color a name and click on OK.

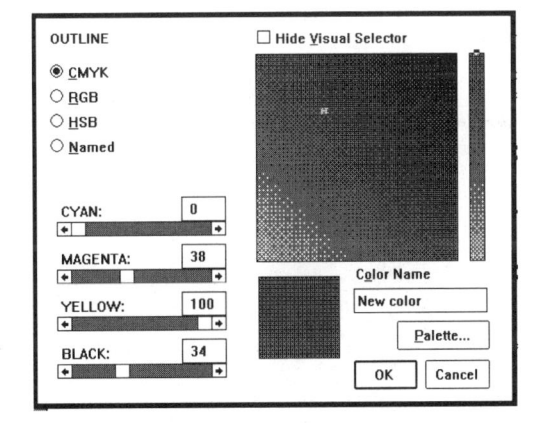

Figure 91. The new color now appears in the *Process* color palette.

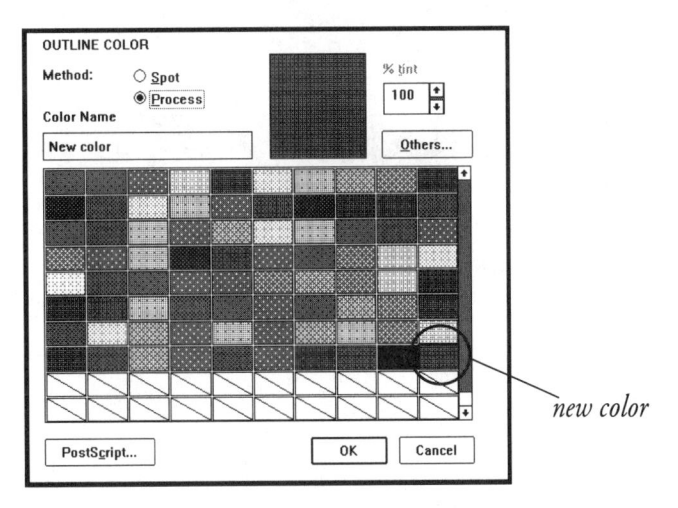

new color

PostScript

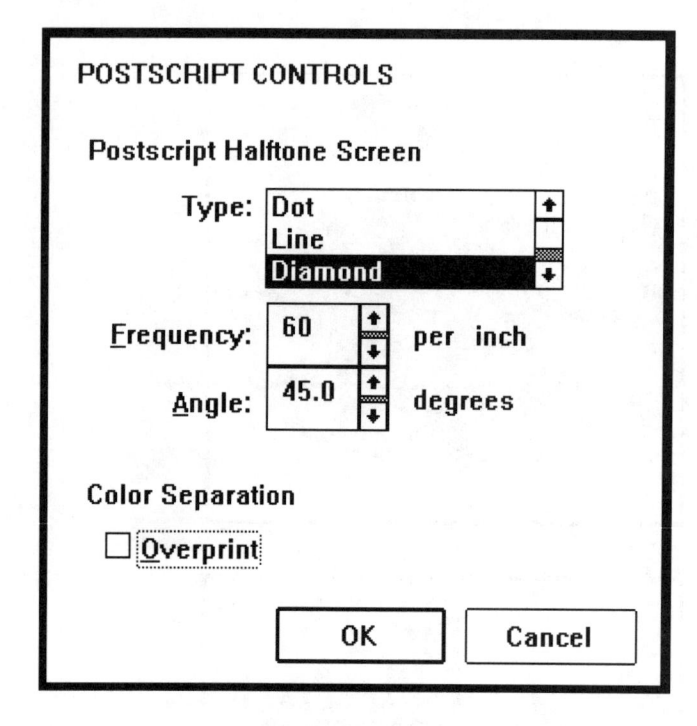

Figure 92. The *PostScript* option in the bottom left of the *OUTLINE COLOR* dialog box of Figure 79, activates the *POSTSCRIPT CONTROLS* dialog box.

The *Postscript Halftone Screen* option works only for Spot colors. By activating the sub-menu next to *Type*, you may choose from a range of effects to apply to a selected outline.

The *Frequency* option determines the number of times the effect will occur per inch.

The *Angle* option determines the angle the effects will be at.

A comprehensive example of these PostScript effects is displayed in the CorelDRAW User's Manual from page 137.

THE FILL TOOL

Figure 93. The Fill Tool is used in conjunction with the Pick Tool to determine the fill of an object. This flyout is activated when the Fill icon in the Toolbox is clicked on with the mouse. A fill may be applied to any closed object.

To apply a predetermined shade of black to a selected object, click on one of the fill options in the bottom row of the Outline Tool flyout.

The other options in the top row of the Fill Tool flyout are discussed below.

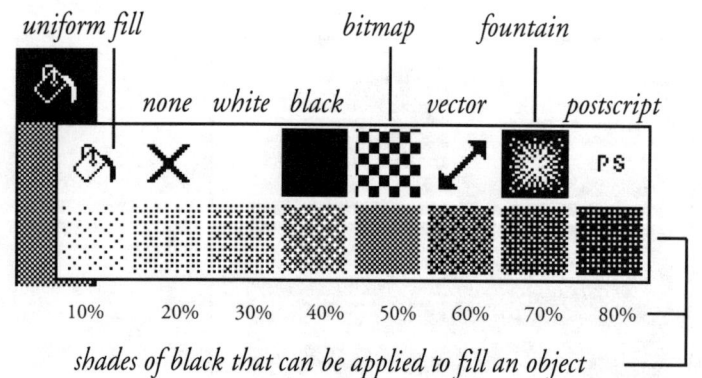

Uniform fill

Figure 94. If you click on the paint tin icon of Figure 93, you will activate the *UNIFORM FILL* color dialog box. This dialog box operates in the same way as the *Outline Color* dialog box described previously in Figures 79 through 92.

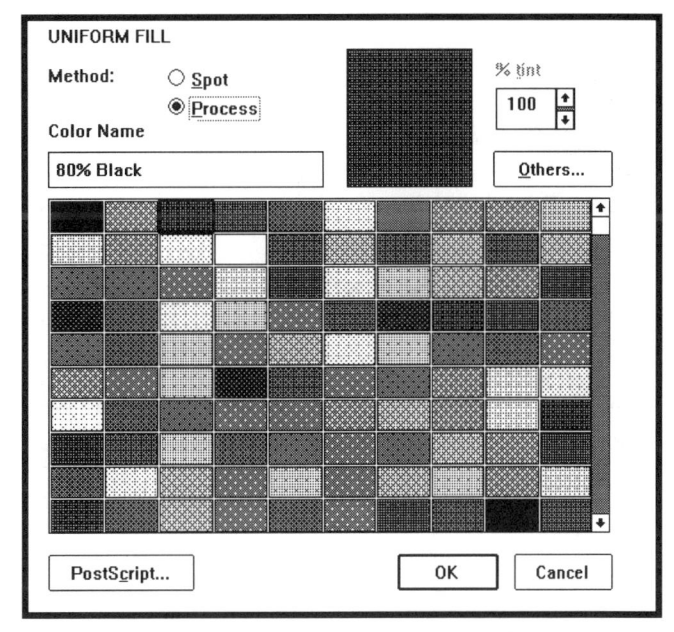

Bitmap fill

Figure 95. The *BITMAP FILL PATTERN* dialog box is activated by clicking on the chess board pattern in the Fill Tool fly-out of Figure 93. In here you may scroll through a variety of predetermined bitmap patterns to fill a selected object. Click on your choice with the mouse, which will display in the top left square.

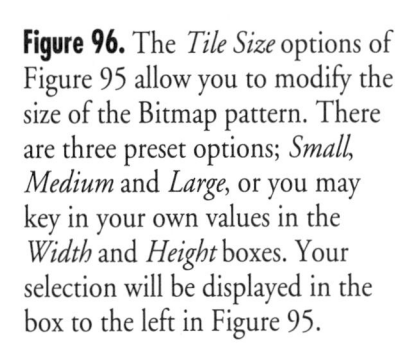

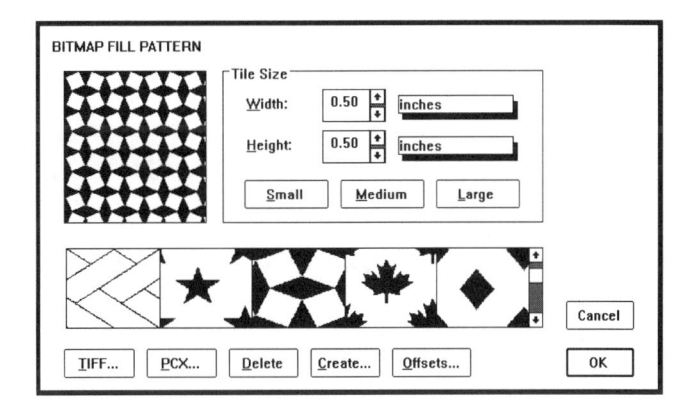

Figure 96. The *Tile Size* options of Figure 95 allow you to modify the size of the Bitmap pattern. There are three preset options; *Small, Medium* and *Large*, or you may key in your own values in the *Width* and *Height* boxes. Your selection will be displayed in the box to the left in Figure 95.

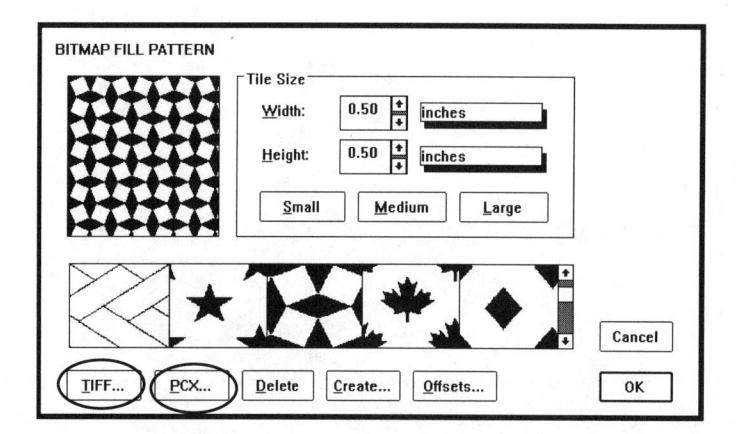

Importing bitmap fills

Figure 97. By selecting either the *TIFF* or *PCX* button, you will activate the *Import Bitmap* dialog box.

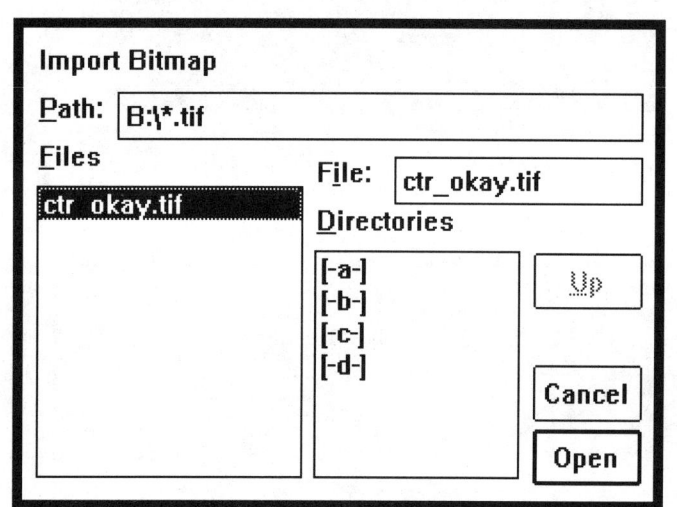

Figure 98. With the *Import Bitmap* dialog box you now have access to all directories and drives on the hard disk. You can choose any TIFF or PCX file (depending on which option you selected) that has been created in an external paint program, or a scanned image, to import into CorelDRAW as a bitmap pattern. Any imported color images will be converted to black and white.

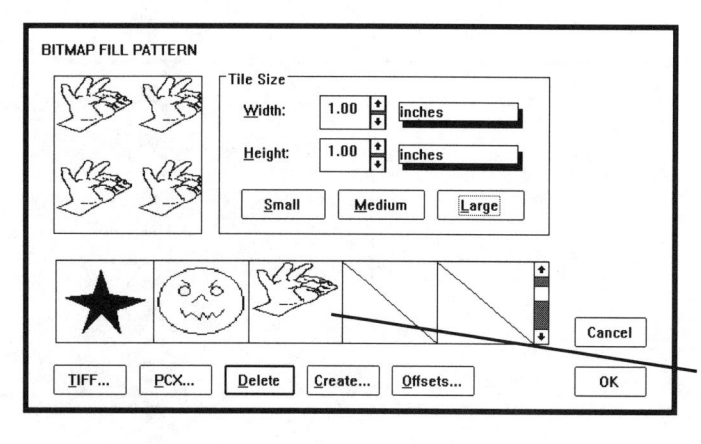

Figure 99. Once you have imported the file and returned to the *BITMAP FILL PATTERN* dialog box, the new bitmap will appear in one of the originally empty bitmap selection boxes.

This is the new TIFF image imported into the BITMAP FILL PATTERN dialog box.

Deleting a bitmap fill

Figure 100. You may delete any bitmap, by first selecting it, and then clicking on the *Delete* button. A screen prompt will appear asking you to confirm your choice.

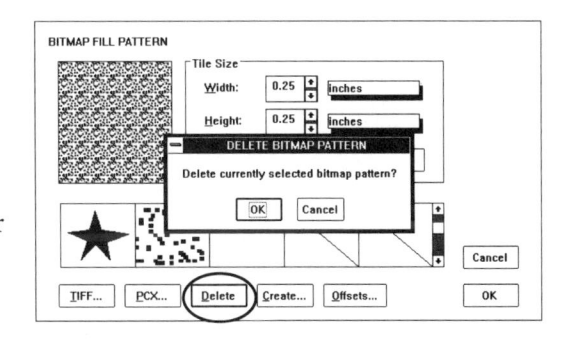

Creating a bitmap fill

Figure 101. One way of creating a bitmap fill is by selecting the *Create* command within the dialog box of Figure 95 to activate the *BITMAP PATTERN EDITOR* dialog box. Here you may click with the mouse to create a pattern, and the *Size* options to modify the size. After selecting OK, the new bitmap fill will appear in one of the previously empty bitmap selection boxes.

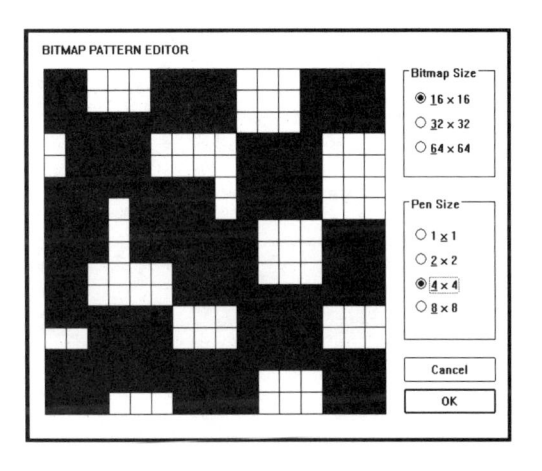

Offsets

Figure 102. (a) By selecting the *Offsets* button from the *BITMAP FILL PATTERN* dialog box of Figure 95, you will activate the *TILE OFFSETS* dialog box (a). Here you can modify the X and Y co-ordinates which will offset the Bitmap patterns. The *Inter Row/Column Offset* will move alternate rows or columns the chosen percentage of the tile size. Compare the patterns of (b) and (c). The pattern in (c) has been offset slightly.

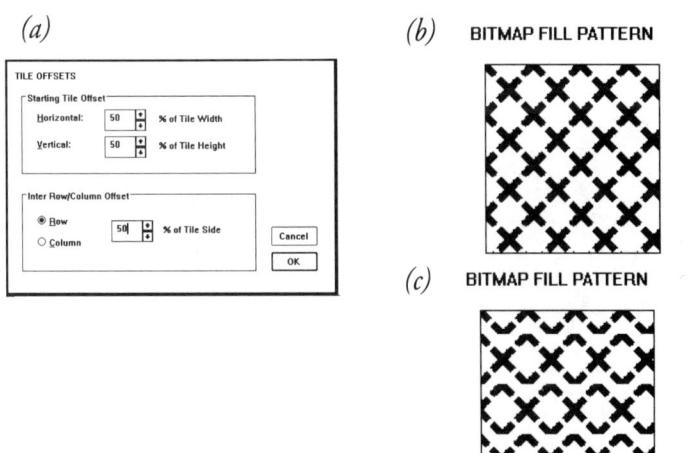

CHAPTER 2: THE TOOLS

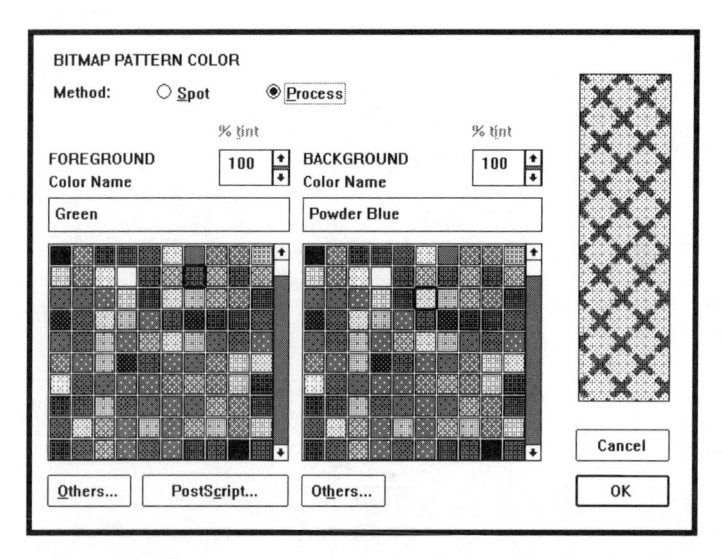

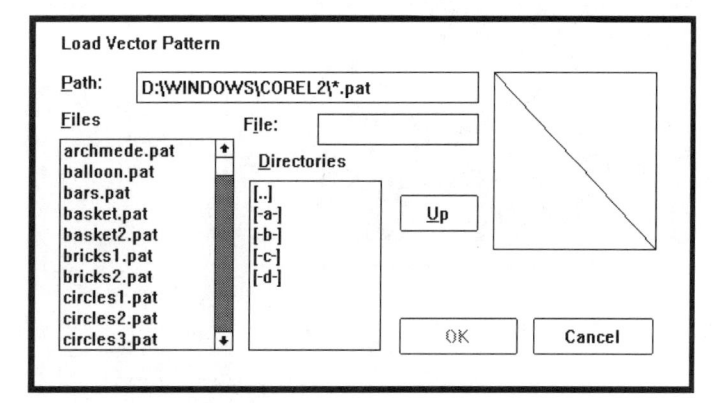

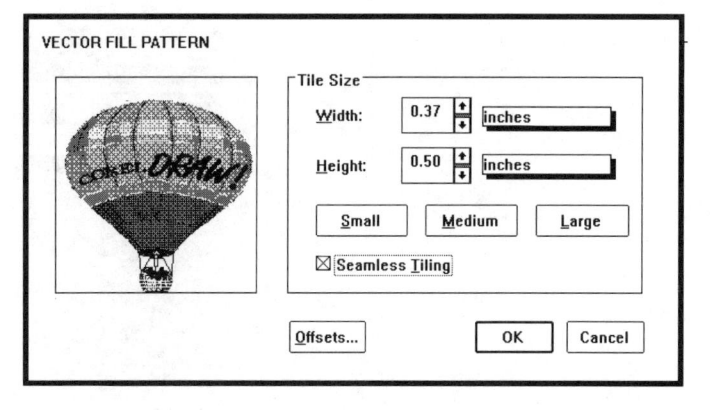

Bitmap color

Figure 103. Once you have selected the Bitmap pattern you wish to use, select OK and the *BITMAP PATTERN COLOR* dialog box will appear. Here you select a color for the foreground and background of the pattern, which will be displayed in the rectangle on the right. Once you return to your page, the chosen bitmap is only visible in the Preview screen.

Vector patterns

Figure 104. The *Load Vector Pattern* dialog box is activated when selecting the Vector icon from the Fill Tool fly-out of Figure 93. Vector patterns can be used as a fill for a closed object. In this dialog box, a list of files with a .PAT extension will be displayed. Make your selection (a bitmap version of this will displayed in the box to the right) and click on OK.

Figure 105. The *VECTOR FILL PATTERN* dialog box is then activated, displaying the Vector pattern in full color. The options you have here determine the size of each tile in the pattern, except for one, the *Seamless Tiling* option. If this option is checked, it will prevent any gaps between tiles in the Preview screen, and when using a printer that is not PostScript.

Editing a vector pattern

Figure 106. You may edit a Vector Pattern in CorelDRAW by opening up the file with the .PAT extension through the *Open* command in the **File** menu. You will need to change the Path extension from .CDR to .PAT via the keyboard.

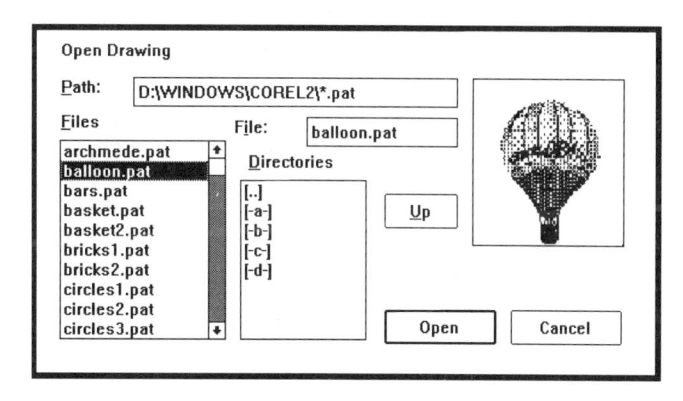

Figure 107. Once you have the file opened, you may edit it as you would any other object within CorelDRAW. Any changes saved will be reflected in the *VECTOR FILL PATTERN* dialog box.

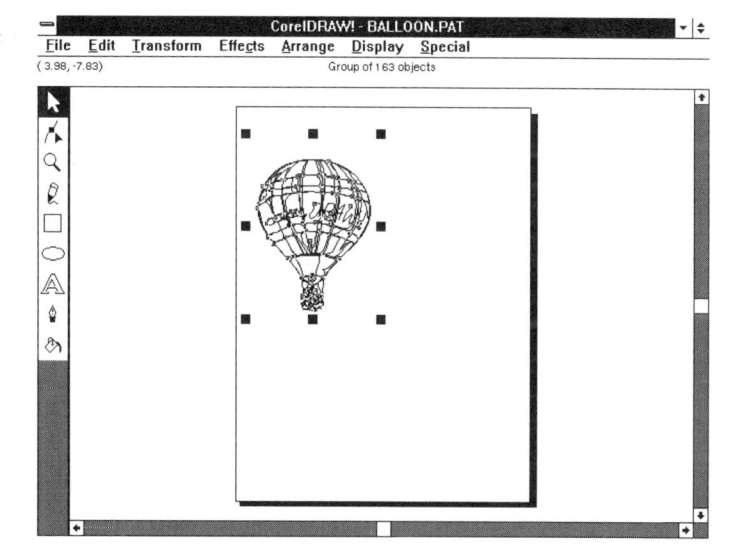

Fountain fills

The *Fountain Fill* dialog box is activated after selecting the Fountain Fill icon from Figure 93. Here you select two colors that will blend together to fill an object. There are two types of fills, *Linear* and *Radial*.

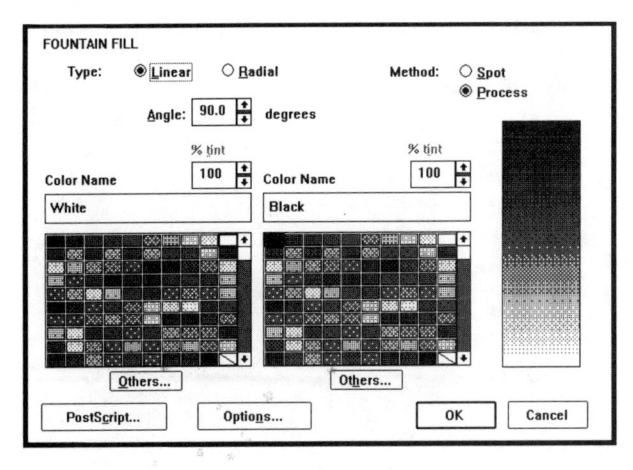

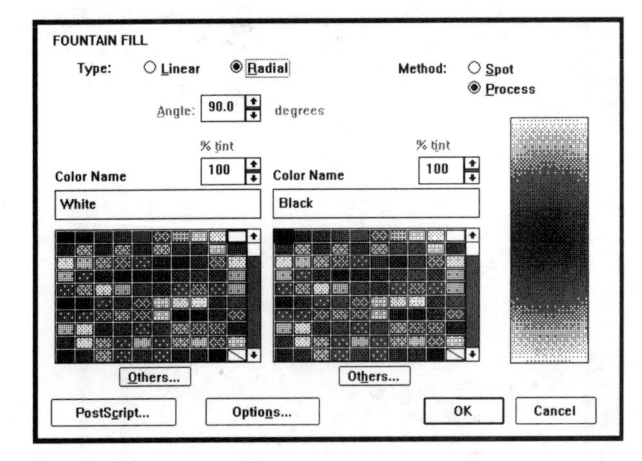

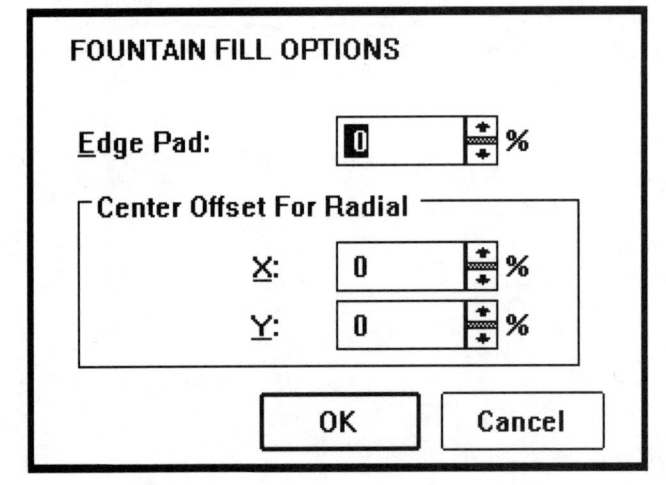

Linear fill

Figure 108. This option will blend two colors within an object in a linear direction, specified in the *Angle* degrees box. The colors and angle selected are displayed in the bar to the right of the dialog box. You must select two different colors in this dialog box, in a similar fashion to that described in the Outline Color section, Figures 79 through 92.

Radial fill

Figure 109. The *Radial Fill* option will blend two colors within an object in a circular direction. The *Angle* option is not available for Radial fills. An example of the fill you have selected is displayed on the right. You must select two different colors in this dialog box, in a similar fashion to that described in the Outline Color section, Figures 79 through 92.

Figure 110. The *Options* button activates the *FOUNTAIN FILL OPTIONS* dialog box. You may change the *Edge Pad* value up to 45%, which will increase the amount of color at the start and end of the specified fill. Because the object acts as a window for a radial fill, this option is useful to apply to asymmetrical objects, where parts of the fill could fall outside of the object. You may also change the center offset of a radial fill by changing the X and Y co-ordinates, which, by default, begin at the center of an object.

PostScript fill

Figure 111. The *PS* option of Figure 93 will activate the *POSTSCRIPT TEXTURE* dialog box. This list of fills allows you to fill the selected object with a variety of patterns, which can only be viewed by printing to a PostScript printer. The options below the list of fills available are used to modify the size and shades of the fills. See Appendix A of the CorelDRAW manual for a comprehensive listing of PostScript fills available.

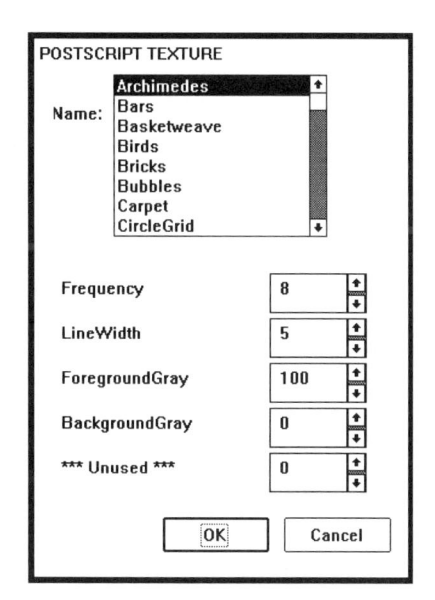

SETTING UP OUTLINE AND FILL DEFAULTS

Figure 112. To set up a default for any outline or fill you wish, select the option with nothing selected on the page. A dialog box similar to this will be activated. Make your selection and select OK.

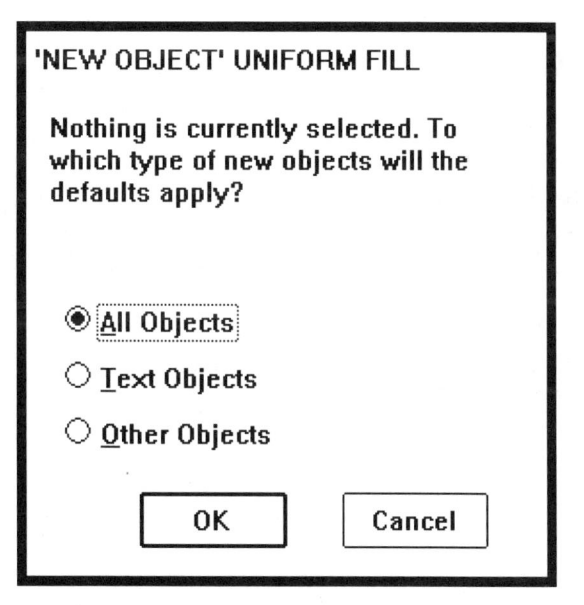

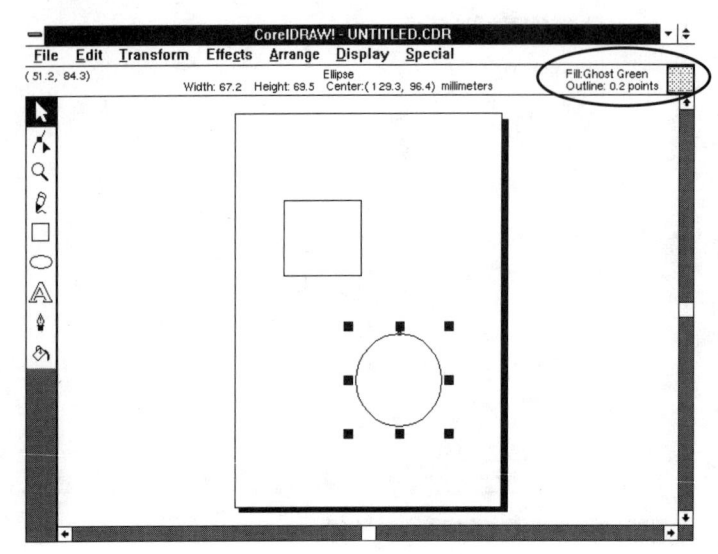

THE FILL INDICATOR

Figure 113. In the top right corner of the Status Line is the *Fill Indicator* which will display the outline and fill of any object selected with the Pick Tool. Use this as your reference point to check the fill and outline details of any object without moving to the Preview screen.

The File Menu   3

The File Menu Commands

The commands contained in the **File** menu are common to most applications that run under Windows. These commands generally relate to a whole CorelDRAW file whereas most of the other commands in the CorelDRAW menus can be used on certain objects on your page.

Figure 1. The File menu.

NEW

Figure 2. This command will give you a completely new CorelDRAW file.

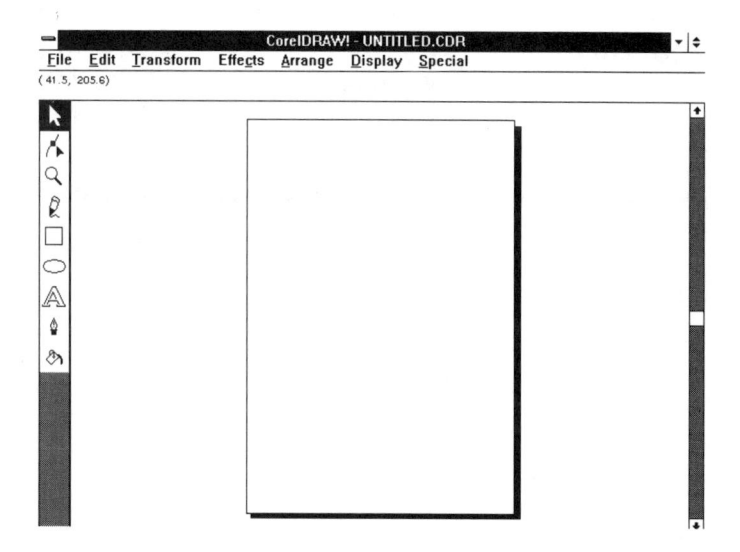

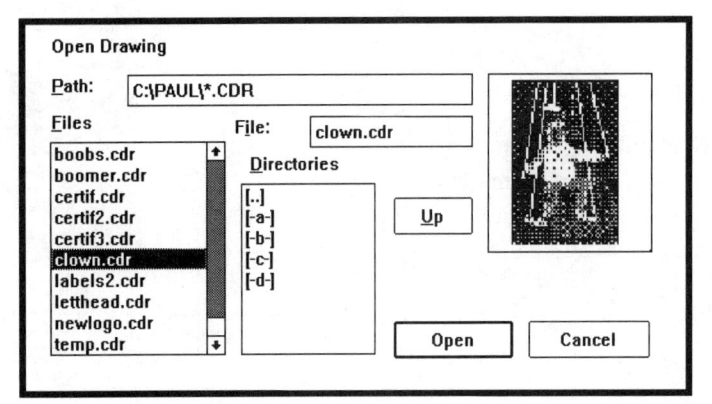

OPEN

Figure 3. The *Open* command will activate the *Open Drawing* dialog box, where you may select the CDR file you wish to open. When you select the file name, if it is a CorelDRAW version 2.0 file, a bitmap image of the file will appear in the box to the right.

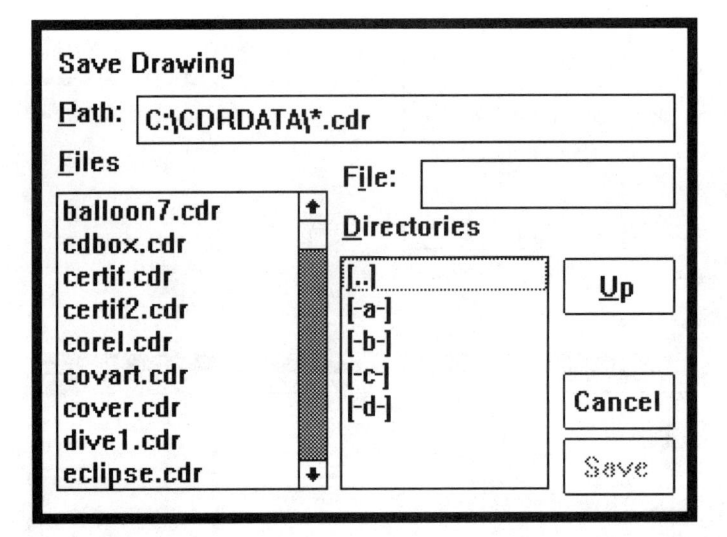

SAVE

Figure 4. The *Save* command will activate the *Save Drawing* dialog box, if you are in an UNTITLED file, or it will save any changes if the file already has a name. In this dialog box you must give your file a name, and choose in which directory and drive you would like to save it.

SAVE AS

Figure 5. The *Save As* command will activate the *Save Drawing* dialog box. If the file has already been saved, it is possible to make a copy of the file by giving it a new name, or saving it into a different directory. If the file is UNTITLED, the *Save As* command produces the same result as the *Save* command.

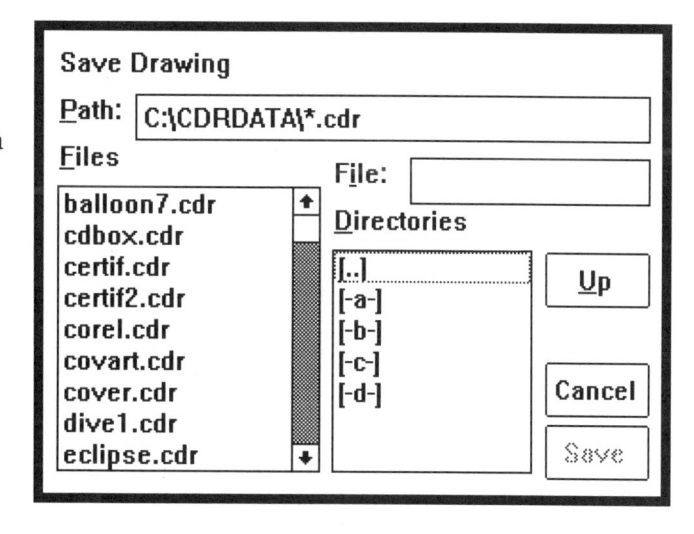

IMPORT

Figure 6. The *Import* command activates the *IMPORT* dialog box. Here you select what type of file you want to import into CorelDRAW. The *For Tracing* option is only available if you are importing a TIF, PCX or BMP file. You choose this option if you plan to trace the image in CorelDRAW.

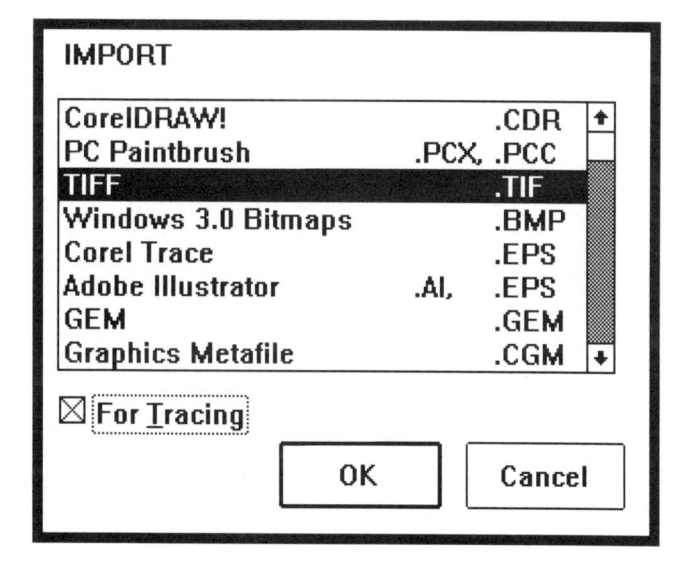

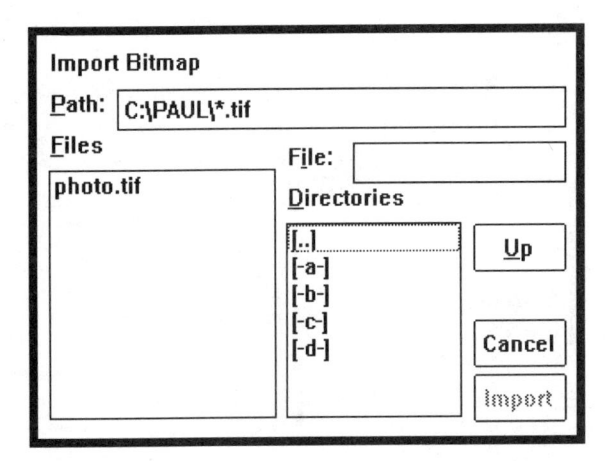

Figure 7. Select OK from the *IMPORT* dialog box of Figure 6 to activate the second *Import Bitmap* dialog box.

CorelDRAW will only display those files in the format that was selected, but from here you have access to all directories and drives on your machine.

EXPORT

Figure 8. The *Export* command allows you to save a file in a variety of different formats for importing into other programs not compatible with the .CDR format. It is also possible to export in CorelDRAW format and if you select the CorelDRAW 1.xx option you can place the file in previous versions of CorelDRAW.

In the *EXPORT* dialog box, select the format of your choice and click on OK.

The *Selected Objects Only* option allows you to export only the section of your drawing that is selected with the Pick Tool.

Include Image Header option gives you a screen representation of the image you exported from CorelDRAW, when you import it into a program such as PageMaker or Ventura. The *Include All Artistic Attributes* option will export the file with all its features included; e.g. fill. The *All Fonts Resident* option, when selected, thinks that all fonts in your CorelDRAW file are fonts available in your printer. The *Resolution* option of the *EXPORT* dialog box is used when creating TIF or PCX bitmaps from your CorelDRAW file. Naturally, the higher the resolution, the better quality the bitmap will be. The *Fixed Size* option is used in conjunction with image header. It gives you three size choices if you are creating an EPS Bitmap image header.

Figure 9. After selecting OK from Figure 8 *EXPORT*, this dialog box appears. In this *Export* dialog box, name the file, and decide where you would like to save it before

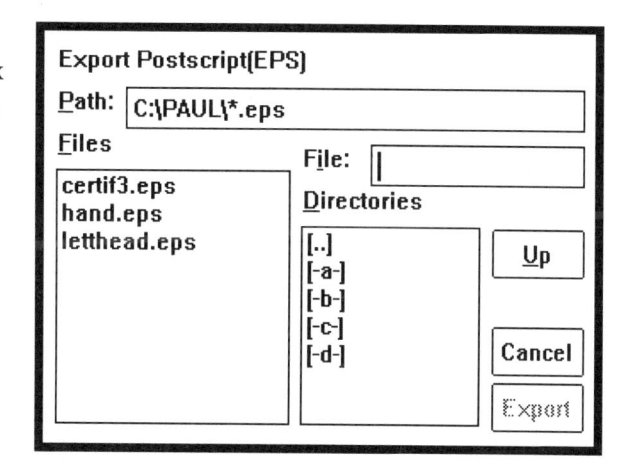

PRINT

Figure 10. The *Print* command activates the *PRINT OPTIONS* dialog box. The first option available in the *PRINT OPTIONS* dialog box is the *Print Only Selected* option. With this checked, only what is selected with the Pick Tool will be printed.

Fit To Page: This will resize your graphic to fill the printed page. *Tile:* Used to print graphics that are larger than the page size in your printer to create posters and large banners.

Figure 11. *Print as Separations:* Will print each different color on a separate page. After selecting OK, the *COLOR SEPARATIONS* dialog box is activated. Here you can make more specific choices about how the color will be printed.

Crop Marks & Crosshairs: (Refer back to Figure 10) Crop marks can be printed on your page but only if the page size is smaller than the printer page size.
Film Negative: This will print your image as a negative. Only available on a PostScript printer.
Include File Info: This option will print the file name, date and time on the page (PostScript only).
All Fonts Resident: By not selecting this option, CorelDRAW will download the relevant fonts enabling the printer to print correctly (PostScript only).
Number of Copies: Specify the number of copies you would like printed.
Scale: You can scale your image by a specific percentage with this option (PostScript only).
Fountain Stripes: The value inserted here determines the number of steps or stripes that will be printed for any fountain fills.
Flatness: This is used to simplify complex images when printing. By increasing the number to 4 or 5 for example, the curves of the drawing may become noticeably rough, as CorelDRAW decreases the number of segments in a curve (PostScript only).
Default Screen Frequency: This option is only available if you have a PostScript printer and will effect the final printed resolution, which will differ depending on the printer.

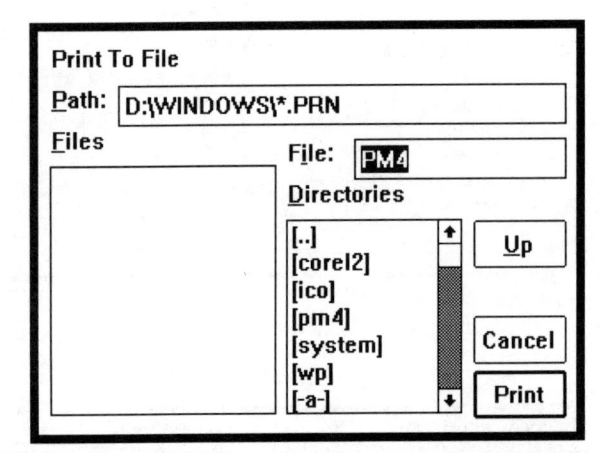

Figure 12. *Print to File:* This option is used when you wish to create a print file to send to a print bureau for typesetting.
For Mac: (Refer to Figure 10) If you select this option in conjunction with the *Print to File* option, it will allow the file to be printed on a Macintosh controlled printer.

Figure 13. *Printer Setup:* In this dialog box, accessed through Figure 10, you can select such things as printer type, page size, orientation, and scaling.

PRINT MERGE

Figure 14. This option is used to combine a word processing document with a CorelDRAW file. This feature is useful for such things as mailing lists, where the image will remain constant, and the name and address will change for each printout. For more details on this procedure consult the CorelDRAW manual on page 188.

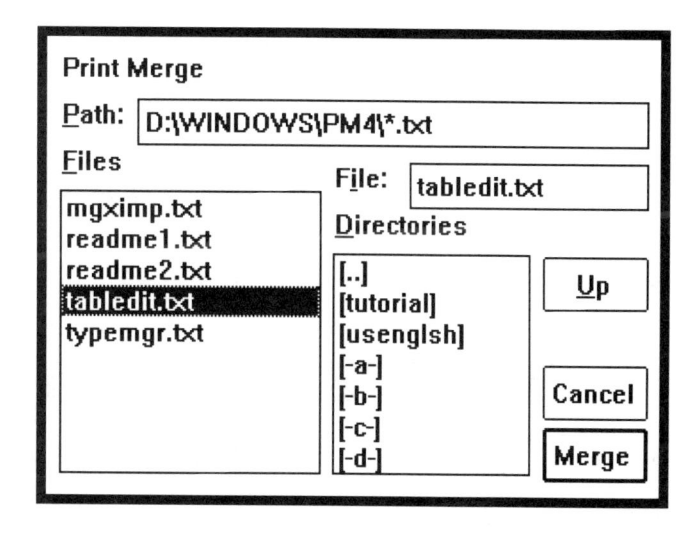

PAGE SETUP

Figure 15. This command is used to set up the page specifications. The *Paper Color* option will activate the *Paper Color* dialog box. This works in the same way the Outline and Fill color dialog boxes work, already explained in Chapter 2. This changes the color of the page on the Preview screen to whatever you select in the *PAPER COLOR* dialog box. It will not print with this color.

Add Page Frame will place a frame the exact dimensions of the page on the screen, which can be filled and outlined and re-sized, as any closed object.

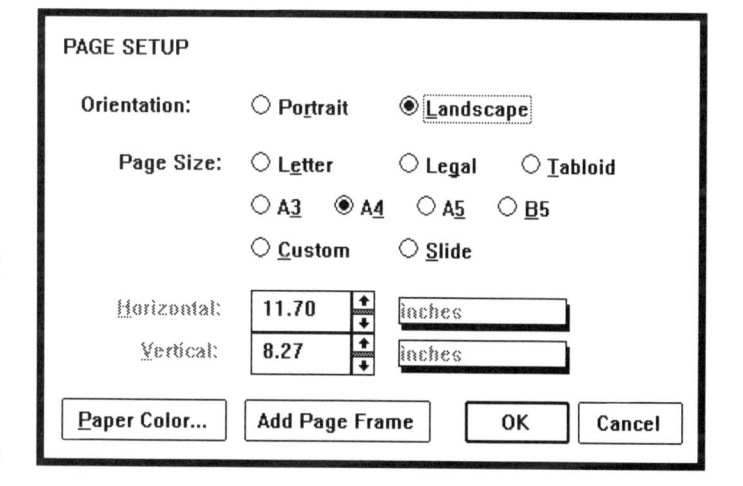

CONTROL PANEL

This command will access the Windows Control Panel. Refer to the Microsoft Windows User's Guide for details.

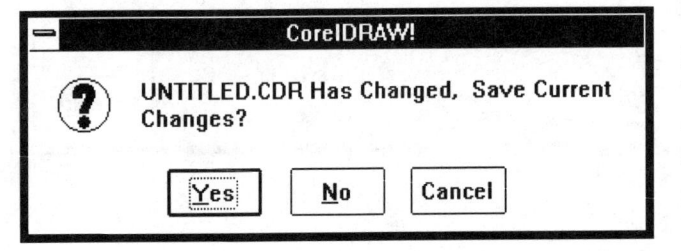

EXIT

Figure 16. This is the command you use when you have finished working with CorelDRAW. If you have made any changes since last saving the current file, you will be given the choice of whether to save these changes or not.

THE EDIT MENU 4

THE EDIT MENU COMMANDS

The commands in the **Edit** menu are used as basic editing options. Some of these commands, such as *Undo, Cut, Copy, Paste, Clear* and *Select All* are common to most Windows applications. It is also the menu used for editing text.

Figure 1. The **Edit** menu.

```
Edit
 Undo              AltBksp
 Redo              AltRet
 Repeat            ^R
 
 Cut               ShiftDel
 Copy              CtrlIns
 Paste             ShiftIns
 Clear             Del
 Duplicate         ^D
 
 Copy Style From...
 Edit Text...      ^T
 Character Attributes...
 
 Select All
```

UNDO

This command will allow you to return the graphic to its previous state before performing the last process. You cannot undo a change of view, any command in the **File** menu, or any selection process.

REDO

The *Redo* command will reinstate whatever was changed by the *Undo* command.

(a)

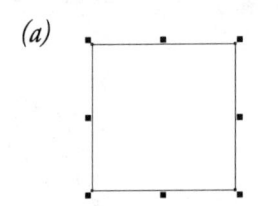

After the square is rotated and duplicated, Repeat is selected.

(b)

(c)

As a result of selecting the Repeat command a third square appears which is rotated to the same degree as the original square.

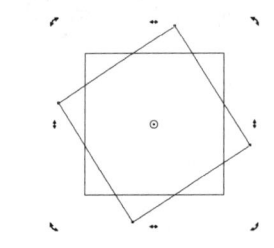

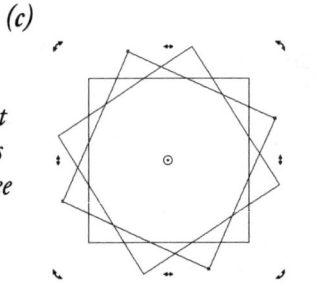

REPEAT

Figure 2. This command will apply the very last process performed on an object, to the currently selected object. See (**a**) and (**b**) for details.

If you rotate a shape with the Pick Tool and leave the original behind (by pressing the + key on the numeric keypad while rotating it) and then select *Repeat*, another square will be rotated to the same degree (Figure **c**).

CUT

The *Cut* command will delete any selected object or objects from the page. It makes a copy of the deleted object to the Windows clipboard, but it will only remain there until the *Cut* or *Copy* command is used again.

COPY

The *Copy* command will make a copy of any selected object or objects to the Windows clipboard leaving the original object behind. It will only remain there until the *Cut* or *Copy* command is used again.

PASTE

This command will allow you to paste back onto the page the last object or objects that had the *Cut* or *Copy* commands applied to them.

CLEAR

The *Clear* command will delete selected objects from the screen permanently, without making a copy of them in the Windows clipboard. You may reverse this command by using the *Undo* command immediately after the *Clear* command.

DUPLICATE

Figure 3. The *Duplicate* command will place a copy of the selected object on the screen. You can alter the position at which the duplicate appears through the *Preferences* command in the **Special** menu. (See Chapter 9, **The Special Menu**.)

(a) The object is selected with the Pick Tool.

(b) The *Duplicate* command is applied.

(c) The text on top has been filled with white to create a shadow effect as seen in the Preview screen.

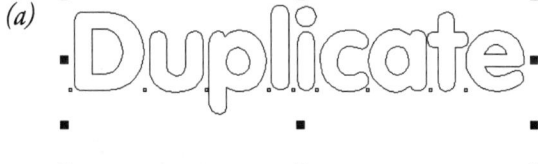

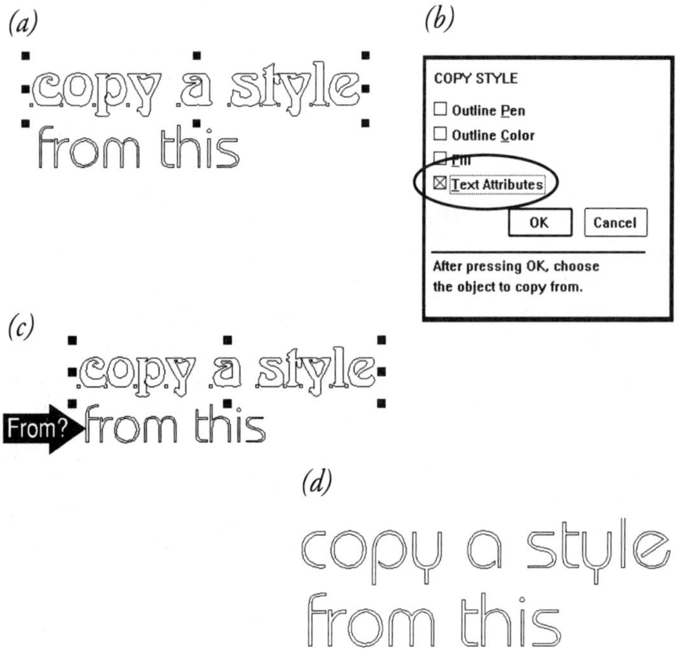

COPY STYLE FROM

Figure 4. This command quickly allows you to copy either *Outline Pen*, *Color*, *Fill* and/or *Text Attributes* from one object to another. This figure illustrates how this is done through the *Copy Style* dialog box. (**a**) Select the object you want to copy the style to (in this case, the top line of text), and choose the *Copy Style From* command. (**b**) Select the required options in this dialog box, and click on OK. (**c**) Select the object to copy the style from (in our case, the bottom line of text). (**d**) The top text string now has the same attributes as the bottom text string.

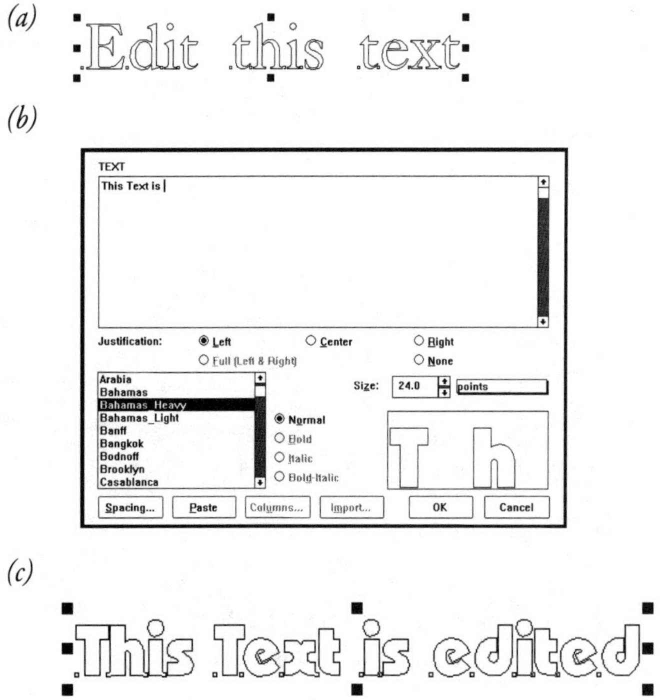

EDIT TEXT

Figure 5. The *Edit Text* command can be used to modify text attributes and/or the spacing of any selected text string. If you have converted a text string to curves, or combined it with another object, you cannot edit it using this command.
(**a**) To use this command, select some text with the Pick Tool, and choose *Edit Text*. (**b**) The *TEXT* dialog box will now appear. The adjustments that can be made in this dialog box are the same as within the *TEXT* dialog box invoked with the Text Tool. (**c**) After editing the text and clicking on OK, the text on the screen will have changed.

CHARACTER ATTRIBUTES

Figure 6. This command can only be used when the Shape Tool has selected a character or characters' nodes.

(**a**) Highlight a node or nodes with the Shape Tool and select this command. The *CHARACTER ATTRIBUTES* dialog box will appear (**b**). Here, you can change the font, style, size, horizontal and vertical position, and the character angle of one or more selected characters in a text string. We selected each letter in turn and changed it slightly. (**c**) Shows the result of these changes.

Note: As an alternative to selecting the Character Attributes command from the Edit menu after highlighting a node(s), you could activate this dialog box by double-clicking on a highlighted node.

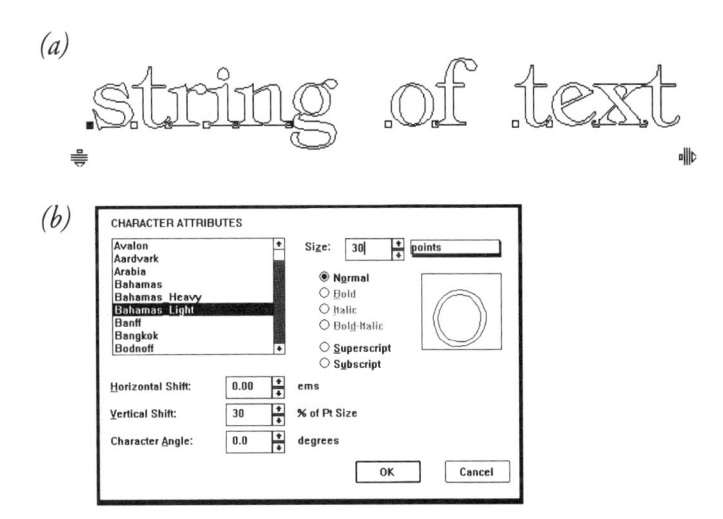

SELECT ALL

Figure 7. This command will select every object on your screen. Once all objects have been selected, you may apply certain commands to them, and all objects will be affected. You must have the Pick Tool selected for this command to be available.

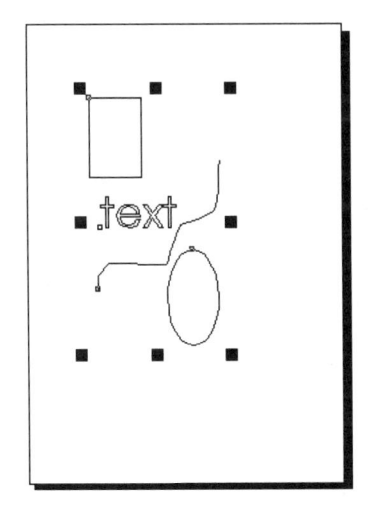

THE TRANSFORM MENU

THE TRANSFORM MENU COMMANDS

The commands in the **Transform** menu deal with the moving, resizing and angle of selected object(s) on your page.

Figure 1. The *Transform* menu.

```
Transform
Move...              ^L
Rotate & Skew...     ^N
Stretch & Mirror...  ^Q
Clear Transformations
```

MOVE

Figure 2. The *Move* command is an alternative process to moving objects with the mouse.
Select the object to be moved with the Pick Tool, and then select the *Move* command.
(a) The *Move* dialog box is invoked when you select this command.
The *Horizontal* and *Vertical* values allow you to move an object to one hundredth of an inch, which is far more accurate than you could do with the mouse and your eye.
The *Leave Original* option, if selected, will make a copy of the object and move it the specified distance.
(b) The *Absolute Coordinates*, if selected, will move the object relative to the ruler measurements

(a)
```
MOVE
Absolute moves are relative
to rulers.
Horizontal: 0.00  inches
Vertical:   0.00  inches
  ☐ Leave Original
  ☐ Absolute Coordinates
     OK      Cancel
```

(b)
```
MOVE
Absolute moves are relative
to rulers.
Horizontal: 3   inches
Vertical:   -4  inches
  ☐ Leave Original
  ☒ Absolute Coordinates
     OK      Cancel
```

CHAPTER 5: THE TRANSFORM MENU

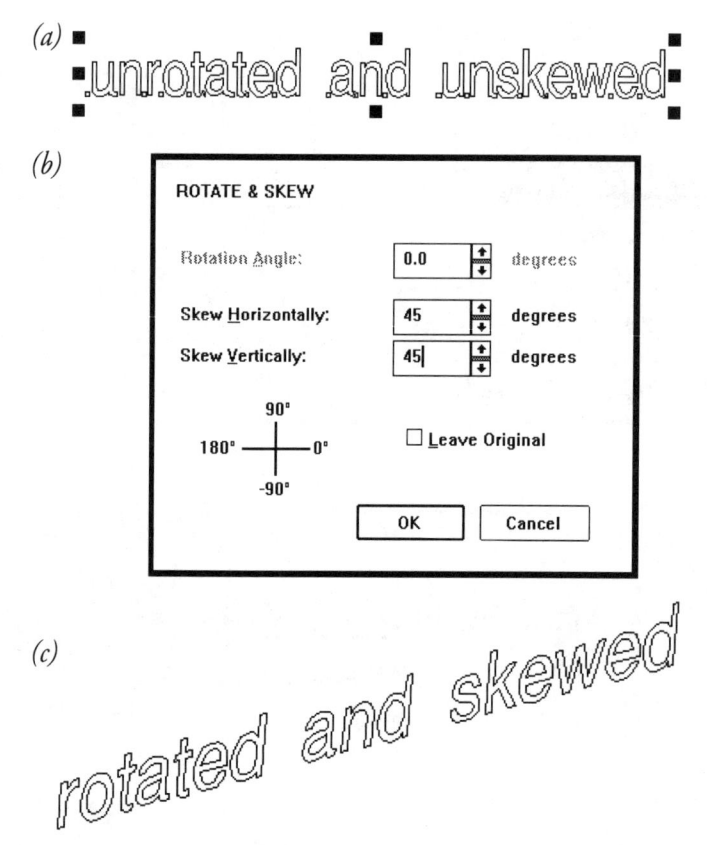

on the page. You must select which node you would like aligned with the co-ordinates from the box that appears.

ROTATE & SKEW

Figure 3. This command gives you an alternative to the rotate and skew handles that are activated by double-clicking with the mouse on an unselected object.

(a) Select the object with the Pick Tool and access the *Rotate & Skew* command.
(b) In the *ROTATE & SKEW* dialog box that appears, you may enter specific values which will effect the angle of rotation and/or skewing of a selected object. If you select the *Leave Original* option, CorelDRAW will make a copy of it, but apply any rotation or skew angles you have specified to the copy.
(c) This is the result of the changes we made in the dialog box of (b).

STRETCH & MIRROR

Figure 4. This command will activate the *STRETCH & MIRROR* dialog box, offering an alternative method of stretching and mirroring with the mouse. Changing the setting in either the *Stretch Horizontally* or *Stretch Vertically* options will stretch the selected object(s) to whatever percentage you insert. The *Horiz Mirror* and *Vert Mirror* options will mirror the selected object(s) in the direction you specify (either horizontal or vertical). The *Leave Original* option leaves the original object behind as well as stretching or mirroring it.

CLEAR TRANSFORMATIONS

The *Clear Transformations* command will return any selected object(s) to its original state before most transformations were applied to it. These include stretching, mirroring, resizing, rotating, skewing, enveloping and changing perspective.

Figure 5. (a) Select the object with the Pick Tool, and then choose the *Clear Transformations* command.

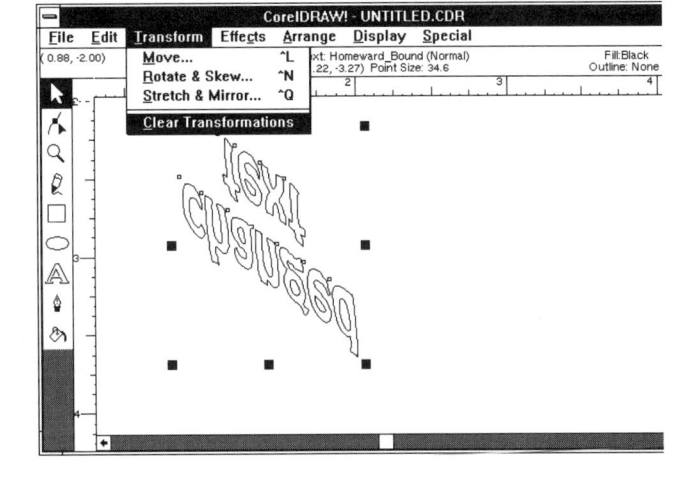

Figure 5. (b) This figure shows the results of using this command on the text in Figure 5 (a).

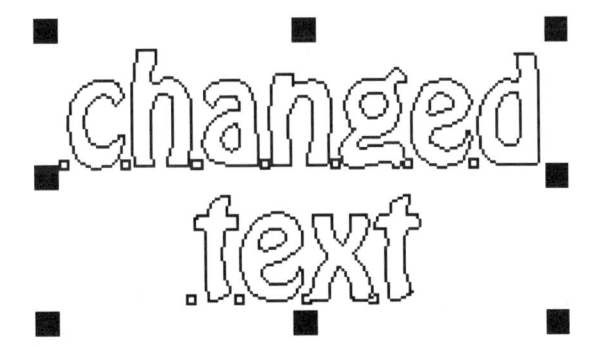

The Effects Menu   6

The Effects Menu Commands

The commands in the **Effects** menu will directly set up an object(s) so that it may be manipulated further with the Shape Tool, after the command has been selected. This is also the menu used to blend objects and give them a 3-D appearance through extruding.

Figure 1. The **Effects** menu.

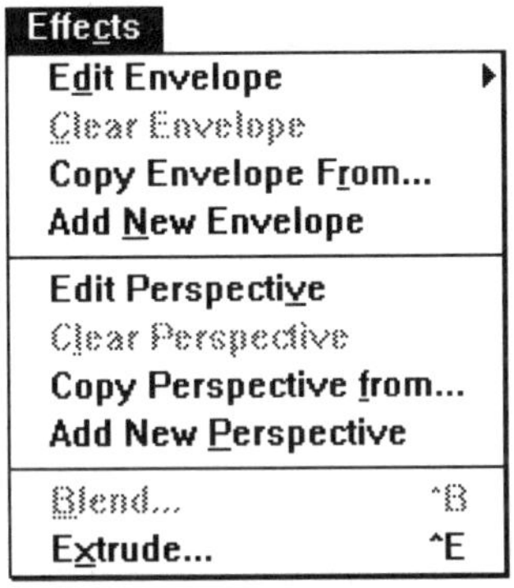

EDIT ENVELOPE

Figure 2. This command activates a sub-menu as shown in this figure.

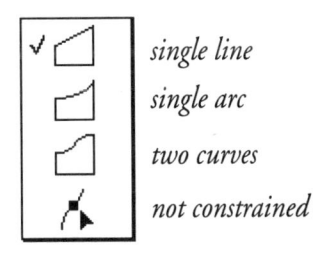

The *Envelope* command is used to change the shape of an object with the Shape Tool. After selecting a specific envelope in the sub-menu, the selected object will appear on screen with a dotted box around it. You can then manipulate the object by moving any of the eight handles around the dotted box, with the Shape Tool.

There are four envelope editing modes, as illustrated here. The last mode is the one you would use to mould an object into an unusual shape, such as text within a circle, or into an asymmetrical shape. The last option also has two control points attached to each node for further manipulation.

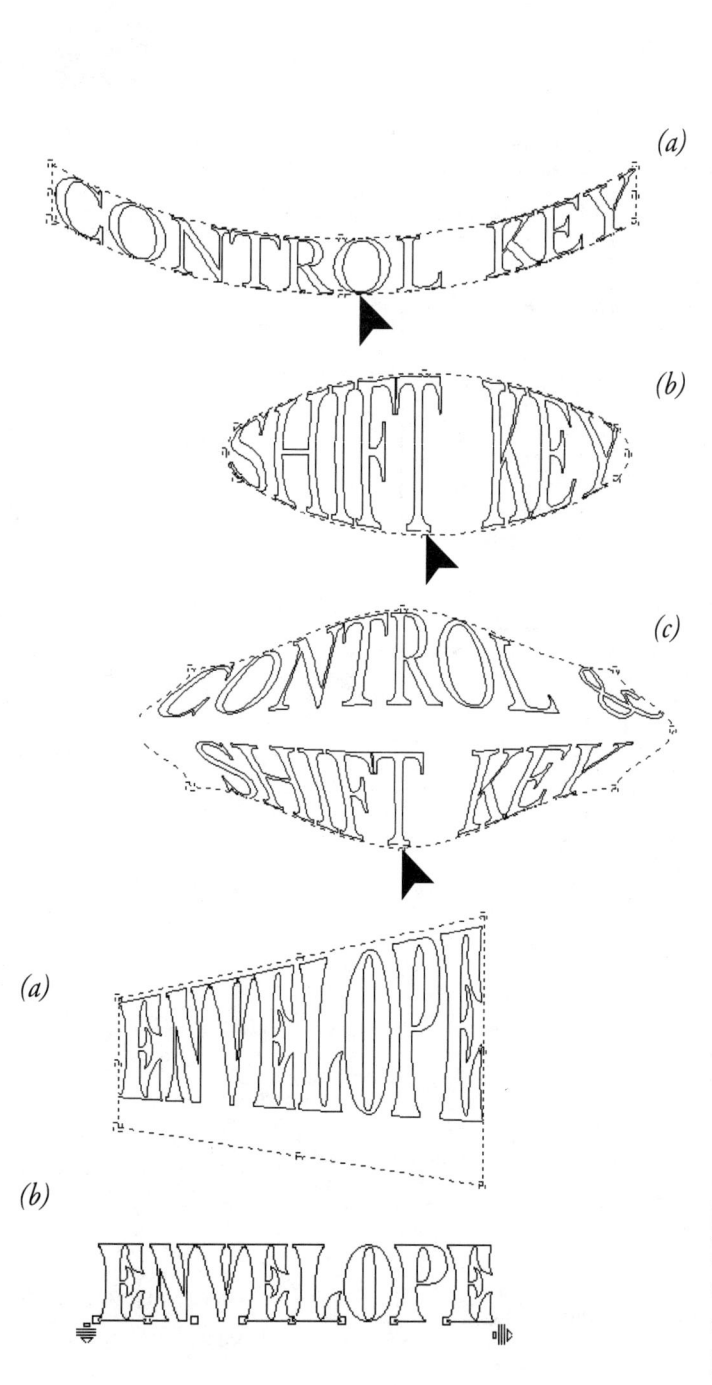

Control and shift keys

Figure 3. Holding these keys down allows you to create mirrored and identical sides of an enveloped object, using the Shape Tool. These keys can only be used with the first three envelope modes.

(a) The Control key will cause handles on the opposite sides to move in the same direction.

(b) The Shift key will cause the handles on the opposite sides to move in the opposite direction.

(c) The Control and Shift keys will cause all handles on all side to move in opposite directions.

CLEAR ENVELOPE

Figure 4. (a) This command can be applied to a selected object that has been enveloped.

(b) This object will then change back to its original shape. If you have applied more than one envelope to this object, it will restore the object back to the previous envelope.

COPY ENVELOPE FROM

This command will copy the shape of one enveloped object to another object.

Figure 5. (a) Select the object that you wish to copy the envelope to and choose the *Copy Envelope From* command. A *From?* arrow head will appear, allowing you to click on the object's outline that you are copying the envelope from.

(b) The envelope of the top text has been copied to the bottom text.

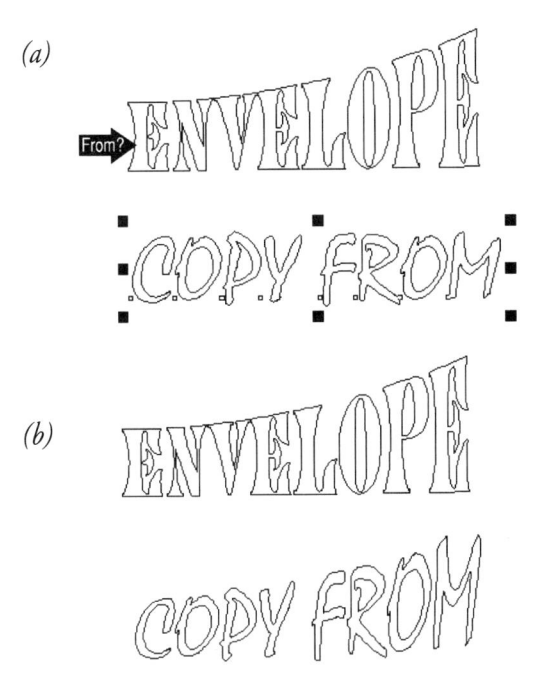

ADD NEW ENVELOPE

Figure 6. This command allows you to add a fresh envelope over an existing one. Once you have applied this command to a selected object, you can then go to the *Envelope* command and choose another envelope mode.

(a) Select the object with the Shape Tool (it can also be selected with the Pick Tool), and click on *Add New Envelope*.

(b) CorelDRAW gives you a fresh envelope around the object without changing the original shape.

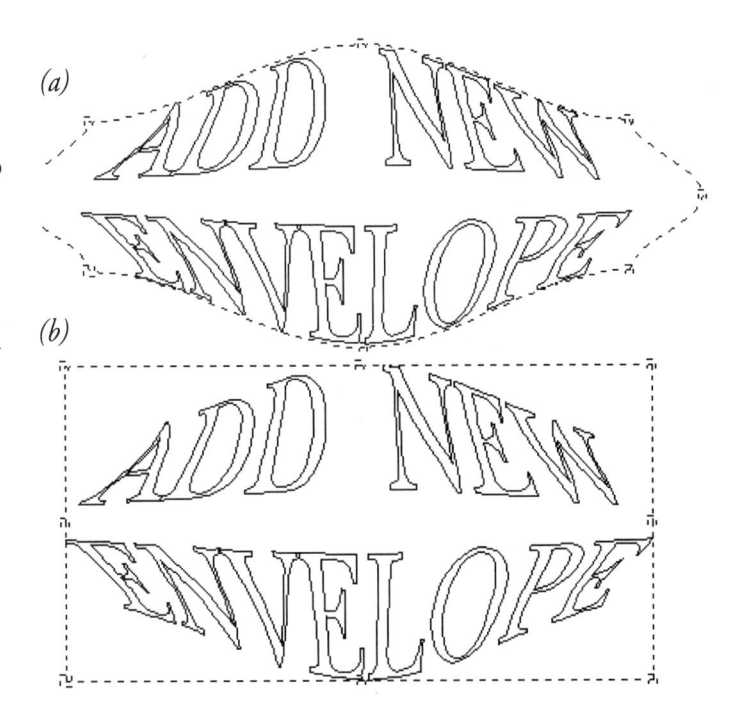

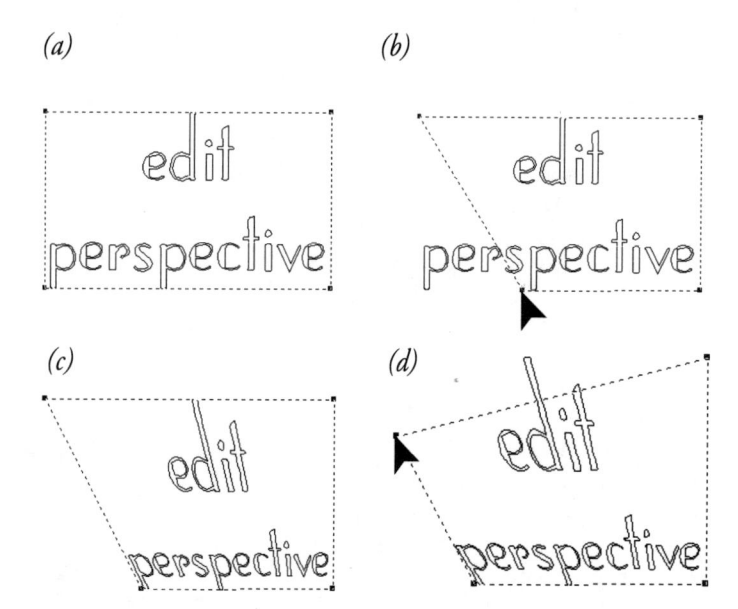

EDIT PERSPECTIVE

The Perspective feature in CorelDRAW allows you to change the sense of depth of an object.

The *Edit Perspective* command, when applied to a selected object, will surround the object with a dotted box.

(a)

(b)

(c)

(d)

Figure 7. (a) This text has had the *Edit Perspective* command applied to it.

(b) The perspective box is being moved with the Shape Tool.

(c) The result of the first move.

(d) You may continue to move the perspective box until you are satisfied with the results. Watch the Status Line to see the position of the vanishing points.

CLEAR PERSPECTIVE

This command will change the object back to its original state before the last perspective was added. If you have applied more than one perspective, it will only erase the last one applied.

Note: This command will not work if the object has since had an envelope applied to it.

COPY PERSPECTIVE FROM

Figure 8. This command allows you to copy the perspective of one object to another.

(a) The top text block is selected with the Pick Tool, and then *Copy Perspective* is selected. The cursor changes to a *From?* arrow, which you must click on the object to copy from.

(b) Shows the results.

(a)

(b)

ADD NEW PERSPECTIVE

This command allows you to add a new perspective outline to any object. If the object has previously had a perspective applied, it will apply a new one, without effecting the current shape. If it has not, it will also apply a new one, as the *Edit Perspective* command does.

Figure 9. (a) This text string has had one perspective box applied to it.

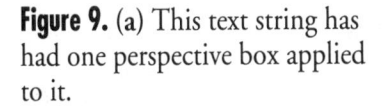

(b) After applying the *Add New Perspective* command, a new perspective outline appears.

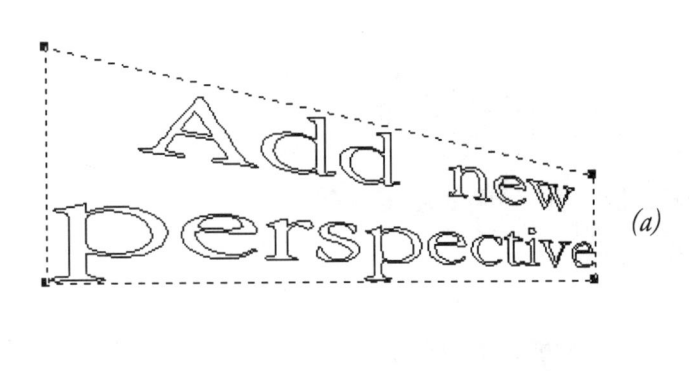

(a)

(b)

BLEND

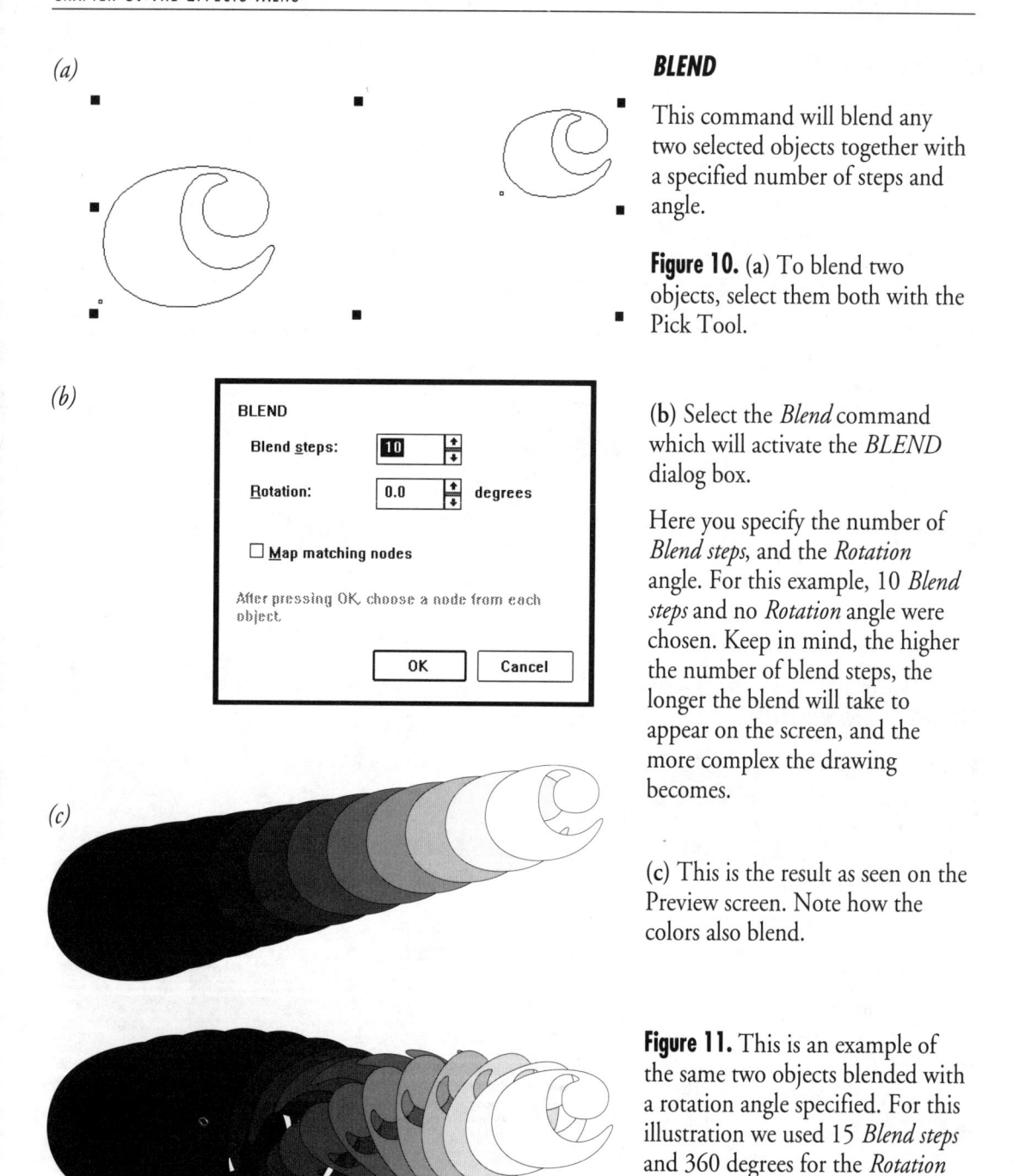

This command will blend any two selected objects together with a specified number of steps and angle.

Figure 10. (a) To blend two objects, select them both with the Pick Tool.

(b) Select the *Blend* command which will activate the *BLEND* dialog box.

Here you specify the number of *Blend steps*, and the *Rotation* angle. For this example, 10 *Blend steps* and no *Rotation* angle were chosen. Keep in mind, the higher the number of blend steps, the longer the blend will take to appear on the screen, and the more complex the drawing becomes.

(c) This is the result as seen on the Preview screen. Note how the colors also blend.

Figure 11. This is an example of the same two objects blended with a rotation angle specified. For this illustration we used 15 *Blend steps* and 360 degrees for the *Rotation* angle.

Figure 12. The *Map matching nodes* option in the *Blend* dialog box of Figure 10(b) allows you to select one node per object, which CorelDRAW will use as the location points for the blend. If you select this option, after clicking on OK in the BLEND dialog box, the nodes of one of the objects will appear and the cursor changes into an arrow as in Figure (**a**). Here you click on the required node.

(**b**) The second object's nodes then become apparent and again you select the required node with the arrow.

(**c**) The two objects will now blend according to the two nodes selected.

Creating highlights

Figure 13. The *Blend* feature is also useful for creating highlights within filled objects.

(**a**) We have drawn two objects that we will blend together to form a highlight.
(**b**) Both objects have had color applied to them.
(**c**) The two objects have been blended together.
(**d**) This is how the blend looks on the Preview screen.

Note: Make sure the lighter colored object is the front object or you will not see the effect.

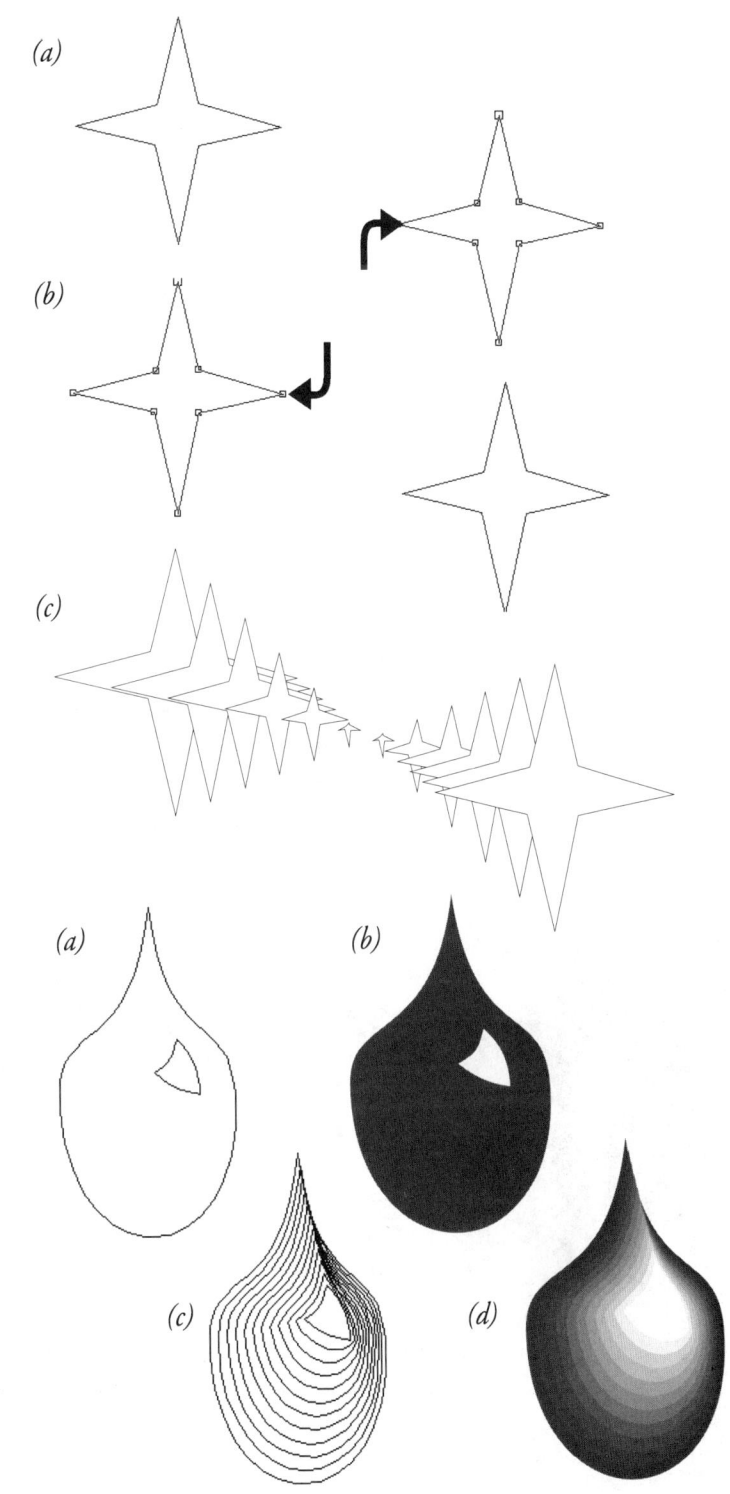

Chapter 6: The Effects Menu

(a)

(b)

(c)

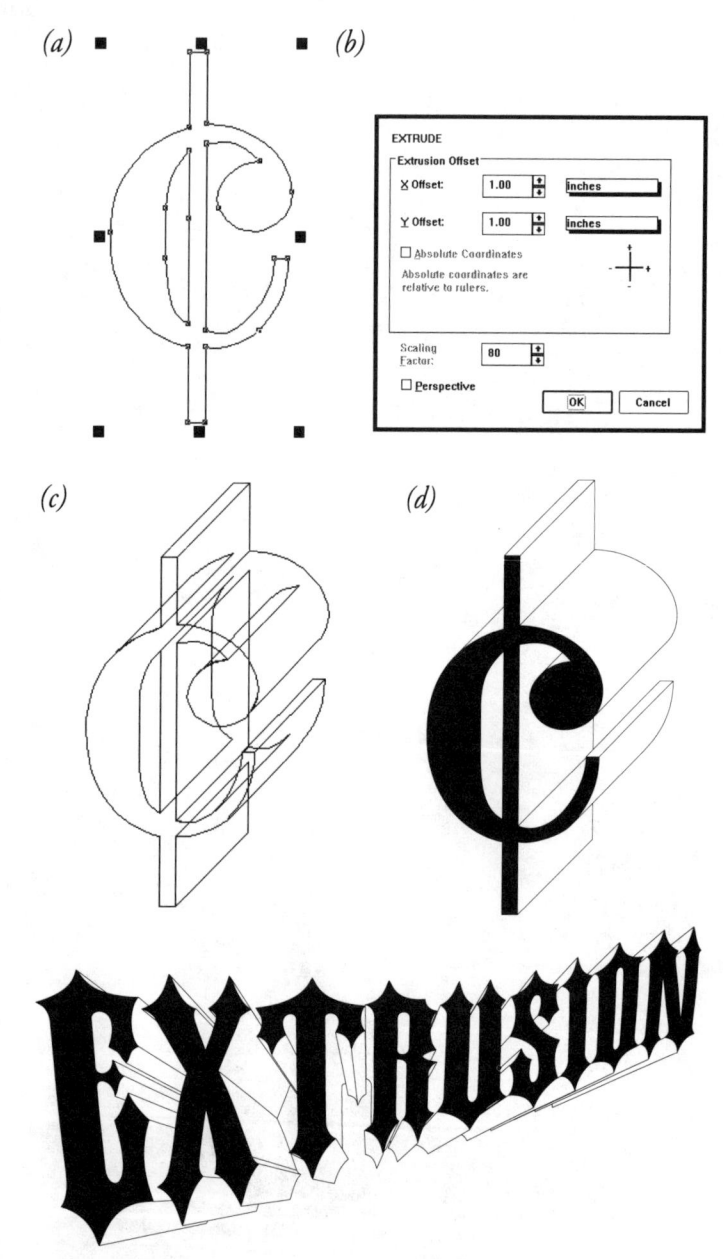

(d)

Figure 15. This text has had its perspective modified and has had an envelope mode applied to it. The *Extrude* specifications were: X = 0 inches, Y = -1 inch, *Scaling Factor* of 60%, and *Perspective* turned on. The extrusion also had a thin black outline and a white fill applied to it.

EXTRUDE

Figure 14. The *Extrude* command can be used to give an object a three dimensional effect. The extruded objects that are created can be filled and outlined independently of the original object.

(**a**) To extrude an object, select it with the Pick Tool. Then select the *Extrude* command, which will activate the *EXTRUDE* dialog box.
(**b**) In this dialog box you must first specify the X and/or Y offset for the extrusion. For example if you have X as 1 inch and Y as 1 inch, this will force the extrusion to go 1 inch to the right and 1 inch above the object.
(**c**) This is the result of our extrusion as seen on the working screen.
(**d**) This is how the object looks on the Preview screen after we have changed the fill of the extrusion.

If you select the *Absolute Co-ordinates* option, the X and Y Offset points will be matched to the rulers on the screen.

Extruded objects will be grouped and can be ungrouped to manipulate or edit each piece of extrusion. An extrusion will always have the same fill and outline as the original object.

76

CHAPTER 6: THE EFFECTS MENU

Figure 16. The *Scaling Factor* percentage of Figure 14(b) determines how big the extrusion will be in relation to the original object. The settings can be from 0 to 400. *Scaling Factor* percentages can only be selected when the *Perspective* has been turned on in the *Extrude* dialog box.

scaling factor of 150%   *scaling factor of 300%*

Figure 17. The *Perspective* option will determine whether the extrusion will project towards a vanishing point, or whether its extrusion lines remain parallel to each other.

(a)

(a) This shows an extrusion with *Perspective* turned on.

(b)

(b) This is the the same extrusion as (a) with *Perspective* turned off.

Figure 18. Lines can also be extruded for an interesting effect.

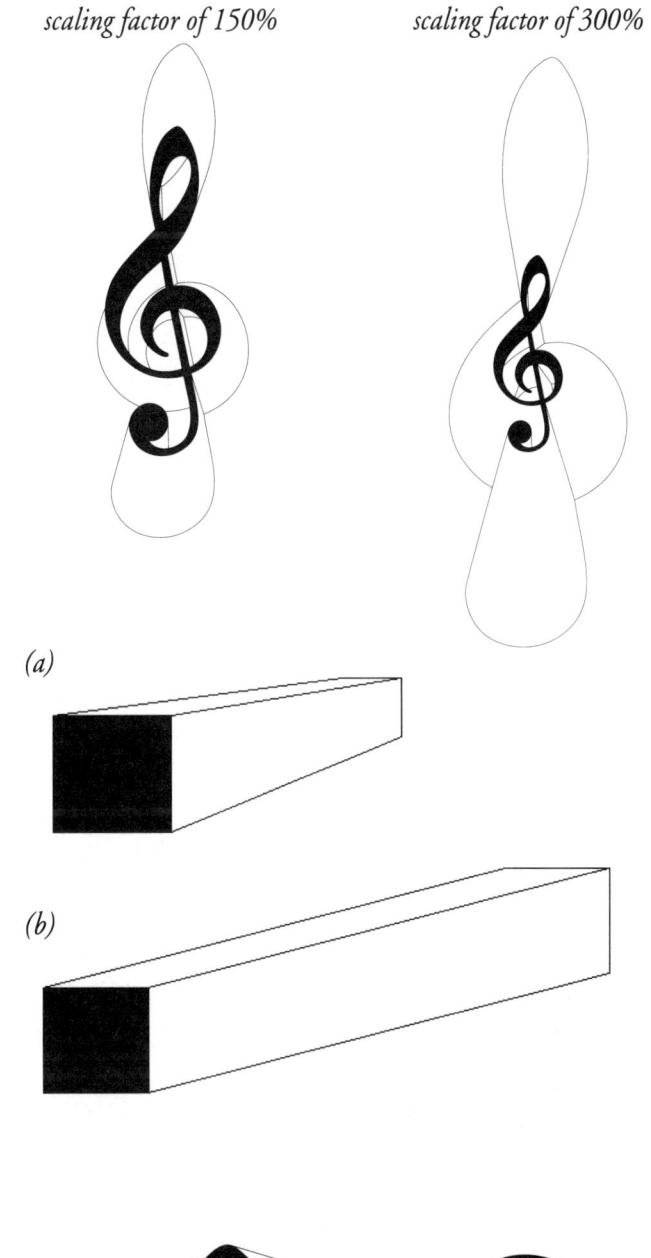

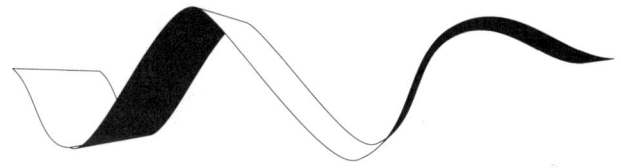

77

THE ARRANGE MENU

7

THE ARRANGE MENU COMMANDS

The commands in the **Arrange** menu will affect the arrangement and drawing position of object(s) in your current file, as well as determining whether the objects are independent or made up of other objects.

Figure 1. The Arrange menu.

```
Arrange
  To Front        ShiftPgUp
  To Back         ShiftPgDn
  Forward One     PgUp
  Back One        PgDn
  Reverse Order
  ─────────────────────────
  Group           ^G
  Ungroup         ^U
  ─────────────────────────
  Combine         ^C
  Break Apart     ^K
  ─────────────────────────
  Convert To Curves ^V
  ─────────────────────────
  Align...        ^A
  Fit Text To Path ^F
  Align To Baseline ^Z
  Straighten Text
```

TO FRONT

Figure 2. By default, in CorelDRAW, the last object drawn or placed on the page is the one that sits on top of any other object.

(a)

(**a**) If you wish to bring an object to the front of all other objects, select it with the Pick Tool, and then choose the *To Front* command.

(b)

(**b**) The results can be seen in this figure. The circle was selected and had the *To Front* command applied to it.

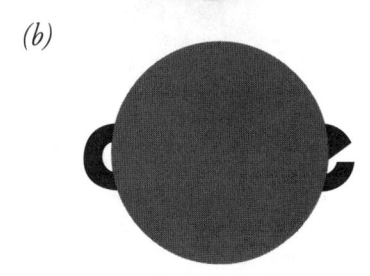

79

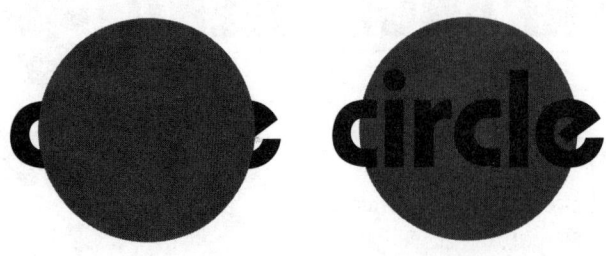

With the circle still selected you can choose the To Back command to send the circle behind the text again.

TO BACK

This command is the opposite to the *To Front* command. If you wish to send any object that is sitting on top of all other objects, select it with the Pick Tool, and then choose the *To Back* command.

FORWARD ONE

This command will move the currently selected object forward one layer.

BACK ONE

This command will move the currently selected object back one layer.

REVERSE ORDER

Figure 3. *Reverse Order*, when applied to two or more selected objects, will reverse the layers in which they appear, from front to back to back to front.

The squares on the left were all selected with the Pick Tool and the Reverse Order command was chosen. The result is shown on the right.

GROUP

Figure 4. This command allows you to 'group' together more than one object so that it can then be treated as a single object. You may color and manipulate the grouped objects, as you would a single object, making this a quick way to apply attributes to more than one object at a time.

To group objects, select them with the Pick Tool and choose the *Group* command. When you select any object of a group, all objects will automatically become selected. The Shape Tool cannot be used on a grouped object, but you can use the Pick Tool to resize and move a grouped object.

You can apply most features to a grouped object, except for the following: *Combine, Break Apart, Edit Text, Fit Text To Path, Straighten Text, Align To Baseline, Blend and Extrude.*

Note: *You may group together grouped objects with other single objects or other groups. You may have up to ten sub-levels of grouping within a group.*

(a) These objects are not yet grouped, as they can be selected as individual objects. The text is the currently selected object.

(b) After selecting all objects and applying the Group command to them, it has become a group of eight objects. Grouping will also conserve memory.

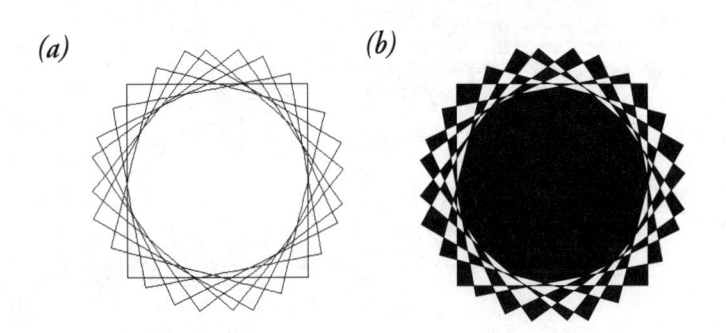

UNGROUP

This command will undo what the *Group* command does, returning each object to its independent status, so that you can manipulate any single object.

COMBINE

The *Combine* command is a different type of grouping, which can be used for a number of effects and reasons. When two or more objects are combined, wherever they overlap will be a gap or window that can be seen through. This can be used to create a mask effect, where one object will be visible through parts of another object on top.

Figure 5. To create this image, the text and the rectangle were selected and then combined together, which created a transparent area where the text and the rectangle overlapped. The image of the unicorn was then placed behind it. If the unicorn was placed on the page last, you would have to use the *To Back* command on it.

Figure 6. (a) These rectangles were created using the *Blend* command. Before combining them, we gave them all a black fill.
(b) Combining them together has created the interesting effect in this figure.

Figure 7. The *Combine* command can also be used to join two separate objects together if you wanted them to be part of the same structure.

(a) Here we want to join the hand to the rest of the body.

(b) Select the two separate objects with the Pick Tool, and apply the *Combine* command to them.

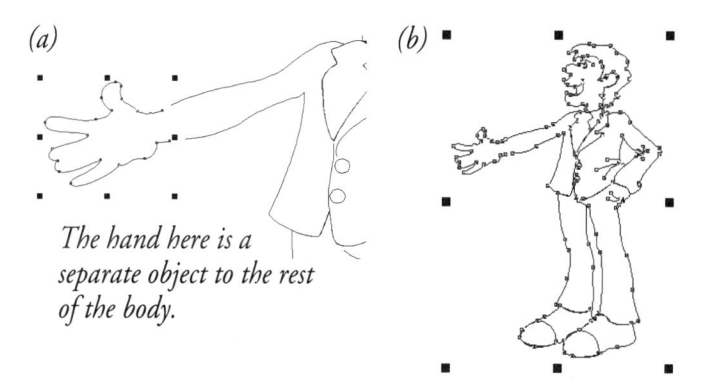

(a)

The hand here is a separate object to the rest of the body.

(b)

Here both the hand and the body were selected with the Pick Tool and then the Combine command was selected. The two objects are now one.

Figure 8. The hand and the body are now part of the same object. You could then go on to further connect them by joining the hand and the arm through the *Node Edit* dialog box. This is done by selecting both nodes you intend to join with the Shape Tool. (Hold down the Shift key to select more than one node at a time.) Then you double-click on one of the nodes to activate the *Node Edit* dialog box, where you select the *Join* option.

Only sections of the same object can be joined, not two different objects. The *Combine* command made the two separate objects one, which allowed us then to join them.

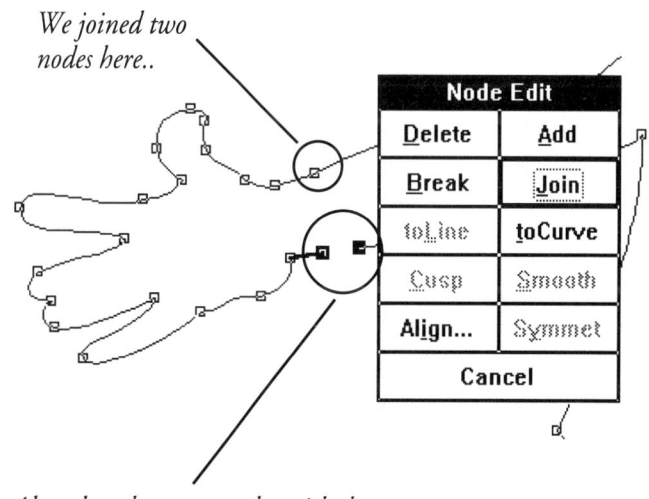

We joined two nodes here..

Also select these two nodes with the Shape Tool and double-click inside one of them to activate the Node Edit dialog box. Here you choose the Join option.

Note: *Once text, circles and squares have been combined with something, they are automatically converted to curves. They cannot be edited as they originally could, and cannot be reverted back to their original state either.*

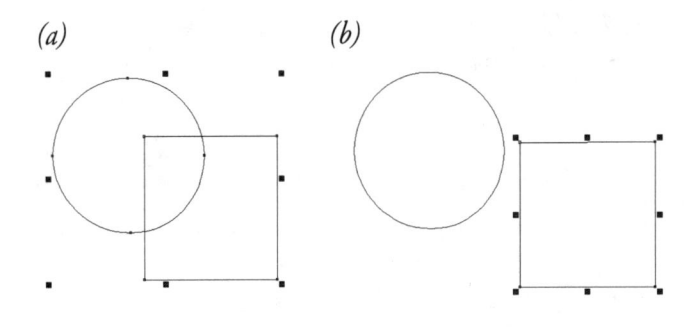

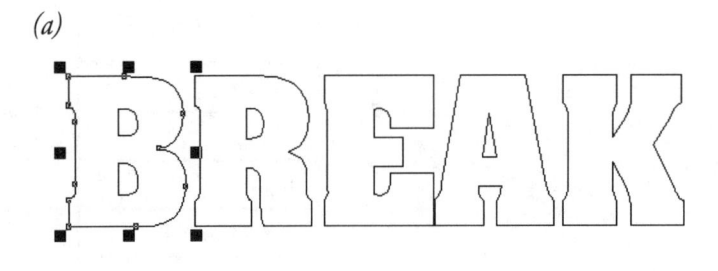

BREAK APART

The *Break Apart* command is applied to objects that have been combined.

Figure 9. (a) This square and circle were combined together to become one object. If you now wanted them to be two separate objects again, select the combined object with the Pick Tool and choose the *Break Apart* command.

(b) The circle and the square are now two separate objects again and can be treated as such. Here the square was selected and dragged away from the circle.

Figure 10. (a) In the case of text, it must be converted to curves before it can be broken apart. (See the *Convert To Curves* command in this menu.) Remember, once text has been converted to curves it cannot be edited as text anymore. Breaking text apart allows you to select each piece of text individually, and apply a different fill to each one.

(b) Here we have applied a different Bitmap Pattern Fill to each piece of text.

Figure 11. Whenever you break text apart, it is important to note that some pieces of text such as an A are made up of two objects. When you do use the *Break Apart* command on these letters, both the objects that make up the letter have to be selected with the Pick Tool and combined, or they will not look like normal letters on the Preview screen or when printed.

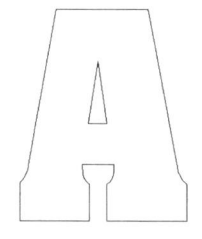

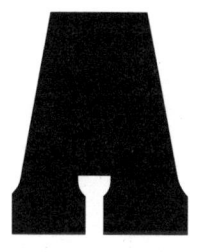

This letter A was converted to curves and then broken apart. See how the middle section of the letter cannot be seen. It also has a black fill.

To solve this problem we selected both sections of the letter A and combined them. This is because, whenever two objects are combined, there will be a gap or cutout where they overlap (see Combine).

CONVERT TO CURVES

Figure 12. The *Convert To Curves* command can be applied to text, ellipses, or rectangles, so they may be manipulated with the Shape Tool as you would any freehand line.

(**a**) Here the command has been applied to a text string, and it is now possible to change the shape of the text pieces by holding the Shape Tool down in one of the nodes and moving it. See how the text is now made up of a series of nodes.

(**b**) In this example the whole text string has been changed, which can be seen clearly on the Preview screen.

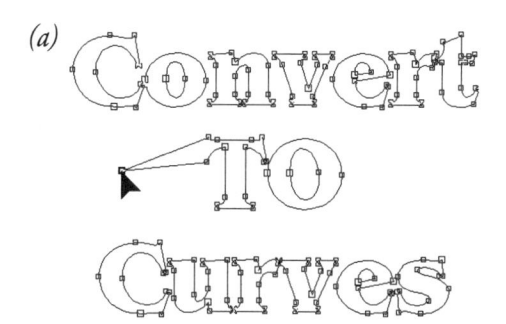

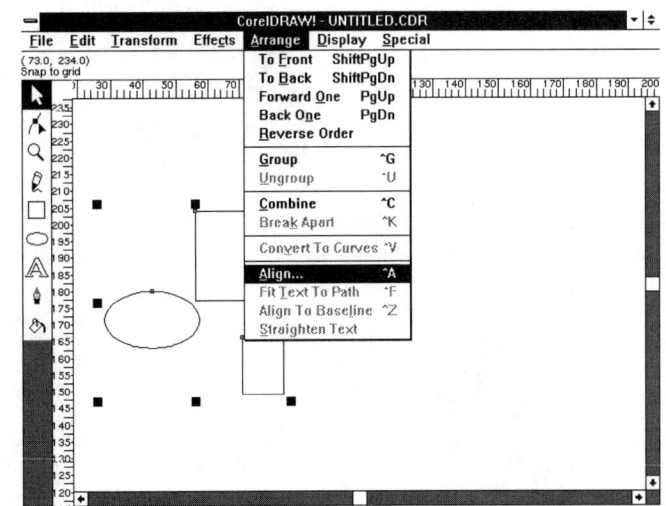

ALIGN

The *Align* command allows you to automatically line up objects on your page.

Figure 15. (a) Select the objects with the Pick Tool you wish to align, and then choose the *Align* command.

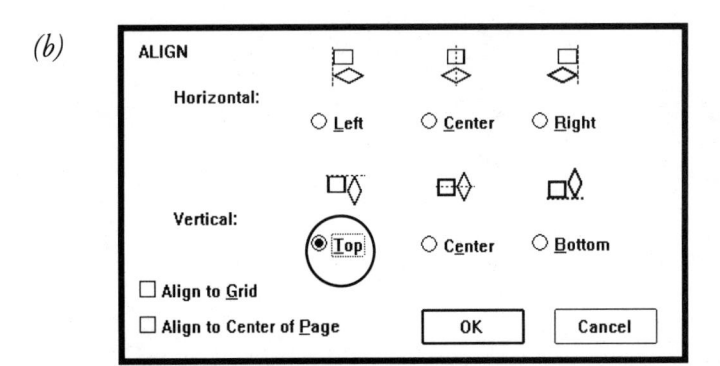

(a)

(b) The *ALIGN* dialog box is activated. Here you have a selection of *Horizontal* and *Vertical* alignment positions. Make your choice and select OK. For this example, the *Top* choice in the *Vertical* option was selected and then we clicked on OK.

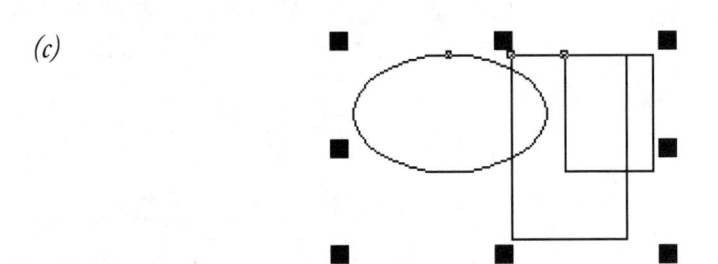

(b)

(c) The selected objects are now aligned as was specified in the dialog box of (b).

(c)

FIT TEXT TO PATH

This command allows you to fit any string of text to a closed or open path in CorelDRAW.

Figure 14. Select both the text string and the path you wish to curve it around, with the Pick Tool. Then select the *Fit Text To Path* command, and the text will flow along or around that path.

Figure 15. In this example a circle was used to flow the text around.

Once the *Fit Text To Path* command has been used, it is then possible to delete the path that was used to flow the text along. This is done by de-selecting the text and the path, by clicking the mouse away from the objects. Then you can re-select the path by clicking on it, making sure you do not select the text by mistake. Then simply press the Delete key on the keyboard.

The direction in which text will flow along a path is determined by the direction you drew that path in. For example: to flow text on the inside of a circle, draw the circle down and to the left. By experimenting with this idea you can come up with the effect you want.

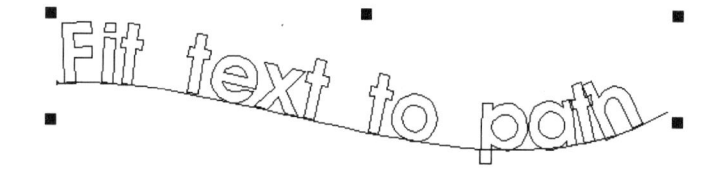

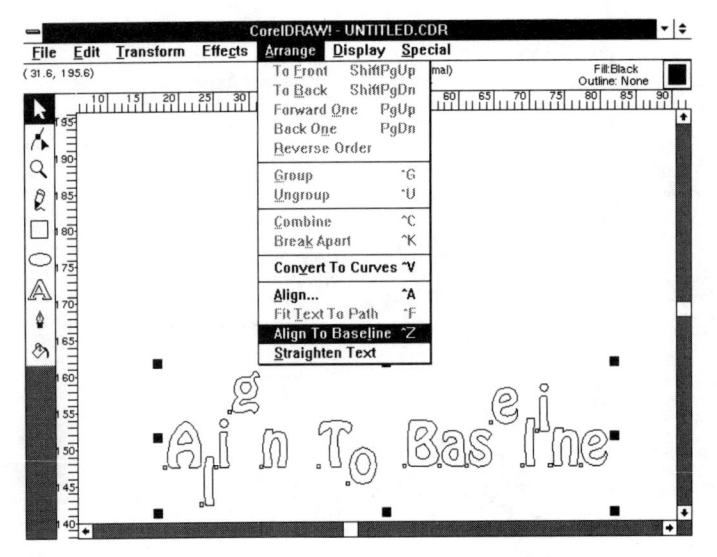

ALIGN TO BASELINE

The baseline is the line that the currently selected text is sitting on. This command will only effect letters that have been individually moved up or down, with the Shape Tool. If these same letters have been shifted to the right or the left, this command will not shift them back.

Figure 16. (a) Select the text string with the Pick Tool that you wish to realign, and then choose the *Align To Baseline* command.

(b) The text is now realigned to its original baseline.

STRAIGHTEN TEXT

The *Straighten Text* command is used to revert text back to its original shape after you have flowed it to a path, shifted it up, down, left, or right, off the baseline, plus any changes you made to the whole string or individual pieces of text in the *Character Attributes* dialog box. It will not straighten text that has been rotated or skewed with the Pick Tool, or through the *ROTATE & SKEW* dialog box.

Figure 17. (a) Select the text, with the Pick Tool or the Shape Tool, that needs straightening, and choose the *Straighten Text* command.

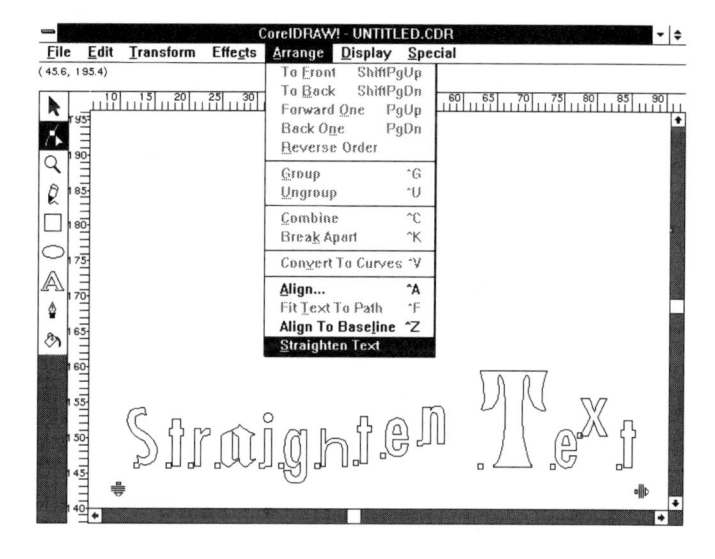

(b) After a few moments the text reverts to its original state.

The Display Menu

The Display Menu Commands

The commands in the **Display** menu will not have a direct affect on any objects on your page, rather they will make changes to the actual screen and its components.

Figure 1. The **Display** menu.

```
Display
  Snap To Grid              ^Y
  Grid Setup...
  Snap To Guidelines
  Guidelines Setup...
  √ Show Rulers
  √ Show Status Line
  √ Show Color Palette
  Show Preview             ShiftF9
  Show Full Screen Preview  F9
  Show Preview Toolbox
  Preview Selected Only
  √ Auto-Update
  √ Show Bitmaps
  Refresh Wire Screen      ^W
```

SNAP TO GRID

When this command is activated, it will force the mouse to stay on the grid points assigned in the *Grid Setup* dialog box (see *Grid Setup*). There are some exceptions to this rule which are as follows: selecting objects, drawing curves with the Pencil Tool and autotracing, rotating and skewing objects, manipulating ellipses with the Shape Tool and using the Zoom Tool.

The Status Line will always indicate if the *Snap To Grid* option is activated. It will also have a tick next to it in the **Display** menu.

Note: The GRID PARAMETERS dialog box can also be accessed by double clicking anywhere on the vertical or horizontal ruler.

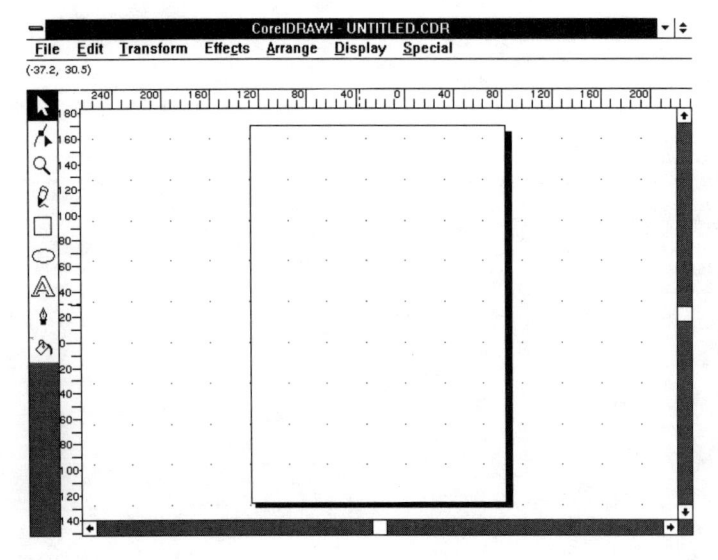

GRID SETUP

Figure 2. This command will activate the *GRID PARAMETERS* dialog box. The first option available in this box is the *Grid Origin* settings. Changing the settings here will determine where the 0 (zero) point of the rulers are situated on your page. By default, the *Grid Origin* will be set at the bottom left of the current page. If, for example, you are working in inches and you change the *Horizontal* and *Vertical Grid Origin* settings to 5 and 5, the 0 point will move up and across the page 5 inches.

The *Grid Frequency* settings determine the spacing of the grid. For example, if you have 1 per inch for both the *Horizontal* and *Vertical* settings, your grid will be made up of 1 inch squares. When changing the unit measurement, the actual settings do not change, so they have to be converted by you every time you change the measurement system.

Figure 3. The *Show Grid* option at the bottom left of the *GRID PARAMETERS* dialog box gives you the option of displaying the grid on the screen. If you have selected this option, the screen and page will be covered in dots that represent the frequency of your grid.

Note: The 0 point of the rulers can also be changed using the mouse. This is done by holding the mouse down in the corner where the two rulers meet and dragging the mouse down and across. Wherever you release the mouse will be the new 0 point.

SNAP TO GUIDELINES

Figure 4. If you have placed any guidelines on your page (see *Guidelines Setup*), objects you are moving or drawing near a guideline will snap to that guideline. The *Snap To Guidelines* command takes precedence over the *Snap To Grid* command.

These are the guidelines discussed in the Guidelines Setup command.

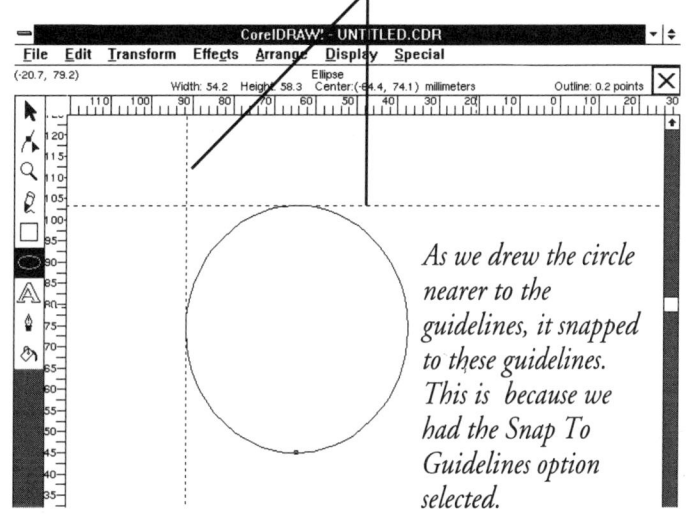

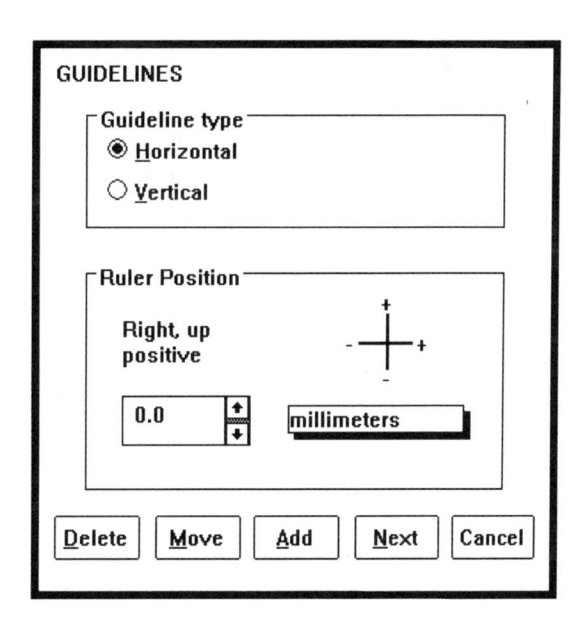

As we drew the circle nearer to the guidelines, it snapped to these guidelines. This is because we had the Snap To Guidelines option selected.

GUIDELINES SETUP

Figure 5. This command activates the *GUIDELINES* dialog box. The first option available here is the *Guideline type* option. You are given the choice of placing a *Horizontal* or *Vertical* guideline. The *Ruler Position* section of this dialog box determines where this horizontal or vertical guideline will be situated on your page. The setting you put in here is in relation to the 0 (zero) point of the rulers.

Once you have put in the desired figure, you click on the *Add* button. The guideline is now on the page. A quick and easy way to activate the *GUIDELINES* dialog box is to double-click on a guideline.

The *Delete* option will remove a guideline from the page, and the *Move* option changes the position of a guideline. If you have multiple guidelines on the page, the *Next* option will display the position of each guideline one by one. Once you have found the guideline you are looking for, you can then move or delete it.

Note: you can also add guidelines to your page by holding the mouse down on the vertical or horizontal ruler, and dragging it out onto the page. Release the mouse where you want the guideline to be situated. You can also move or remove guidelines from the page by holding the mouse down on a guideline and dragging it to a new position, or back into the ruler to remove it.

SHOW RULERS

This command will either turn on or off the horizontal and vertical rulers that appear on the screen.

SHOW STATUS LINE

Figure 6. By default, the Status Line in CorelDRAW will be on. It is possible to deactivate this line by selecting the *Show Status Line* command. To turn it on again, simply select the same command. It is always good to keep the *Status Line* active, as it provides vital information about what you are creating.

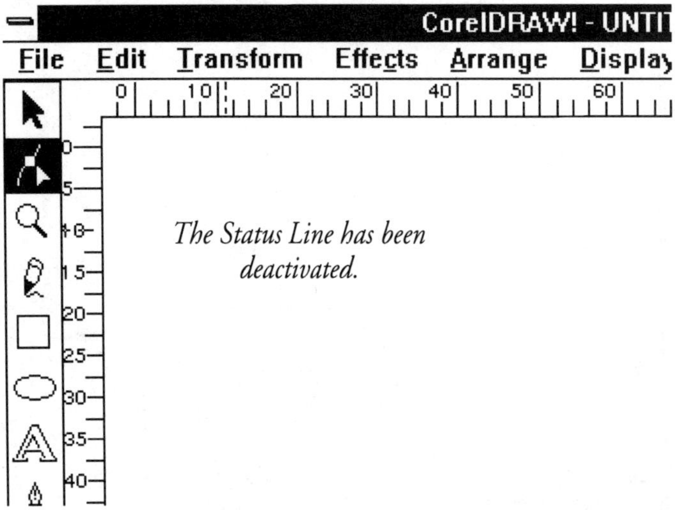

The Status Line has been deactivated.

SHOW COLOR PALETTE

Figure 7. The *Color Palette* is a strip of colors that runs along the bottom of your CorelDRAW screen. This lets you quickly and easily apply a different color fill to a selected object(s). At each side of the palette is an arrow that, when clicked on with the mouse, will give you access to the rest of the colors available in this palette.

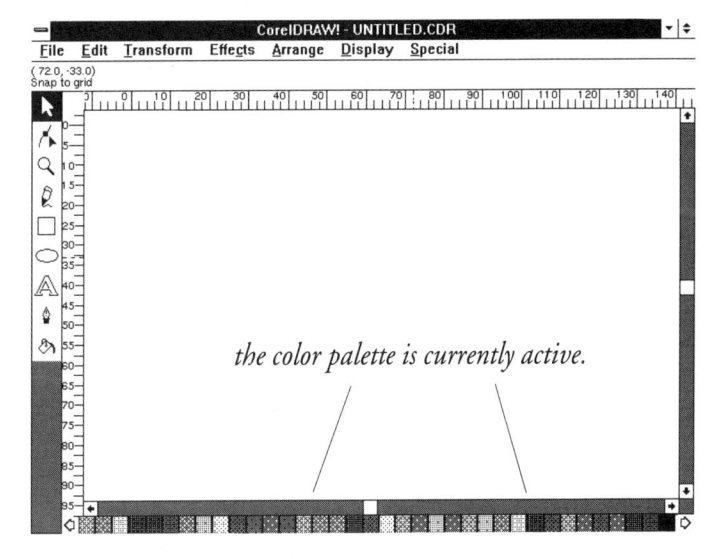

the color palette is currently active.

SHOW PREVIEW

Figure 8. The *Show Preview* command activates the Preview screen which displays how the page will look when printed. Note the Preview screen to the right of this figure.

Shift and F9 is a quick keyboard way of activating the Preview screen.

FULL SCREEN PREVIEW

This option allows you to activate the Preview screen with out the page boundaries, Toolbox, Status Line or menu bar. F9 is a quick keyboard way of activating *Full Screen Preview*.

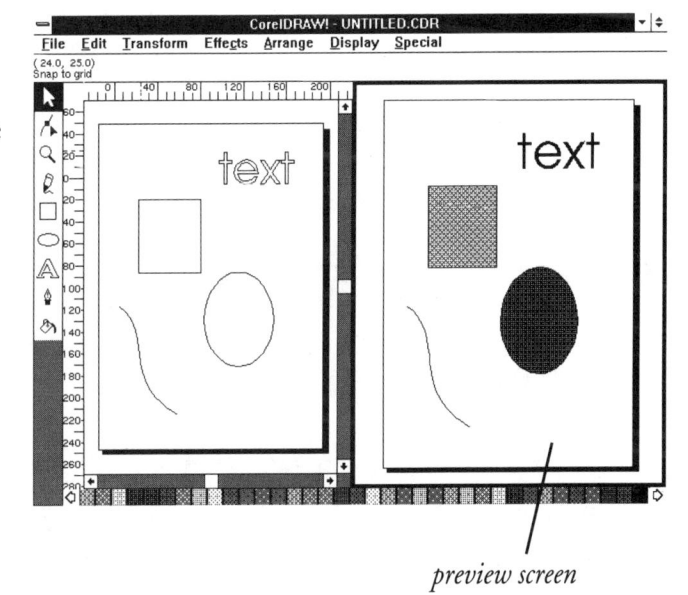

preview screen

CHAPTER 8: THE DISPLAY MENU

(a)

The options available in the Preview Screen Toolbox flyout are the same as the options available in the Working Screen Toolbox.

(b)

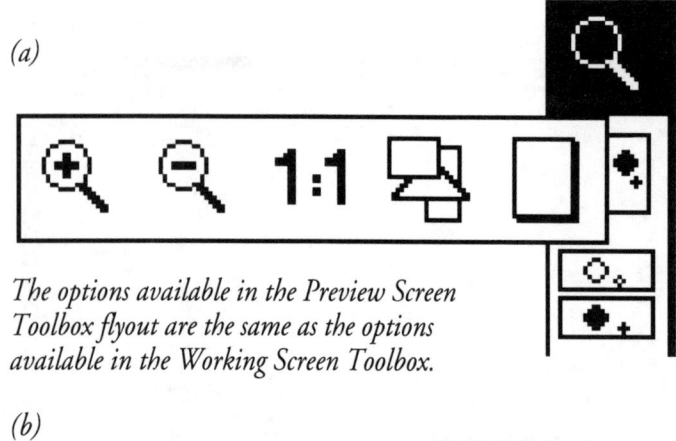

The above option when clicked on will display the Working Screen and the Preview Screen running vertically side by side as in Figure 8.

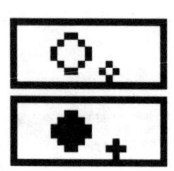

The above option will change the view of the two screens so that they are running horizontally, as in Figure (c).

(c)

SHOW PREVIEW TOOLBOX

Figure 9. This command can only be used when the Preview screen is on (not the *Full Screen Preview*).

(**a**) It activates a toolbox that lets you change the viewing size of the Preview screen, without affecting the Working screen. The Zoom Tool fly-out has the same options available as the Working screen Zoom Tool.

(**b**) The other two options available in the Preview screen Toolbox change the position of the two screens from vertical to horizontal and vice versa.

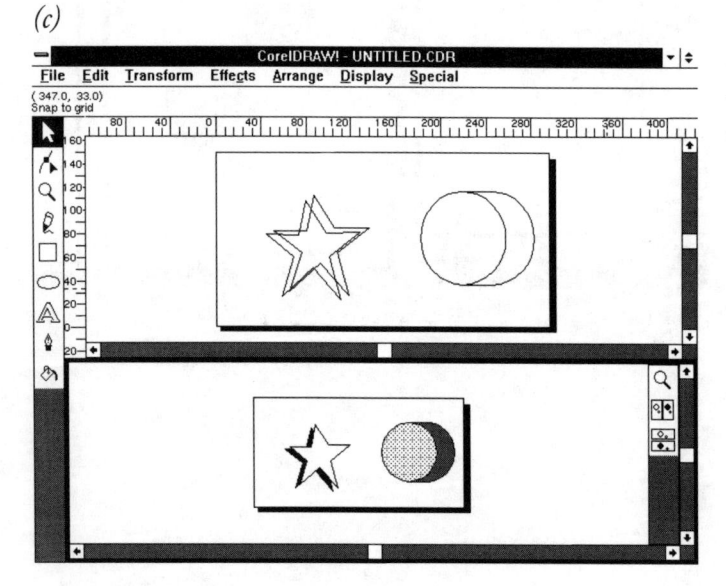

(**c**) This is the result of changing the Preview screen viewing options in Figure 9(b).

PREVIEW SELECTED ONLY

Figure 10. With this command, you have the option of only displaying, in the Preview screen, objects that have been selected with the Pick Tool on the Working screen. Here we have selected the circle on the Working screen and, as you can see, it is the only thing that appears on the Preview screen. This feature will also work with the *Full Screen Preview* option active.

AUTO UPDATE

By default this option will be on. It makes sure that any changes you make to the file will automatically re-draw on the Preview screen. When turned off, re-drawing on the Preview screen will only take place when you click the mouse on the Preview screen.

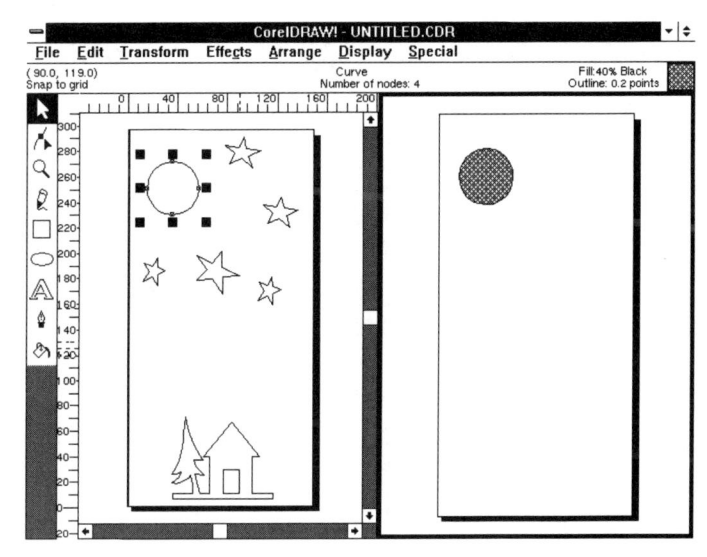

Here we have selected one object only on the Working Screen, and it is the only object that appears on the Preview Screen. This is because the Preview Selected Only command is active.

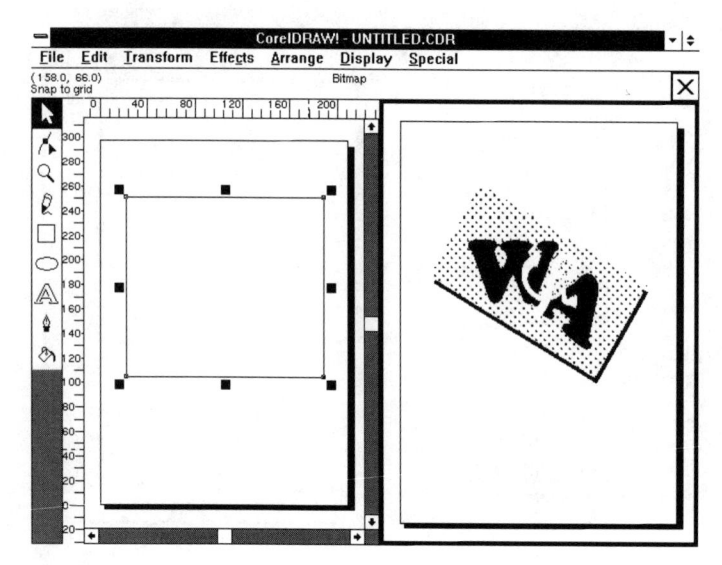

SHOW BITMAPS

Figure 11. If you have any bitmaps on your page that are slow to redraw, you can deselect the *Show Bitmaps* option, and the square containing the bitmap on the Working screen will be empty.

REFRESH WIRE SCREEN

If you have interrupted the re-drawing of objects on the Working screen, you can have them re-drawn by selecting the *Refresh Wire Screen* command.

The Special Menu   9

The Special Menu Commands

The commands in the **Special** menu offer a variety of options. With this menu you have the ability to export and re-import text as well as creating patterns and arrowheads that can be saved in the CorelDRAW system. You can also alter, through the *Preferences* command, a number of features that determines how CorelDRAW operates..

Figure 1. The Special menu.

```
Special
 Extract...
 Merge-Back...

 Create Pattern...
 Create Arrow...

 Preferences... ^J
```

EXTRACT

Figure 2. This command lets you save text created in CorelDRAW as an ASCII file, which can then be edited in a word processing program. The *Extract* dialog box is where you name the file and decide where you are going to save it.

Once you have loaded the extracted text into a word processing program, do not change any of the text or numbers that CorelDRAW has added to the beginning of the file and with each paragraph, as these are identification markers. Once you have finished making any changes to the extracted text, save it as an ASCII file again and return to CorelDRAW

```
Extract
Path: C:\CARRIE\*.txt
Files               File: info
publish.txt         Directories
steve.txt           [..]        Up
                    [-a-]
                    [-b-]
                    [-c-]       Cancel
                    [-d-]
                                Extract
```

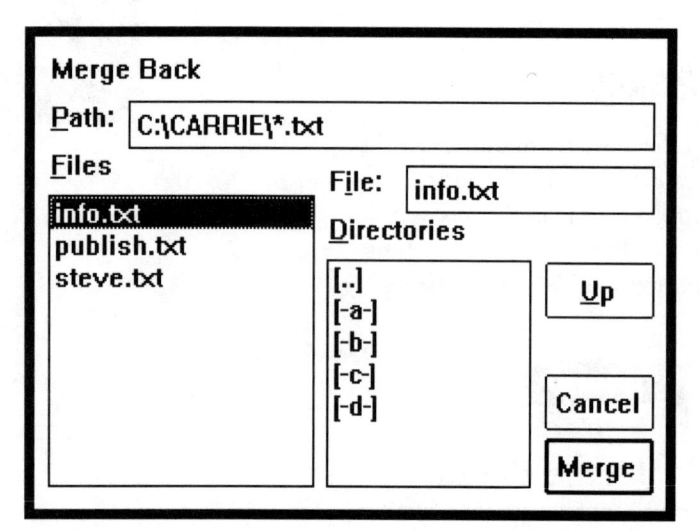

MERGE BACK

Figure 3. The *Merge Back* command will bring the text back into CorelDRAW that was earlier extracted. Select the file from the *Merge Back* dialog box, and click on OK. Any minor editing changes, to do with alignment or overlapping of text that you may have added, can be fixed in CorelDRAW

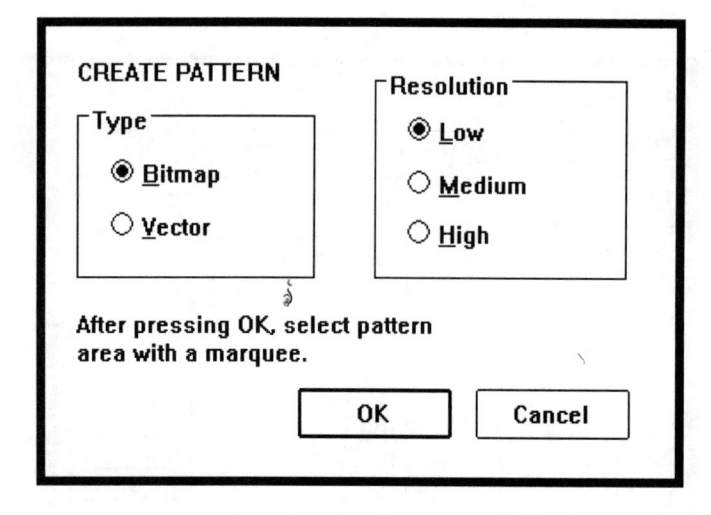

CREATE PATTERN

Figure 4(a). The *Create Pattern* command allows you to create patterns from an image you have drawn on your page. This image or drawing will then become part of the Bitmap or Vector fill pattern dialog boxes.

This option can only be chosen if you have an object selected with the Pick Tool. It will activate the *CREATE PATTERN* dialog box. The first option available here is *Type*. After selecting either *Bitmap* or *Vector*, click on OK. (If you have selected Bitmap you must also select a *Resolution*.)

Figure 4(b). Once you return to the page, your cursor will have turned into a crosshair that spans the whole screen. Select the graphic marquee fashion; i.e. draw an imaginary box around the object with your finger on the mouse.

Release the mouse and the *CREATE PATTERN* screen prompt appears. Click OK here if you have selected the graphic properly. Next time you go into the *BITMAP FILL PATTERN* or *LOAD VECTOR PATTERN* dialog box (depending on the type you chose), the graphic you selected will be one of the patterns.

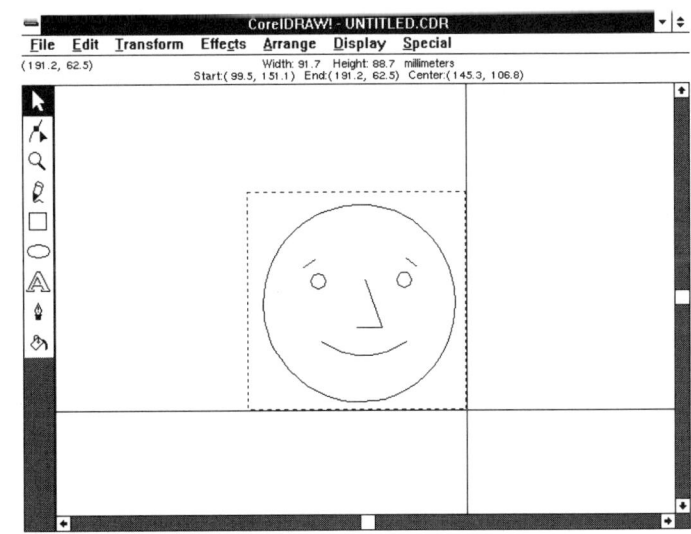

CREATE ARROW

Figure 5. This command can only be chosen if you have an object selected. It will activate the *CREATE ARROW* screen prompt, which asks you whether or not you want to create an arrowhead with the selected object. Clicking on OK will insert the selected object in the *ARROWHEAD SELECTION* dialog box, obtainable through the *OUTLINE PEN* dialog box (see description of the Outline Tool in Chapter 2, **The Tools**).

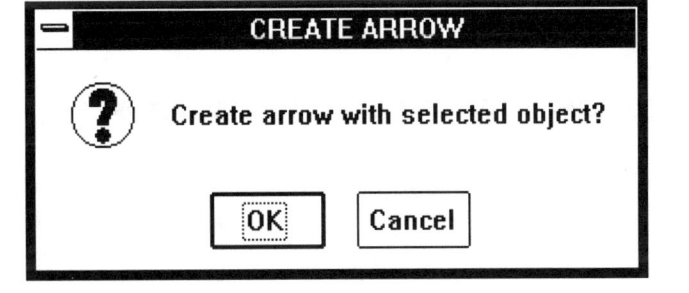

Chapter 9: The Special Menu

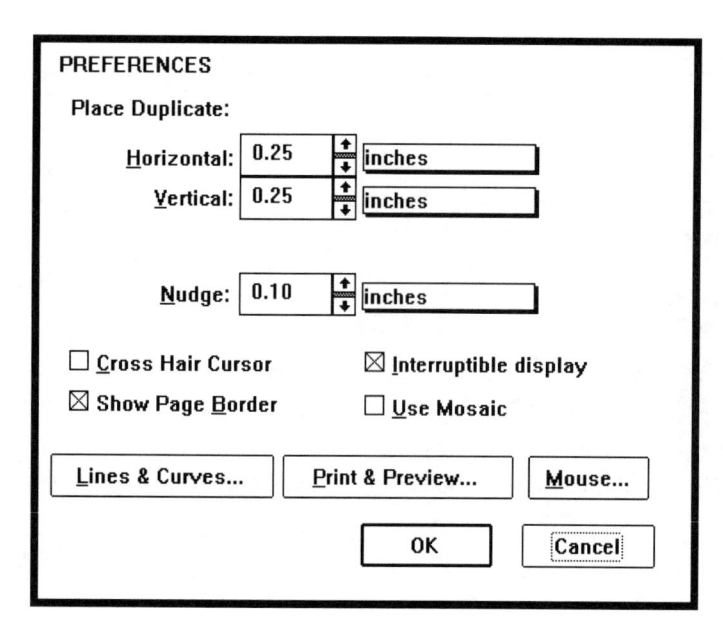

PREFERENCES

Figure 6. On selecting this command, the *PREFERENCES* dialog box is activated.

The first option in this dialog box is *Place Duplicate*. Changing the settings here will affect where a duplicated object will appear, after using the *Duplicate* command in the **Edit** menu.

The *Nudge* option lets you determine the amount of space a selected object can be moved using the arrow keys on your keyboard.

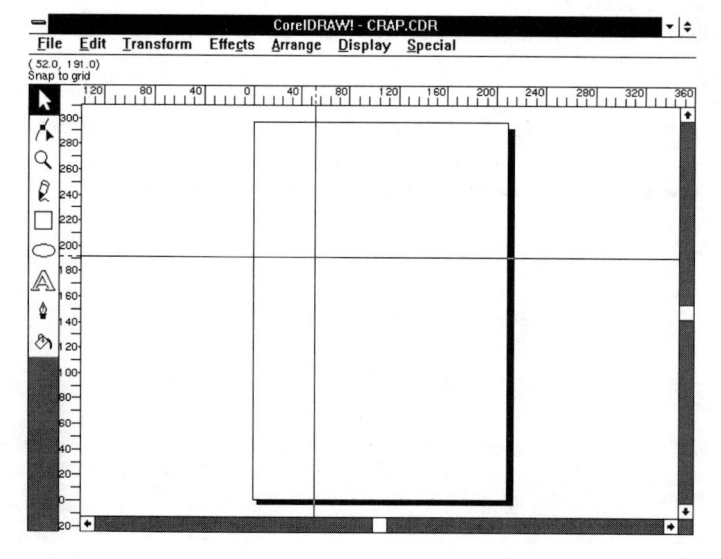

Figure 7. If you select *Cross Hair Cursor*, your mouse will turn into a crosshair that covers the whole screen.

Figure 8. If you do not want the Page Border to appear on the Working screen, deselect the *Show Page Border* option. This figure shows the result.

The *Interruptible display* option is checked on by default. This lets you interrupt the redrawing on the Working screen, by clicking the mouse or pressing a key.

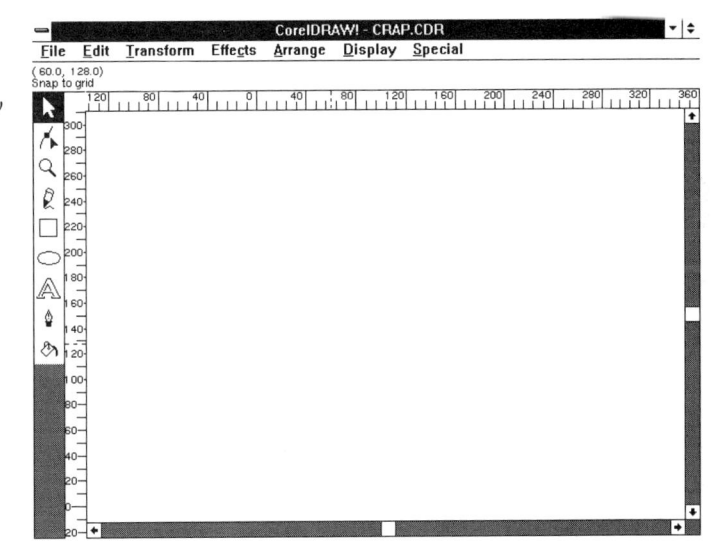

Figure 9. If you have the *Use Mosaic* option turned on, every time you *Open* or *Import* a CorelDRAW file, the MOSIAC utility that comes with CorelDRAW will be activated. This lets you view the files before performing the option on them you selected. It also allows for some options selected (such as *Print*) to be performed on more than one file at once.

For more information see Chapter 11, **MOSIAC**.

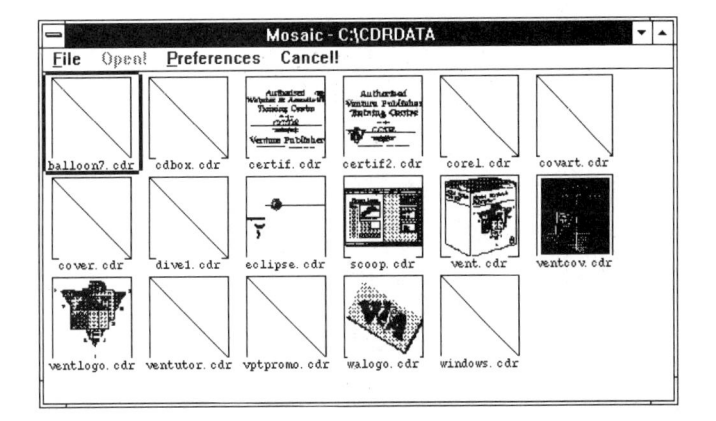

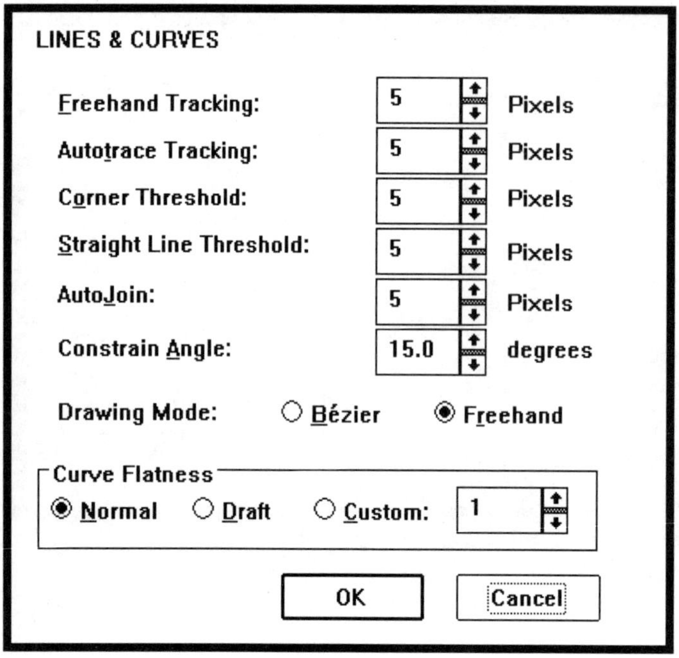

Figure 10. The *Lines & Curves* button of Figure 6 will activate the *LINES & CURVES* dialog box. The first six options here, including *Freehand Tracking, Autotrace Tracking, Corner Threshold, Straight Line Threshold, AutoJoin* and *Constrain Angle*, determine how CorelDRAW treats lines created with the Pencil Tool, and when autotracing. The default settings usually serve the purpose, but if for some reason you want to create a drawing with a certain effect, you have the option to change these settings.

With the *Drawing* Mode option of Figure 10, you have a choice between *Bezier* or *Freehand*. These choices affect the way the Pencil Tool draws (see the Pencil Tool description in Chapter 2, **The Tools**).

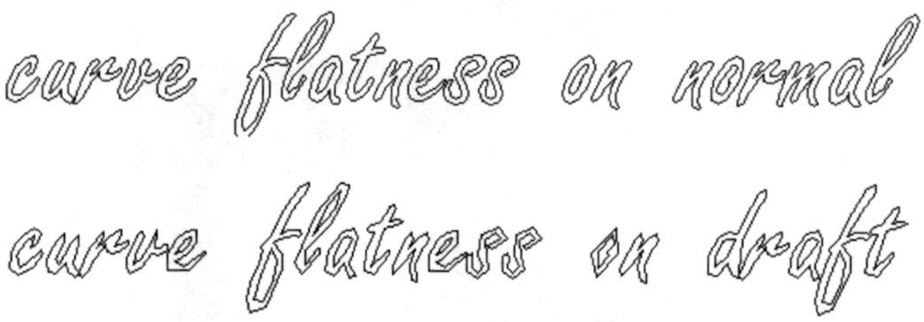

Figure 11. The *Curve Flatness* option determines the number of line segments in your drawing or text, on the screen, and on non-PostScript printers.

Increasing this figure can speed up redrawing and printing time. *Normal* is the lowest (on 1), and *Draft* is the highest (on 10); *Custom* lets you choose any setting in between.

Clicking on OK or Cancel in the *LINES & CURVES* dialog box will take you back to the *PREFERENCES* dialog box of Figure 6.

CHAPTER 9: THE SPECIAL MENU

Figure 12. Click on the *Print & Preview* button of Figure 6 to get the *PRINT & PREVIEW* dialog box. The *Miter Limit* controls the sharpness of the corners of your objects. This option is available to ensure that corners do not extend past where they are supposed to.

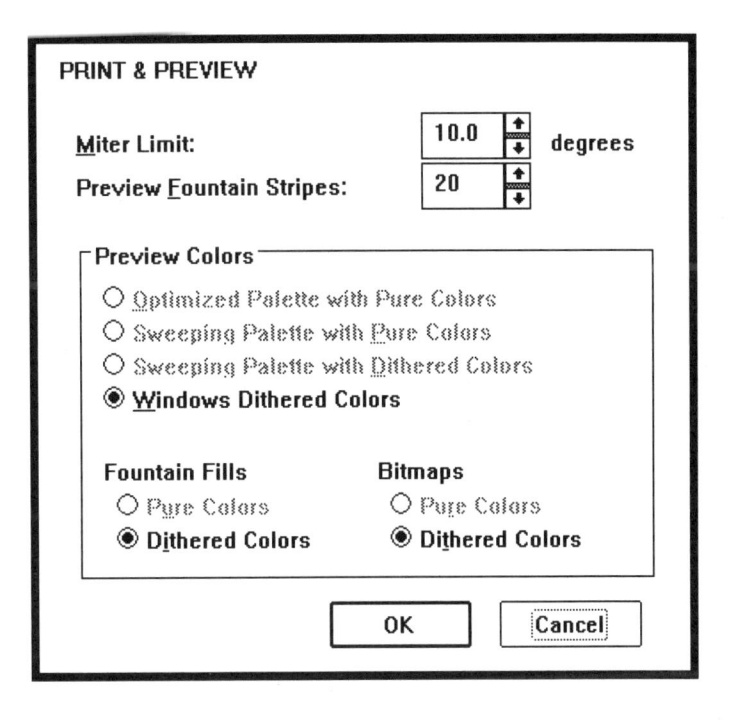

Figure 13. The *Preview Fountain Stripes* option lets you set how many sections make up a fountain filled object on the Preview screen. The less stripes you have, the faster it will redraw on the Preview screen. This option has no effect on the printing.

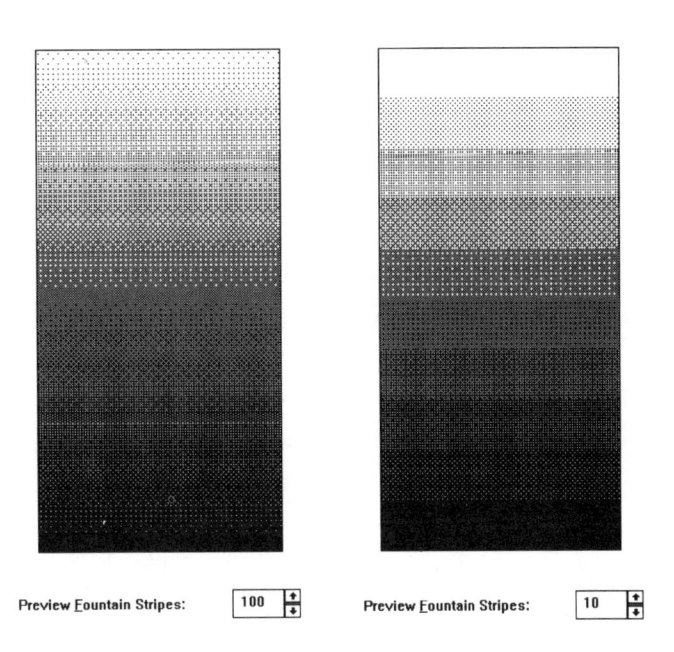

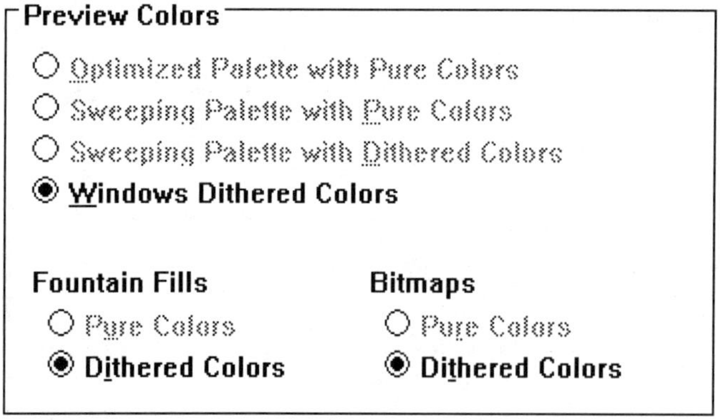

Figure 14. The *Preview Colors* section of the Figure 12 dialog box can only be modified if you have the ability to display 256 colors on your screen. The *Optimized Palette with Pure Colors* option displays the Preview screen with a palette made up of all the colors in the present drawing. If there is not a wide range of colors in your drawing, the palette will be limited, therefore the colors might not be accurate.

The *Sweeping Palette with Pure Colors* and *Sweeping Palette with Dithered Colors* are the same in the sense that both options fill the palette with a wide range of colors. The *Pure Colors* choice displays the screen using the closest matching color from the current palette. The *Dithered Colors* option uses a dithering effect, that will use as many colors as possible to create a smoother looking fill, which is the best looking option in the case of fountain fills.

The *Windows Dithered Colors* option is the only choice available if you do not have the ability to display 256 or more colors on your screen.

At the bottom of the *PRINT & PREVIEW* dialog box is the *Fountain Fills* and *Bitmaps* choices, where you can select either *Pure* or *Dithered colors*. The combination of choices, combined with the palette choices above, will give you a number of different ways of viewing the Preview screen.

After you have finished with the *PRINT & PREVIEW* dialog box, click on OK or Cancel to return to the *PREFERENCES* dialog box of Figure 6.

Figure 15. Click on the *Mouse* button in Figure 6 to get the *MOUSE* dialog box. Here you can assign the right mouse button to perform any one of the choices indicated in this dialog box.

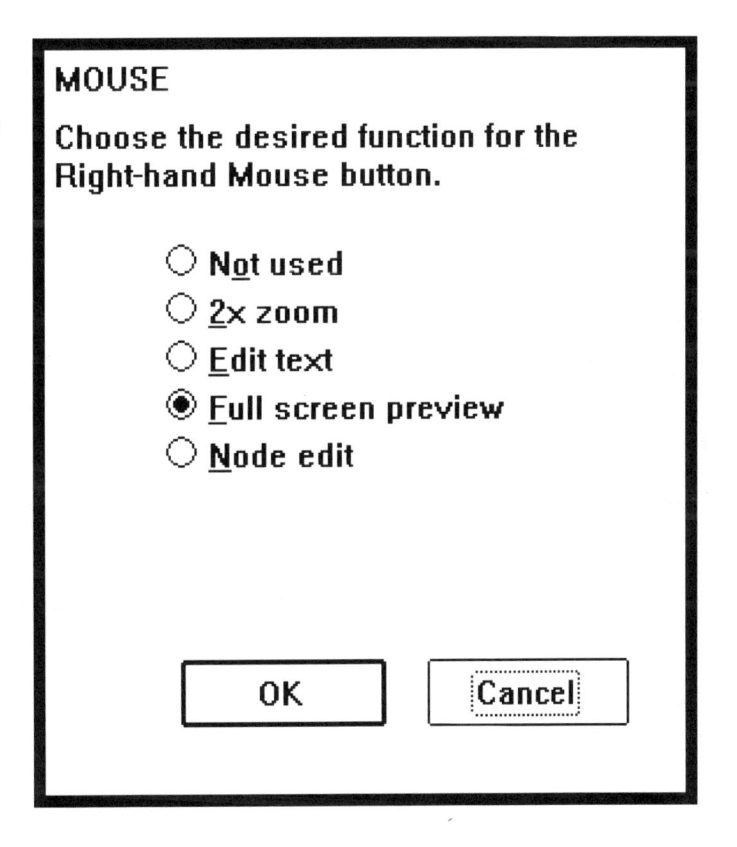

CorelTRACE 10

Using CorelTRACE

CorelTRACE is an extra utility that comes with CorelDRAW. If you have loaded CorelTRACE on your machine, you have the ability to trace black and white, gray scale and color bitmaps. You can then use these traced images in CorelDRAW for further manipulation, or leave them as is.

Figure 1. If CorelTRACE is installed on your machine, it is activated through the Windows Program Manager by double-clicking on the relevant icon.

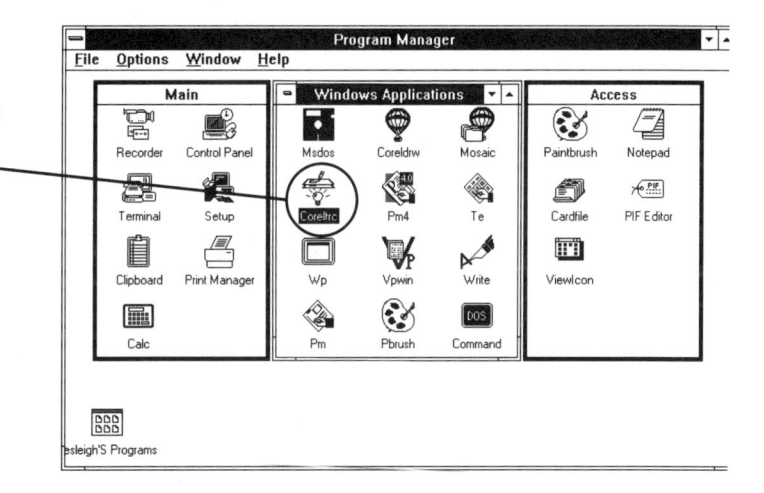

Figure 2. The CorelTRACE window allows you to search through your computer's hard drive and directories for the appropriate file(s) you want to trace. CorelTRACE will only trace TIF or PCX files, and the currently available files in the active directory (Path) will be listed in the box to the left of the dialog box. Once a file has been selected from this list, it will appear in the *File Selected* frame.

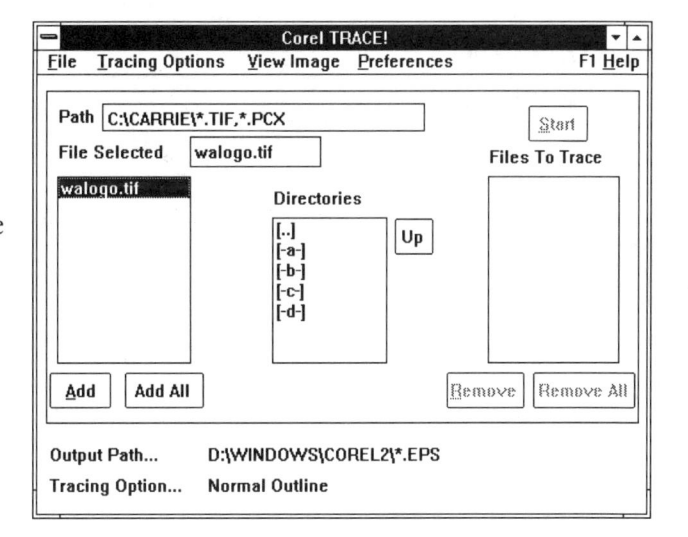

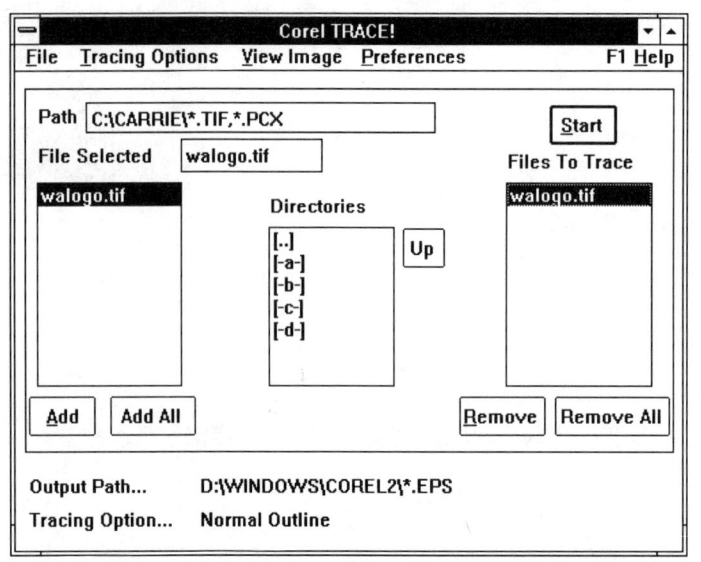

Figure 3. Once you have selected the file you want to trace, click on the *Add* button below the list of files. This will place the name of the file in the *Files To Trace* list. The *Add All* button will add all files here. The *Remove* and *Remove All* buttons work in the opposite way. They will clear the *Files To Trace* list of any selected files, or all files respectively.

Figure 4. Once you have added your files to the *Files To Trace* list, you may select where your file is to be placed after tracing, which is indicated by the Output *Path*. To change this, select the *Output Options* command from the **File** menu.

The *On name conflict* options are there if you happen to be tracing the same file again, and the output path is the same, you are able to either replace the file with the newly traced version, or you can let CorelTRACE prompt you to change the name of the file.

The *Saved Traced File in* option is what determines the output path. Click the cursor in the frame and backspace over the current path, so you are able to key in a new one.

THE TRACING OPTIONS MENU

Figure 5. Before you begin to trace the file, you are able to set up your own personalized tracing options. This can be done through the **Tracing Options** menu. The *Normal Outline* and *Normal Centerline* options are two default options that come with CorelTRACE. To create your own style, drag the mouse down the menu until it covers one of the eight sets of three dots. This will activate the *Tracing Options* dialog box of Figure 6.

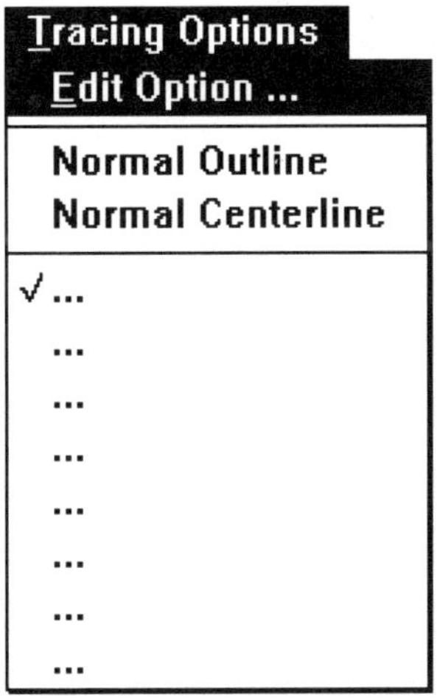

Figure 6. The *Tracing Options* dialog box gives you a range of selections to choose from that will have a final result in the tracing of your file(s). Once you have set up the dialog box to your required choices, place a name in the *Type New Name* frame in the bottom left of the dialog box, and click on OK. This style will now be saved in the **Tracing Options** menu. Only eight at a time can be saved. For more information on *Tracing Options* refer to the CorelTRACE manual that comes with CorelDRAW

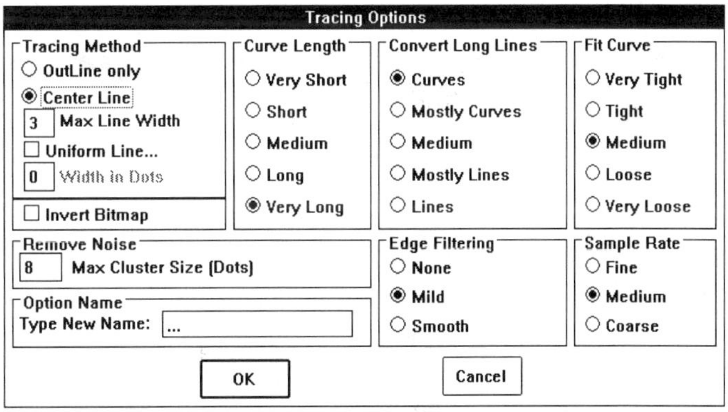

To edit a style you have previously saved, make sure it is the currently selected style in the **Tracing options** menu (the tick mark next to the style name indicates this), and choose the *Edit Option* command from the **Tracing Options** menu.

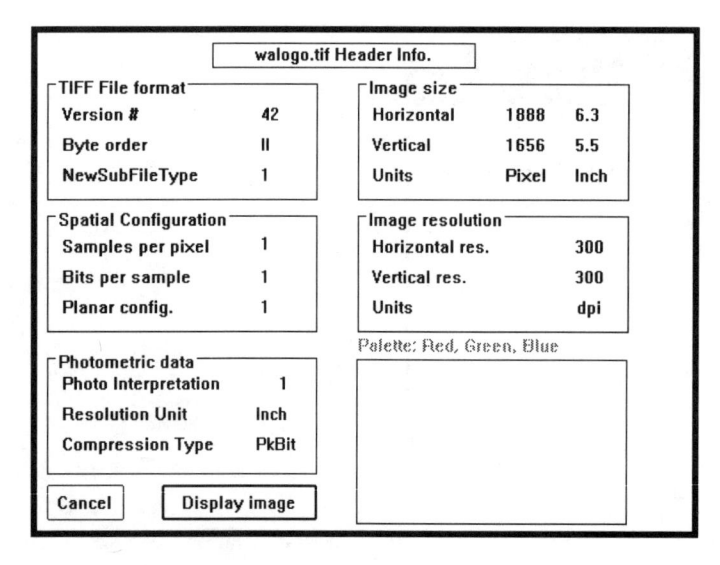

THE VIEW IMAGE MENU

Figure 7. The *View File Information* command is the first option available in the **View Image** menu. Selecting this command will activate the *View File Information* dialog box. This dialog box displays current technical information about the selected file.

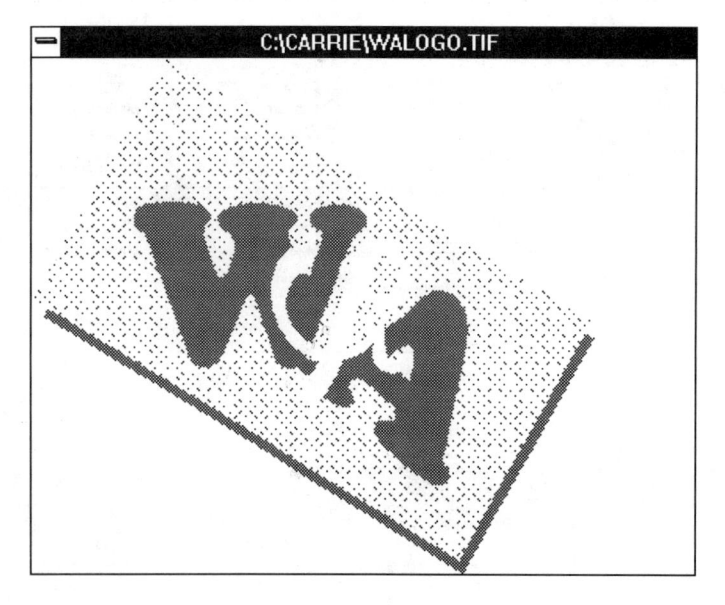

Figure 8. The *Display Image* command in the **View Image** menu will let you look at the file before you trace it.

THE PREFERENCES MENU

Figure 9. The last choices you have available, before you begin to trace the file, are in the **Preferences** menu. The first four options in this menu can be turned on or off at any time before the trace. The tick to the left of the options indicate they are on.

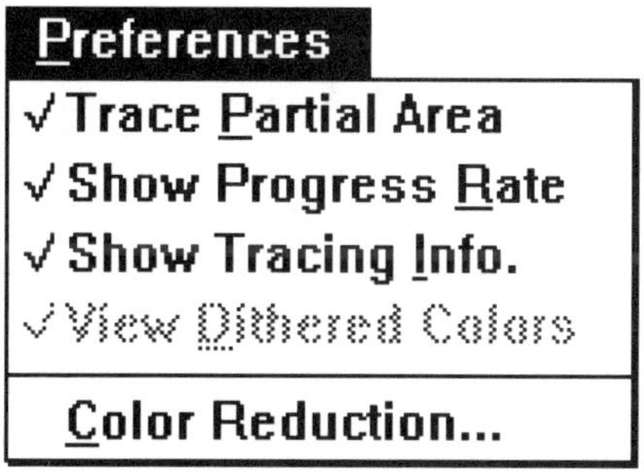

> Preferences
> ✓ Trace Partial Area
> ✓ Show Progress Rate
> ✓ Show Tracing Info.
> ✓ View Dithered Colors
> Color Reduction...

Figure 10. The *Trace Partial Area* option allows you to select a certain section of the file, if you do not want the whole file traced. After you click on the *Start* button to begin tracing, the file will appear in a box with eight selection handles. These handles are used in conjunction with the mouse to cover the section of the file you want traced.

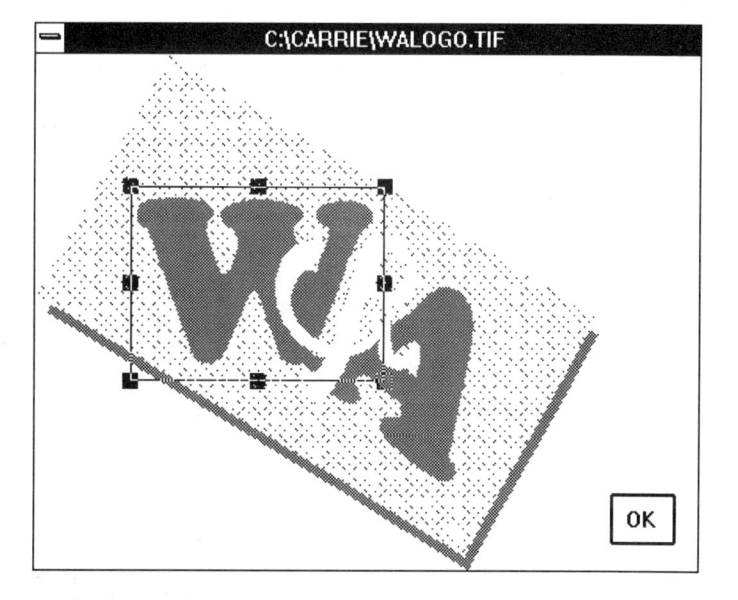

Figure 11. The *Show Progress Rate* choice, if active, will place a percentage gauge below the file as it is being traced. This will indicate the progress of the trace.

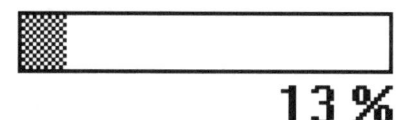

13 %

Figure 12. The *Show Tracing Info* command tells you the size of the file, as well as the number of nodes and the tracing time, after the file has been traced.

Size 844 x 629, 758 Nodes 43 Obj. Trace time 7:39

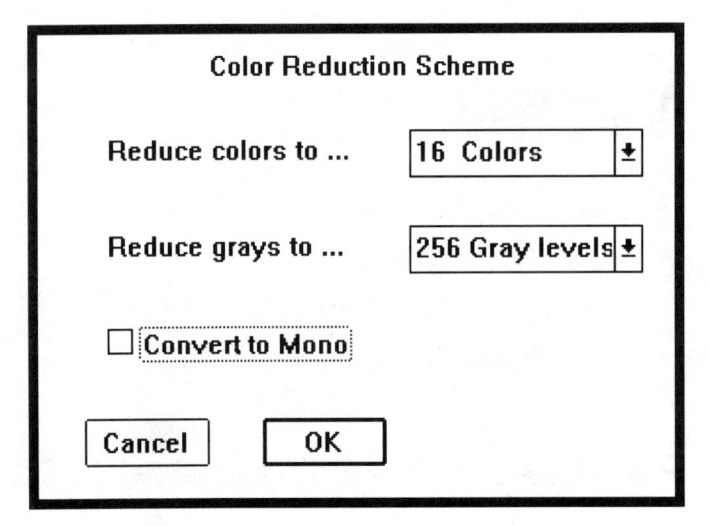

The *View Dithered Colors* option is only available if you have the ability to display 256 or more colors on your screen. It gives you the option of displaying the traced image in pure or dithered colors, and only works on gray scale or colored images.

Figure 13. The *Color Reduction* command gives you access to the *Color Reduction Scheme* dialog box.

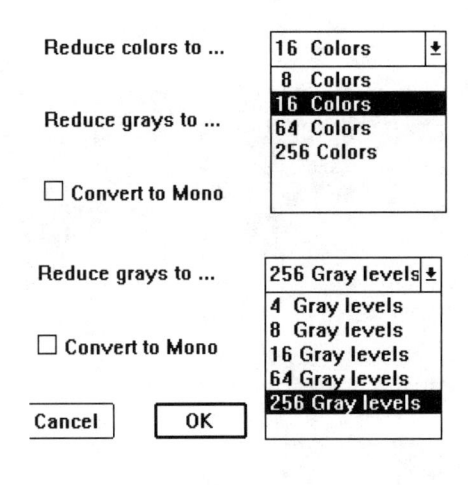

Figure 14. The *Reduce colors to* and the *Reduce grays to* options in the *Color Reduction Scheme* dialog box let you select the amount of colors and gray levels your drawing will be traced with. These options are only available if the image you are tracing is in color or has gray scales.

The *Convert to Mono* option in the *Color Reduction Scheme* dialog box, when selected, will convert color or images with gray scales to black and white line art.

Once you have changed any or all of the settings in CorelTRACE, you may begin to trace the image. If you do not change any of the settings or options discussed, your image will be traced in one of the default settings. To begin tracing the file, make sure the name of the file is in the *Files To Trace* list (Figure 3) and click on the *Start* button above the *Files To Trace* list. After a few moments, (depending on the size and complexity of the file), the image will be traced.

Figure 15. Once your file has been traced, CorelTRACE will display the image. In this example we selected the *Convert to Mono* command in the *Color Reduction Scheme* dialog box (Figure 13), and we only traced a certain area of the file.

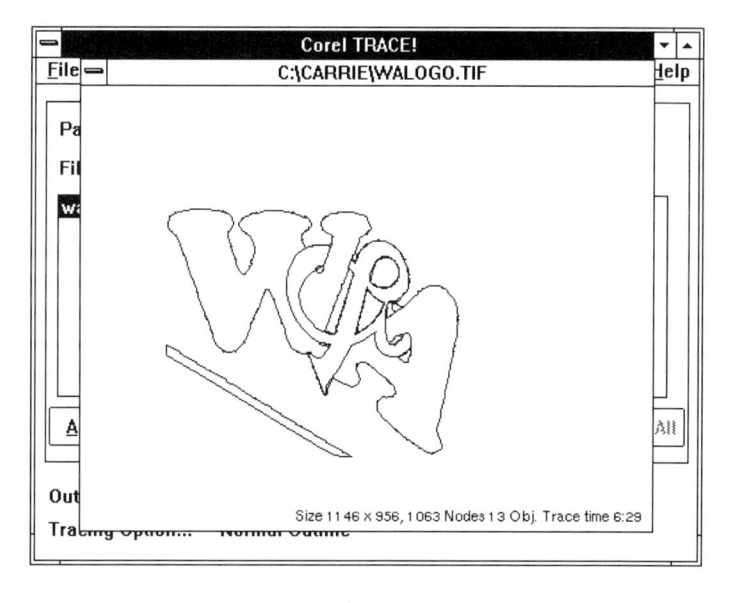

Figure 16. Once the file has been traced, select the *Exit* command from the **File** menu. You can now either load this file into a program that accepts EPS files, or import it into CorelDRAW for further manipulation.

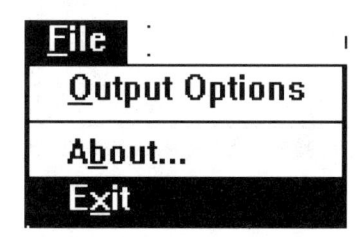

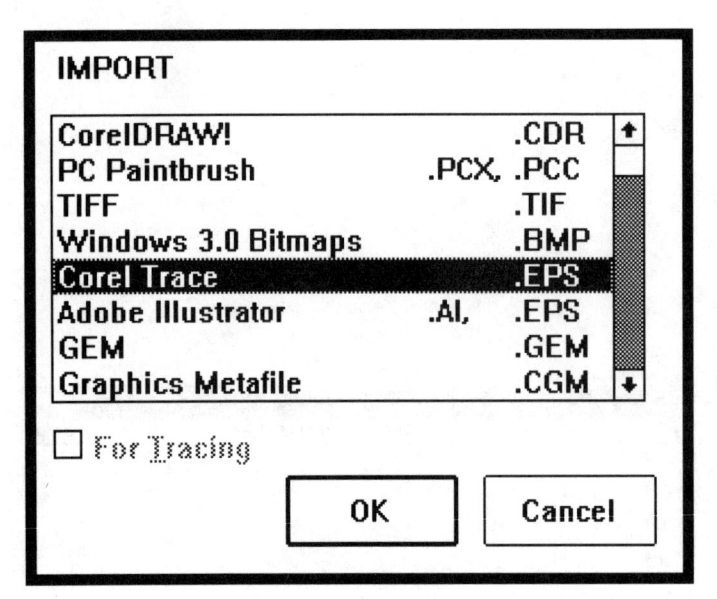

Importing CorelTRACE Images into CorelDRAW

Figure 17. To place the file into CorelDRAW, select the *Import* command from the **File** menu, once in CorelDRAW. In the *IMPORT* dialog box, choose the *Corel Trace* option and click on OK.

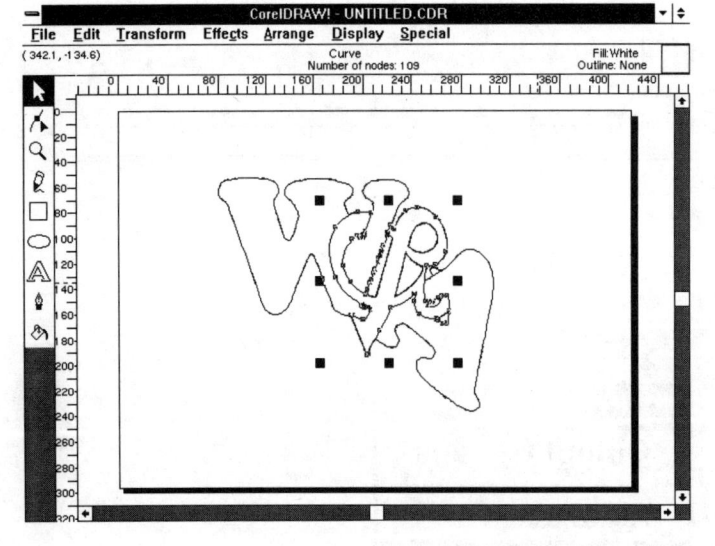

Figure 18. Once you locate the file and load it into CorelDRAW, you are free to manipulate or edit this drawing in any way you wish. You can then go on to export this file in any of the export formats available in CorelDRAW.

MOSAIC 11

USING MOSAIC

MOSAIC, an extra utility that comes with CorelDRAW, can be used to visually select bitmap versions of CDR files before opening them. It is also possible to select more than one file so that options like exporting and printing, can be performed on multiple files at once.

MOSAIC can be accessed directly from the Windows Program Manager (Standalone mode) or through CorelDRAW (CorelDRAW mode). There are slight differences between these two modes which will be discussed.

Figure 1. To open MOSAIC through Windows, double-click on the relevant icon.

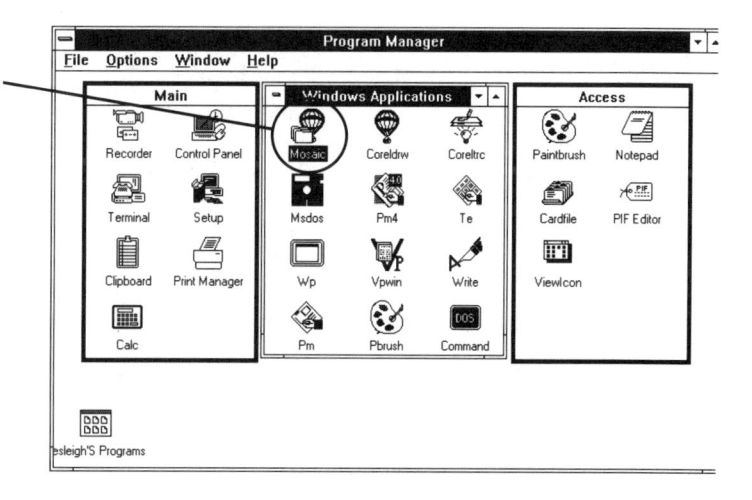

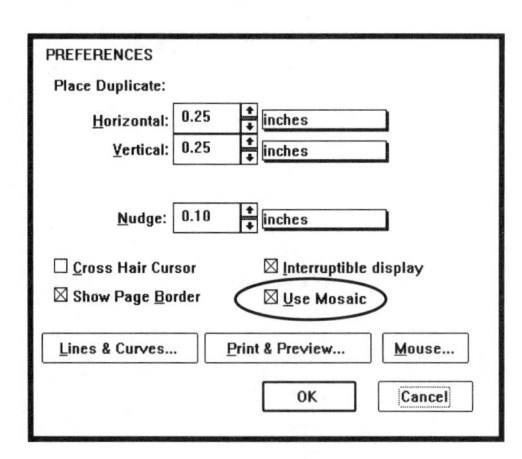

Figure 2. To open MOSAIC through CorelDRAW, the *Use Mosaic* option in the *Preferences* dialog box from the **Special** menu must be on. Now, whenever you select *Open* or *Import* from the **File** menu, MOSAIC will be activated.

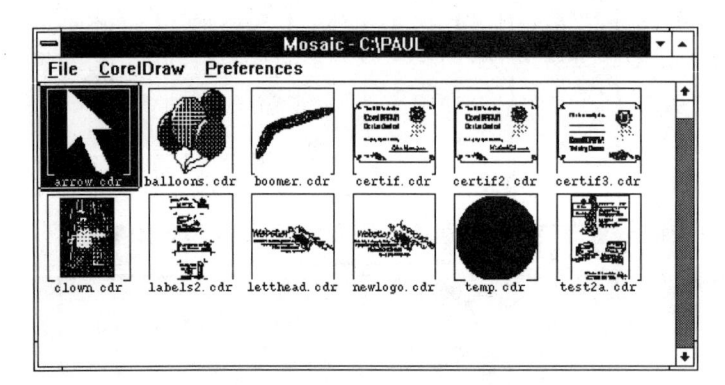

Figure 3. Here MOSAIC has been opened from Windows. If the currently active directory has any CDR files in it, a bitmap representation of the file is displayed in a box. CDR files created in a earlier versions of CorelDRAW (before 2.0) will have a diagonal line through the box. The title of the file is also displayed under each box.

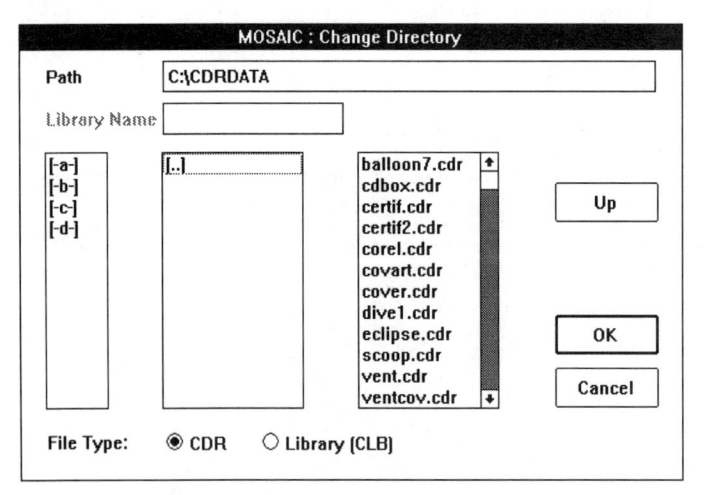

Figure 4. To change the currently active directory, select the *Change Dir* command from the **File** menu. This will activate the *Change Directory* dialog box where you have access to the machine's drives and directories. Once you find the drive and the directory you require, click on the OK button and the CDR files in this

THE FILE MENU

Figure 5. The first option in the File menu is the *Delete* command. On choosing this command, any files selected in the current directory will be removed.

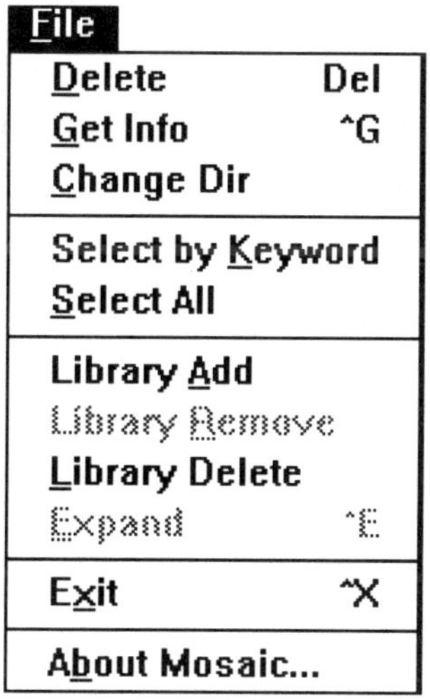

Figure 6. The *Get Info* command is only available if you have a file selected. It will activate the *Information* dialog box. This dialog box will give you information on the current file, such as *Name* and *Size*. The *Keywords* option allows you to insert certain words to cross reference or select files with the same or similar keywords (see *Select by Keyword*). Words placed in here must be separated by a comma.

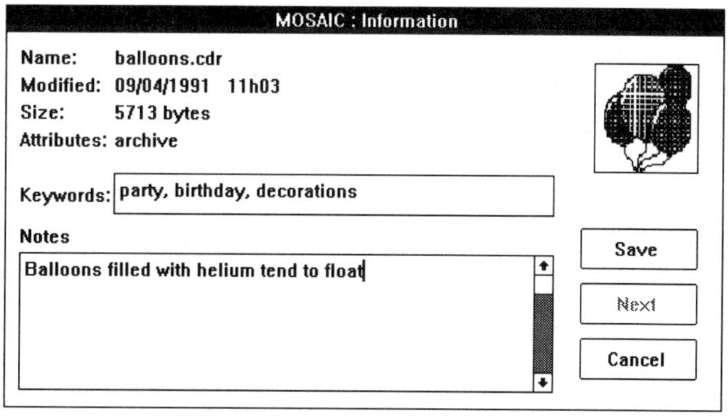

The *Notes* frame is there for inserting text about the file that you may like to remember, such as reasons for the drawing, or any information you may think relevant.

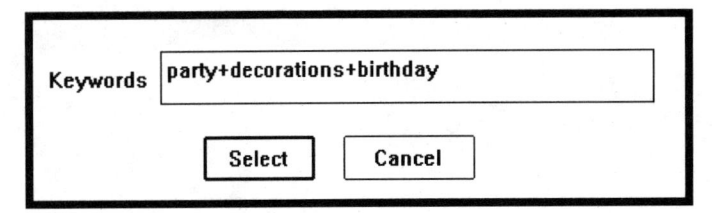

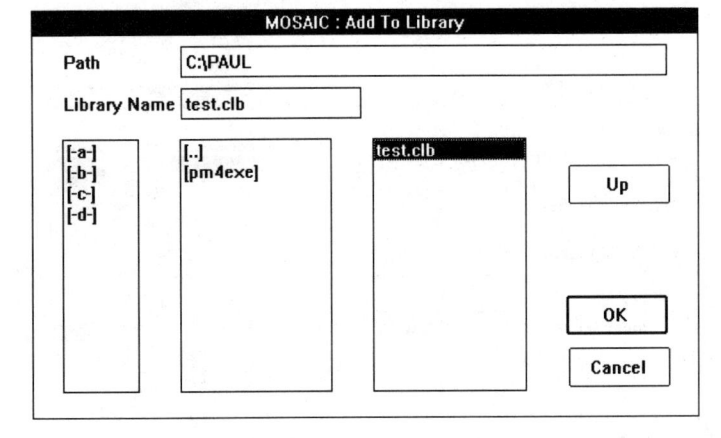

Figure 7. The *Select by Keyword* option will display a small dialog box, that lets you insert any keywords that will relate to your CDR files. The words must be separated by either a comma (which means "or") or a + (which means "and"). After clicking on OK, all CDR files in the current directory that have the same keywords in their *Information* dialog box will become selected.

The *Select All* option will select all CDR files in the currently active directory.

Figure 8. The *Library Add* command activates the *Add To Library* dialog box. MOSAIC allows you to create libraries of compressed CDR files. A library can contain CDR files from different directories. This command can only be accessed if you have two or more files selected. You give the library a name in the *Library Name* frame and the *Path* option determines where the Library is saved.

Adding new files to an already existing library is also done through this dialog box. When creating libraries and adding to existing ones, DOS is activated and the files are compressed using a program called LHARC. Once this compressing is complete, MOSAIC returns to the screen. A library contains a .CLB and a .CLH version of each file in the library. These files must stay in the same directory for correct operation.

Figure 9. To display a library of files, select the *Library (CLB)* option in the *Change Directory* dialog box. Then click on the library you want and then select OK.

The *Library Remove* command in the **File** menu (Figure 5) will remove any selected files from the currently active library.

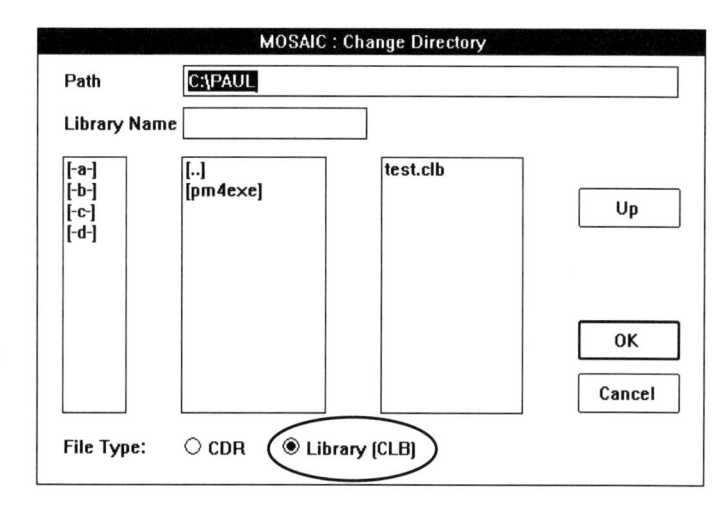

Figure 10. The *Library Delete* command from Figure 5 activates the *Delete Library File(s)* dialog box, where you may select a whole library to be deleted.

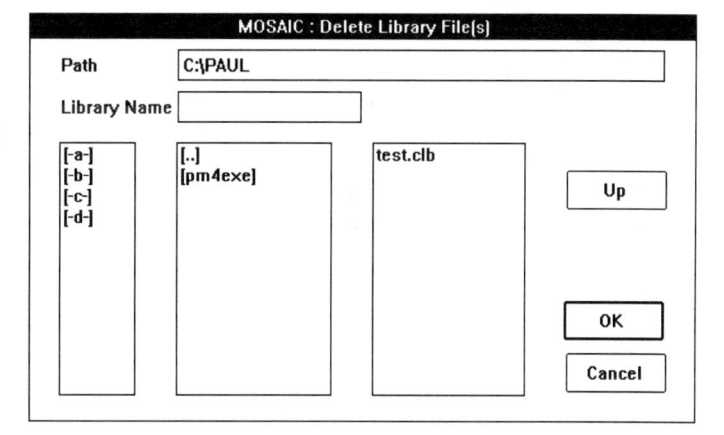

CHAPTER 11: MOSAIC

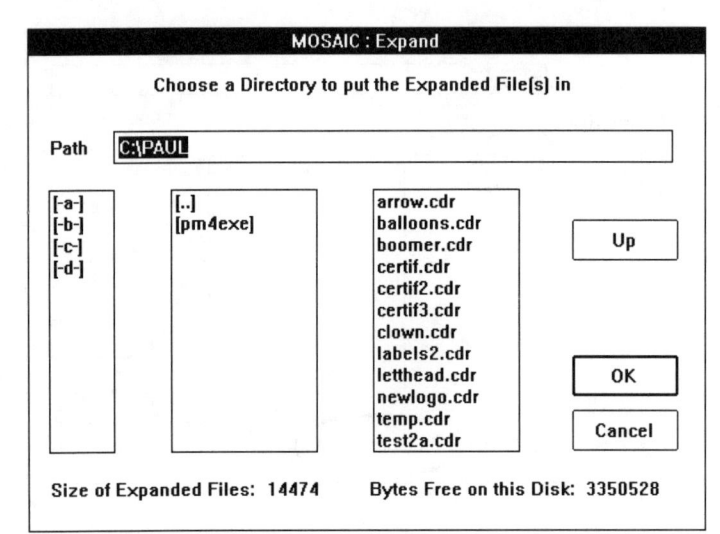

Figure 11. The *Expand* command from the **File** menu will decompress library files back to CDR files. In the *Expand* dialog box, you select a drive and directory where you want the files to be saved. Compressing files will in no way effect the original CDR files.

The *Exit* command from the **File** menu will quit MOSAIC.

The next menu in MOSAIC after **File** will vary, depending on which mode you are running MOSIAC in.

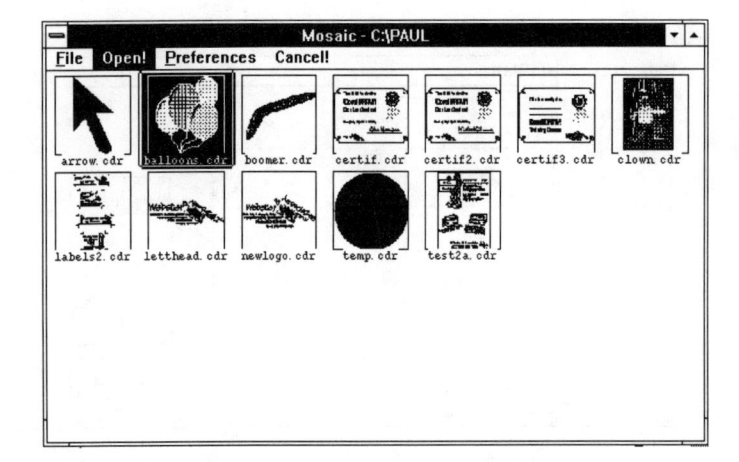

THE OPEN/IMPORT MENU

Figure 12. If you had started MOSIAC from inside CorelDRAW, the menu will read either **Open** or **Import**, depending on whether you chose the *Open* or *Import* command from the **File** menu in CorelDRAW. In this case all you do is select the relevant file in MOSIAC, and click on the **Open** or **Import** name in the menu bar. This will either open the CorelDRAW file, or import the image into the currently open CorelDRAW file.

THE CORELDRAW MENU

Figure 13. If you have opened MOSAIC from Windows, the second menu will be the **CorelDraw** menu.

The first command in the **CorelDraw** menu is the *Open* command. You would choose this command after you have selected a file in MOSAIC. If the file is a library file, it will be decompressed in a directory of your choice. CorelDRAW will now be opened with the selected file active.

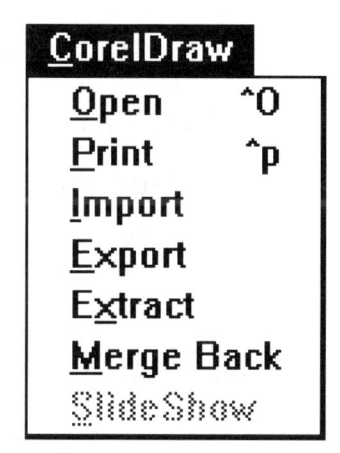

The *Print* command will print all selected file(s), opening CorelDRAW as it prints each file. Again all library files will be decompressed into a directory of your choice. The *Import* command will open CorelDRAW, importing all selected files one at a time. Library files are treated in the same way as you would with the *Open* and *Print* commands.

The *Extract* and *Merge Back* options perform the same function as they do in the **Special** menu of CorelDRAW. With MOSAIC you are able to select more than one file for extracting and merging back.

Figure 14. The *SlideShow* command activates the *Slide Show* dialog box. This lets you display any selected CDR files in MOSAIC one at a time for presentation purposes. The *Continuous slideshow* option will display all the selected files one at a time, over and over, until you press a key. The *Non-interruptible* option displays all the selected files only once and the cycle cannot be interrupted. The *Time delay between slide (s.)* option lets you determine the amount of time each file will display for.

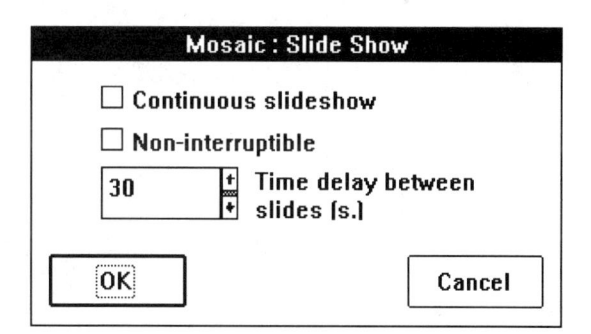

THE PREFERENCES MENU

Figure 15. The last menu in MOSAIC is the **Preferences** menu.

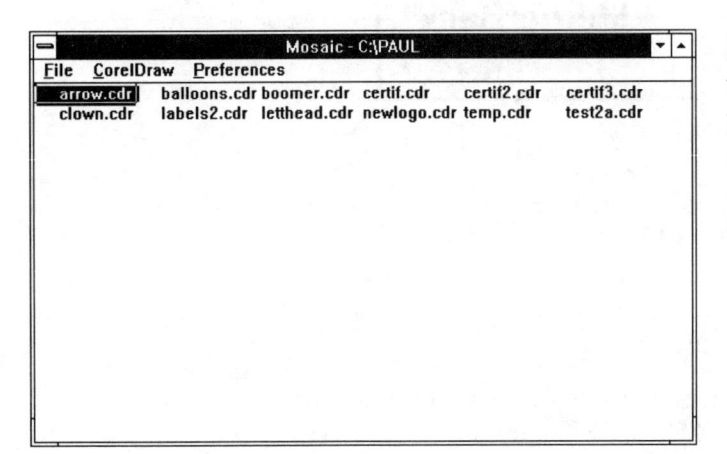

Figure 16. By default MOSAIC will display all files as bitmaps. If you select the *Icon display* option (which is the default setting), the CDR files will only appear as their title in MOSIAC.

Figure 17. The *Large Icons* option makes the size of the file bitmap representation larger.

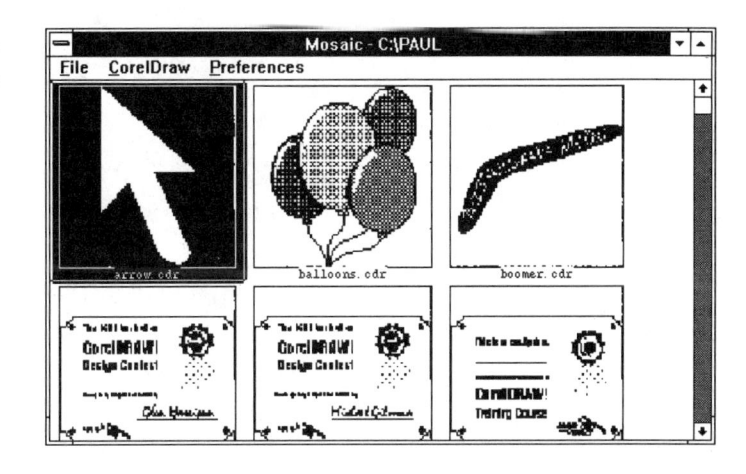

Figure 18. The *Detailed text* option lists current information about the file.

Figure 19. If you have the *Confirm each selected file* option on, it will activate a screen prompt asking you to confirm every time you perform a command (such as *Print*), on a file.

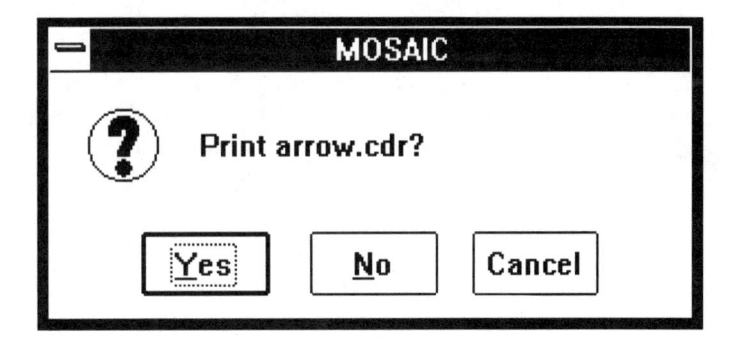

Dialog Boxes   A

Locating Dialog Boxes

Many CorelDRAW menu commands and fly-out options will activate a dialog box. The following pages provide a quick summary on how to access these dialogs boxes.

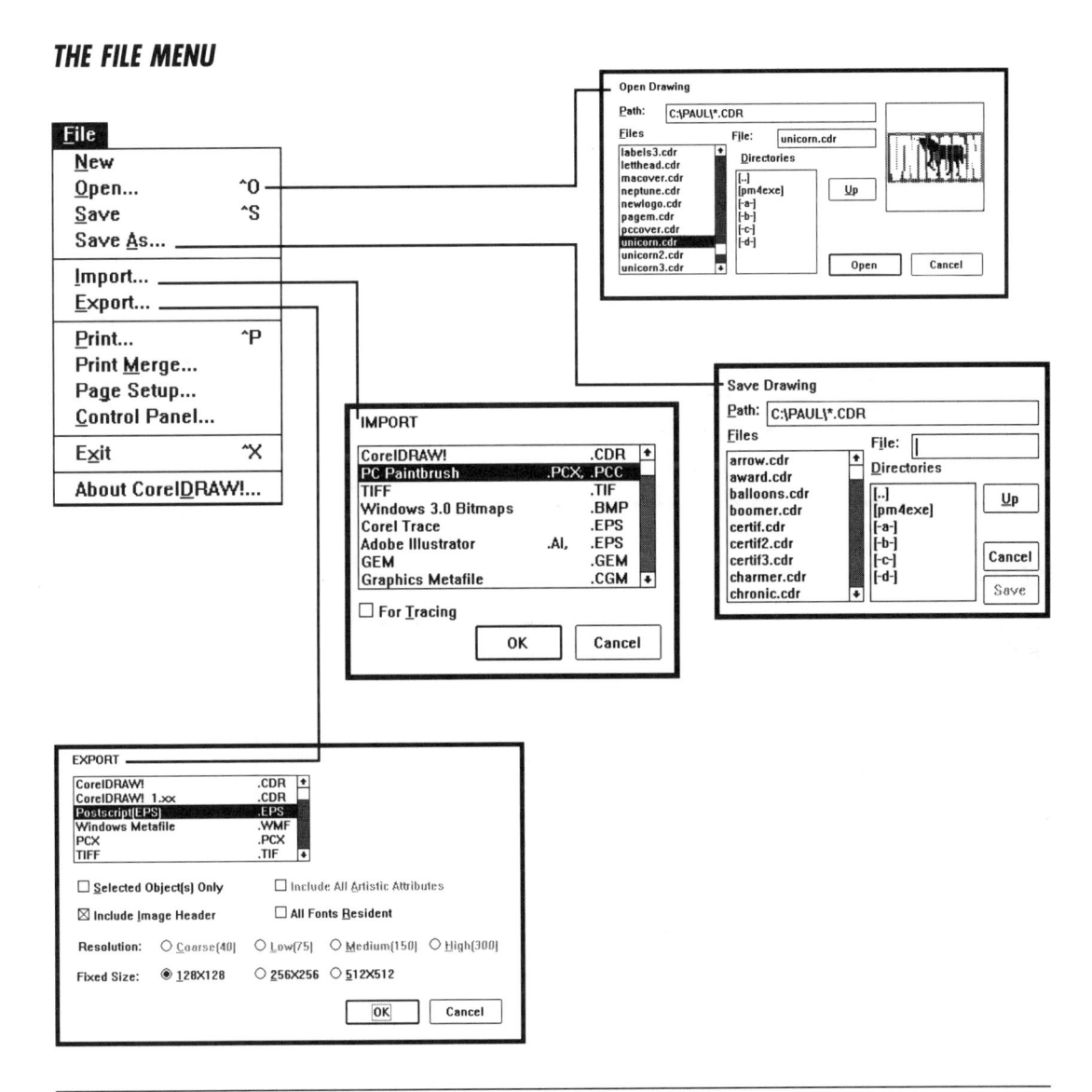

THE FILE MENU

File
- New
- Open...   ^O
- Save   ^S
- Save As...
- Import...
- Export...
- Print...   ^P
- Print Merge...
- Page Setup...
- Control Panel...
- Exit   ^X
- About CorelDRAW!...

Open Drawing
Path: C:\PAUL*.CDR
Files: labels3.cdr, letthead.cdr, macover.cdr, neptune.cdr, newlogo.cdr, pagem.cdr, pccover.cdr, unicorn.cdr, unicorn2.cdr, unicorn3.cdr
File: unicorn.cdr
Directories: [..], [pm4exe], [-a-], [-b-], [-c-], [-d-]
Up | Open | Cancel

IMPORT
CorelDRAW!	.CDR
PC Paintbrush	.PCX, .PCC
TIFF	.TIF
Windows 3.0 Bitmaps	.BMP
Corel Trace	.EPS
Adobe Illustrator .AI,	.EPS
GEM	.GEM
Graphics Metafile	.CGM

☐ For Tracing   OK | Cancel

Save Drawing
Path: C:\PAUL*.CDR
Files: arrow.cdr, award.cdr, balloons.cdr, boomer.cdr, certif.cdr, certif2.cdr, certif3.cdr, charmer.cdr, chronic.cdr
File:
Directories: [..], [pm4exe], [-a-], [-b-], [-c-], [-d-]
Up | Cancel | Save

EXPORT
CorelDRAW!	.CDR
CorelDRAW! 1.xx	.CDR
Postscript[EPS]	.EPS
Windows Metafile	.WMF
PCX	.PCX
TIFF	.TIF

☐ Selected Object(s) Only   ☐ Include All Artistic Attributes
☒ Include Image Header   ☐ All Fonts Resident
Resolution: ○ Coarse(40) ○ Low(75) ○ Medium(150) ○ High(300)
Fixed Size: ⦿ 128X128   ○ 256X256 ○ 512X512

OK | Cancel

127

Appendix A: Dialog Boxes

File
- New
- Open... ^O
- Save ^S
- Save As...
- Import...
- Export...
- Print... ^P
- Print Merge...
- Page Setup...
- Control Panel...
- Exit ^X
- About CorelDRAW!...

PRINT OPTIONS (POSTSCRIPT)
- ☐ Print Only Selected
- ☐ Fit To Page
- ☐ Tile
- ☐ Print As Separations
- ☐ Crop Marks & Crosshairs
- ☐ Film Negative
- ☐ Include File Info
  - ☐ Within Page
- ☐ All Fonts Resident

Number Of Copies: 1
☐ Scale: %
Fountain Stripes: 128
Flatness: 1.00

Default Screen Frequency
- ◉ Device's
- ○ Custom: Per Inch

Destination
PostScript Printer
LPT1:

☐ Print to File ☐ For Mac

[Printer Setup...] [OK] [Cancel]

PAGE SETUP

Orientation: ◉ Portrait ○ Landscape

Page Size:
- ○ Letter ○ Legal ○ Tabloid
- ○ A3 ◉ A4 ○ A5 ○ B5
- ○ Custom ○ Slide

Horizontal: 210.1 millimeters
Vertical: 297.2 millimeters

[Paper Color...] [Add Page Frame] [OK] [Cancel]

Print Merge

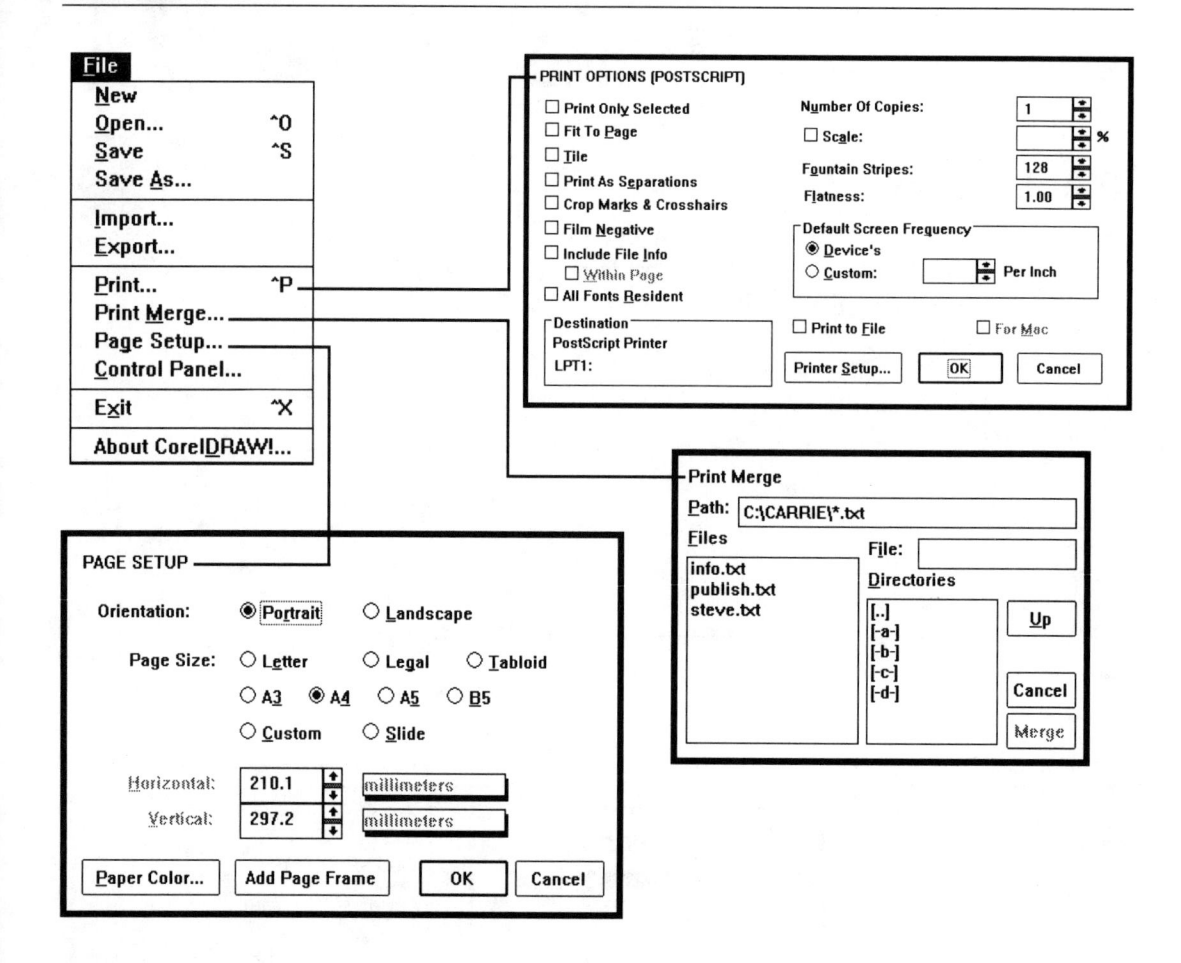

Path: C:\CARRIE*.txt

Files:
info.txt
publish.txt
steve.txt

File:

Directories:
[..]
[-a-]
[-b-]
[-c-]
[-d-]

[Up] [Cancel] [Merge]

THE EDIT MENU

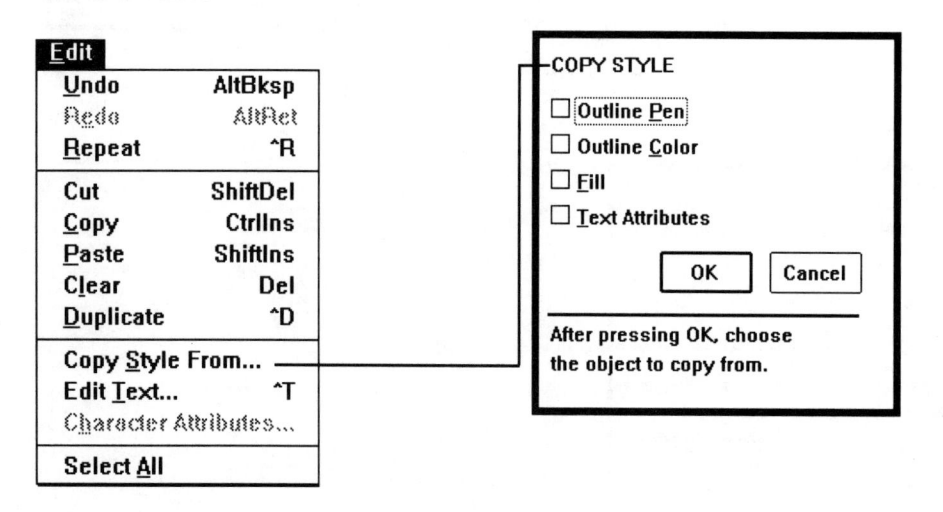

Edit
- Undo AltBksp
- Redo AltRet
- Repeat ^R
- Cut ShiftDel
- Copy CtrlIns
- Paste ShiftIns
- Clear Del
- Duplicate ^D
- Copy Style From...
- Edit Text... ^T
- Character Attributes...
- Select All

COPY STYLE
- ☐ Outline Pen
- ☐ Outline Color
- ☐ Fill
- ☐ Text Attributes

[OK] [Cancel]

After pressing OK, choose the object to copy from.

APPENDIX A: DIALOG BOXES

Edit
Undo	AltBksp
Redo	AltRet
Repeat	^R
Cut	ShiftDel
Copy	CtrlIns
Paste	ShiftIns
Clear	Del
Duplicate	^D
Copy Style From...	
Edit Text...	^T
Character Attributes...	
Select All	

TEXT

Justification: ● Left ○ Center ○ Right
○ Full (Left & Right) ○ None

Fonts: Avalon, Aardvark, Arabia, Bahamas, Bahamas_Heavy, Bahamas_Light, Banff, Bangkok, Bodnoff

● Normal
○ Bold
○ Italic
○ Bold-Italic

Size: 228.1 points

[Spacing...] [Paste] [Columns...] [Import...] [OK] [Cancel]

CHARACTER ATTRIBUTES

Fonts: Avalon, Aardvark, Arabia, Bahamas, Bahamas_Heavy, Bahamas_Light, Banff, Bangkok, Bodnoff

Size: 228.1 points

● Normal
○ Bold
○ Italic
○ Bold-Italic

○ Superscript
○ Subscript

Horizontal Shift: 0.00 ems
Vertical Shift: 0 % of Pt Size
Character Angle: 0.0 degrees

[OK] [Cancel]

THE TRANSFORM MENU

Transform
Move...	^L
Rotate & Skew...	^N
Stretch & Mirror...	^Q
Clear Transformations	

MOVE

Absolute moves are relative to rulers.

Horizontal: -0.31 inches
Vertical: -3.35 inches

☐ Leave Original
☒ Absolute Coordinates

[OK] [Cancel]

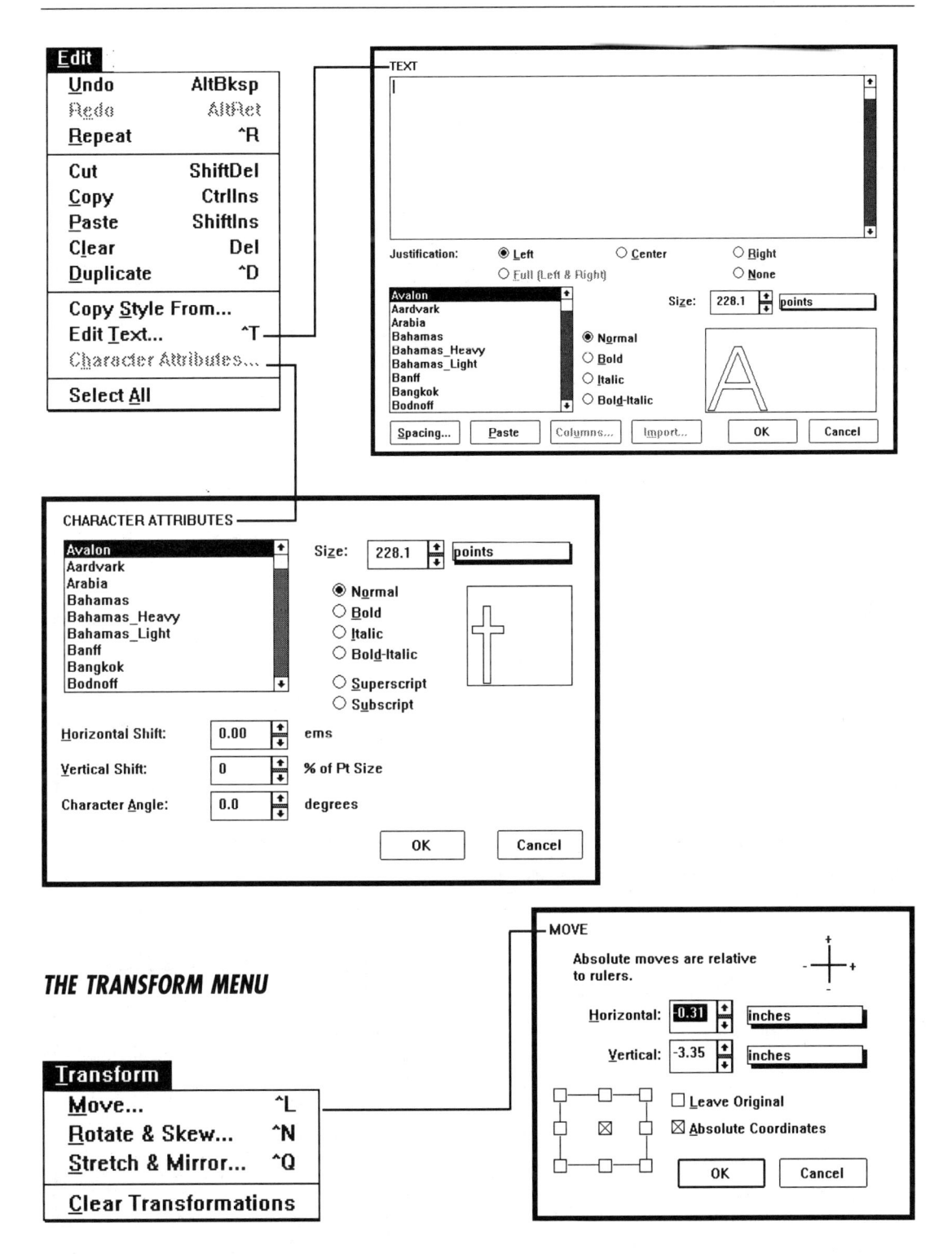

129

APPENDIX A: DIALOG BOXES

Transform
- Move... ^L
- Rotate & Skew... ^N
- Stretch & Mirror... ^Q
- Clear Transformations

ROTATE & SKEW

Rotation Angle: 0.0 degrees
Skew Horizontally: 0.0 degrees
Skew Vertically: 0.0 degrees

☐ Leave Original

[OK] [Cancel]

STRETCH & MIRROR

Stretch Horizontally: 100 %   [Horz Mirror]
Stretch Vertically: 100 %   [Vert Mirror]

☐ Leave Original

[OK] [Cancel]

THE EFFECTS MENU

Effects
- Edit Envelope ▶
- Clear Envelope
- Copy Envelope From...
- Add New Envelope
- Edit Perspective
- Clear Perspective
- Copy Perspective from...
- Add New Perspective
- Blend... ^B
- Extrude... ^E

BLEND

Blend steps: 20
Rotation: 0.0 degrees

☒ Map matching nodes

After pressing OK, choose a node from each object.

[OK] [Cancel]

EXTRUDE

Vanishing Point
X Offset: 0.00 inches
Y Offset: 0.00 inches

☐ Absolute Coordinates
Absolute coordinates are relative to rulers.

Scaling Factor: 80
☒ Perspective

[OK] [Cancel]

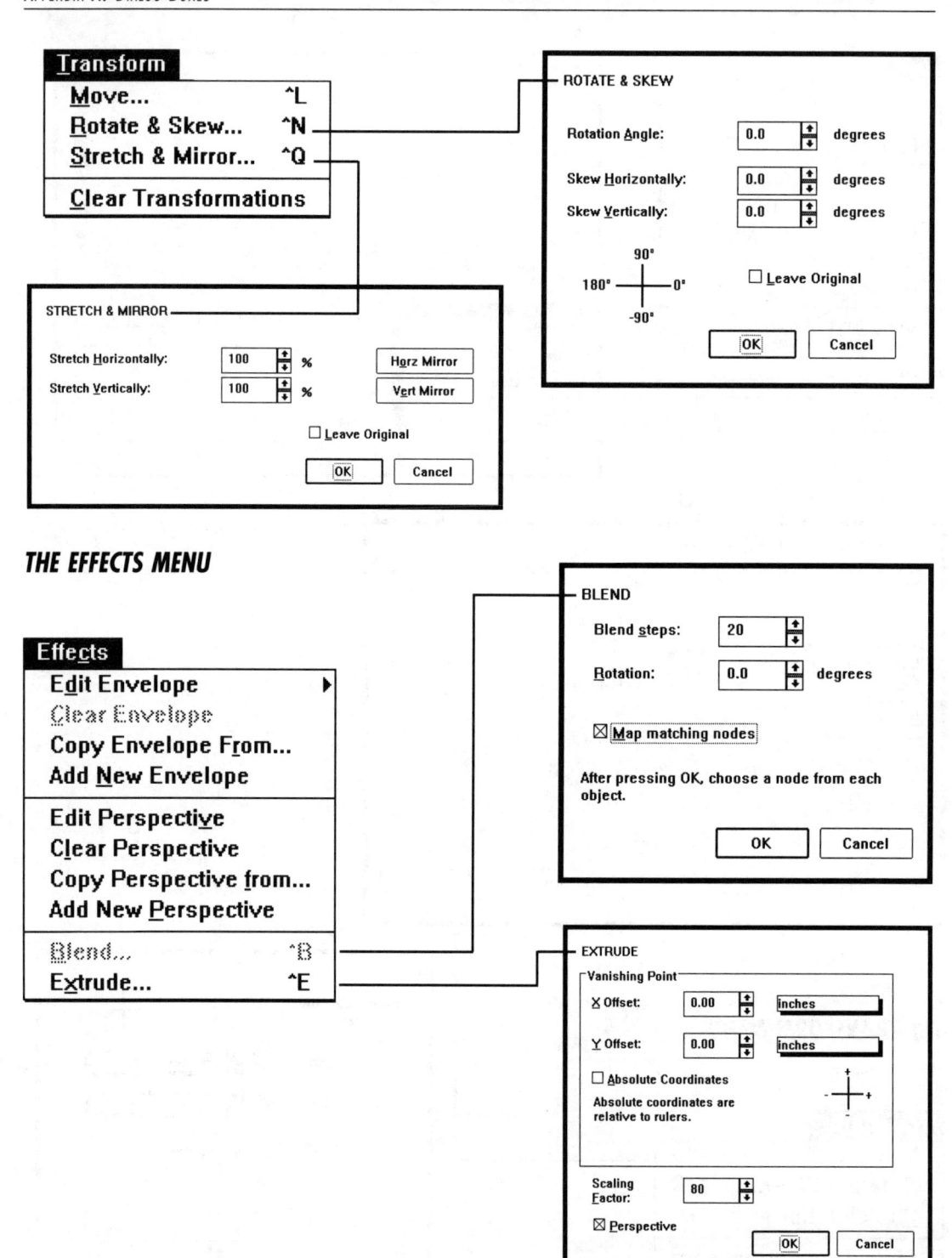

APPENDIX A: DIALOG BOXES

THE ARRANGE MENU

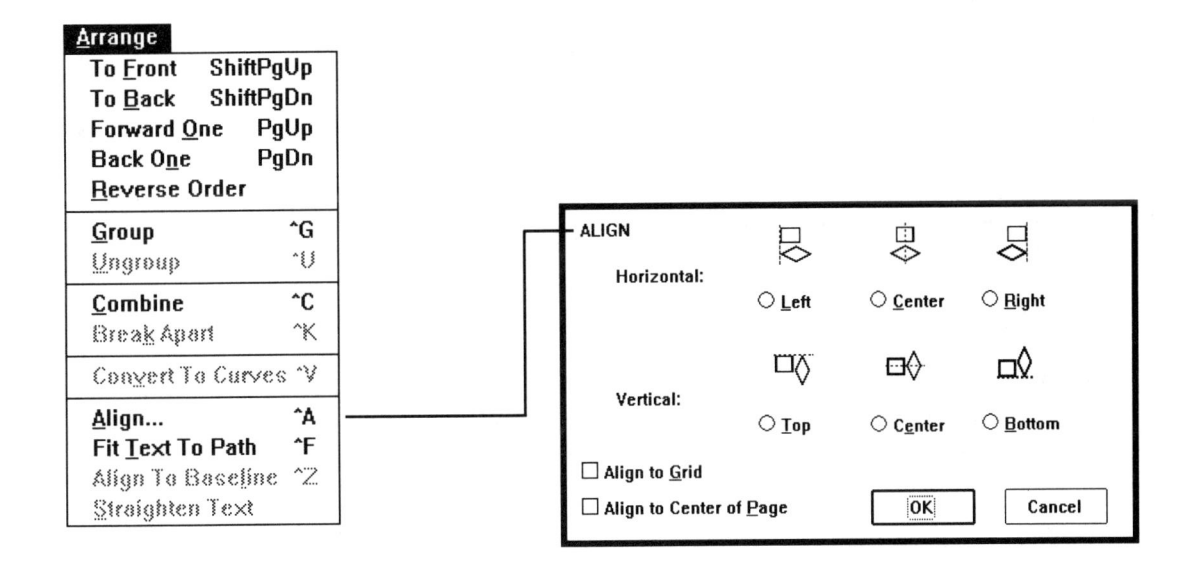

Arrange
To Front	ShiftPgUp
To Back	ShiftPgDn
Forward One	PgUp
Back One	PgDn
Reverse Order	
Group	^G
Ungroup	^U
Combine	^C
Break Apart	^K
Convert To Curves	^V
Align...	^A
Fit Text To Path	^F
Align To Baseline	^Z
Straighten Text	

ALIGN

Horizontal: ○ Left   ○ Center   ○ Right

Vertical: ○ Top   ○ Center   ○ Bottom

☐ Align to Grid
☐ Align to Center of Page   [OK]   [Cancel]

THE DISPLAY MENU

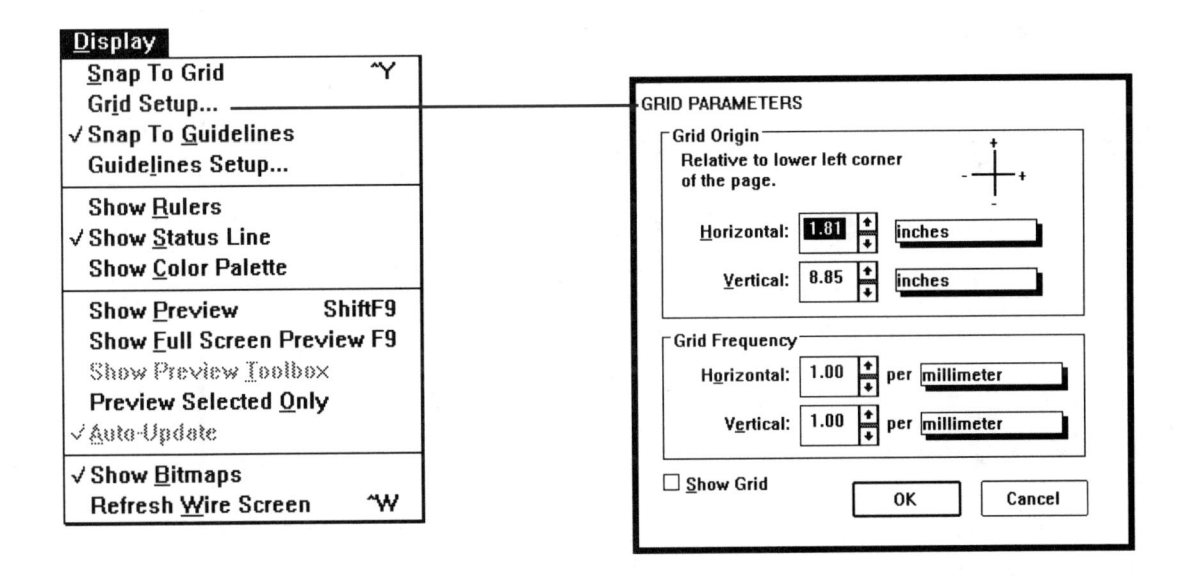

Display
Snap To Grid	^Y
Grid Setup...	
√ Snap To Guidelines	
Guidelines Setup...	
Show Rulers	
√ Show Status Line	
Show Color Palette	
Show Preview	ShiftF9
Show Full Screen Preview	F9
Show Preview Toolbox	
Preview Selected Only	
√ Auto-Update	
√ Show Bitmaps	
Refresh Wire Screen	^W

GRID PARAMETERS

Grid Origin
Relative to lower left corner of the page.

Horizontal: [1.81] inches
Vertical: [8.85] inches

Grid Frequency
Horizontal: [1.00] per [millimeter]
Vertical: [1.00] per [millimeter]

☐ Show Grid   [OK]   [Cancel]

131

Appendix A: Dialog Boxes

Display
- Snap To Grid ^Y
- Grid Setup...
- √ Snap To Guidelines
- Guidelines Setup...
- Show Rulers
- √ Show Status Line
- Show Color Palette
- Show Preview ShiftF9
- Show Full Screen Preview F9
- Show Preview Toolbox
- Preview Selected Only
- √ Auto-Update
- √ Show Bitmaps
- Refresh Wire Screen ^W

GUIDELINES

Guideline type:
- ● Horizontal
- ○ Vertical

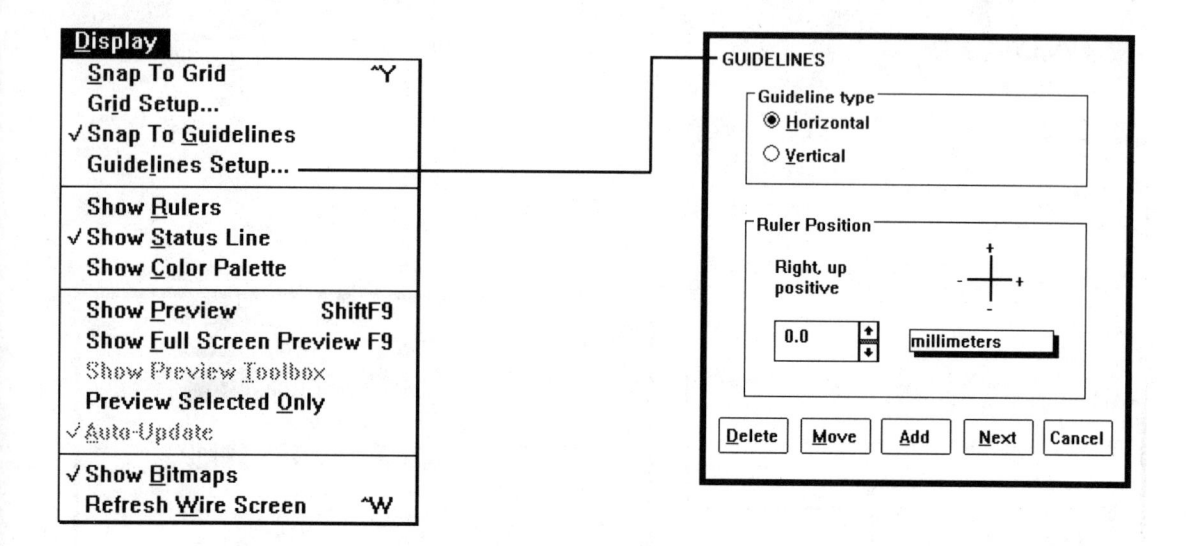

Ruler Position

Right, up positive

0.0   millimeters

[Delete] [Move] [Add] [Next] [Cancel]

THE SPECIAL MENU

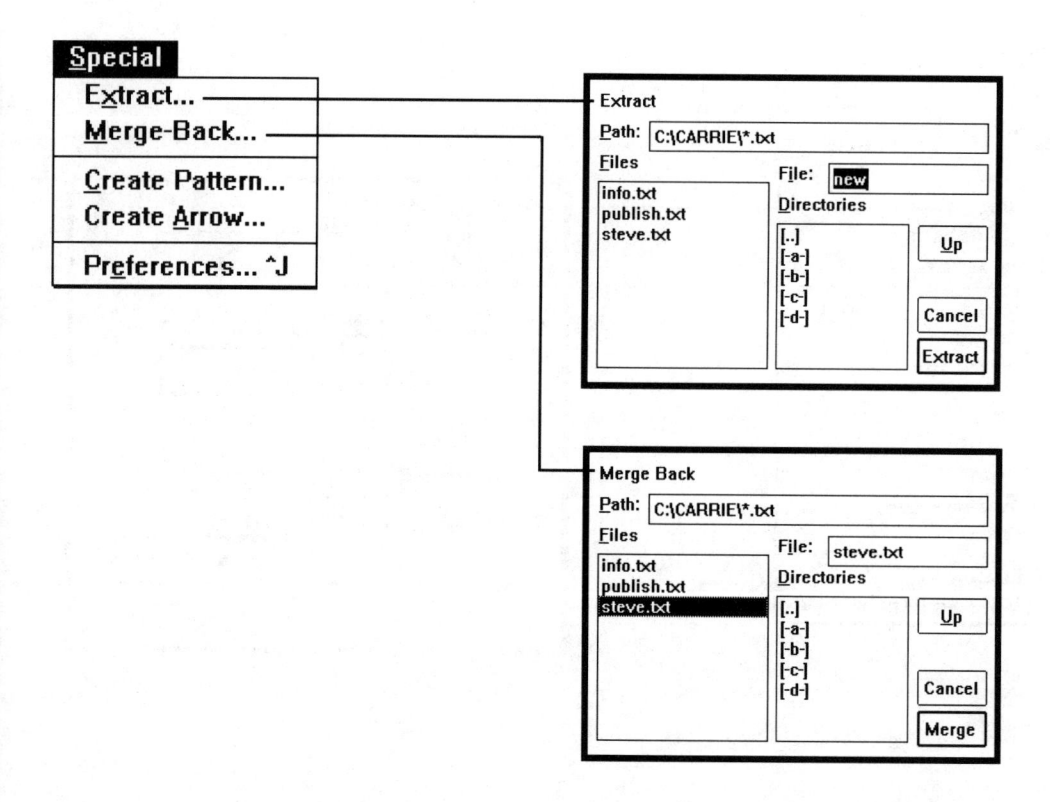

Special
- Extract...
- Merge-Back...
- Create Pattern...
- Create Arrow...
- Preferences... ^J

Extract

Path: C:\CARRIE*.txt

Files:
- info.txt
- publish.txt
- steve.txt

File: new

Directories:
- [..]
- [-a-]
- [-b-]
- [-c-]
- [-d-]

[Up] [Cancel] [Extract]

Merge Back

Path: C:\CARRIE*.txt

Files:
- info.txt
- publish.txt
- **steve.txt**

File: steve.txt

Directories:
- [..]
- [-a-]
- [-b-]
- [-c-]
- [-d-]

[Up] [Cancel] [Merge]

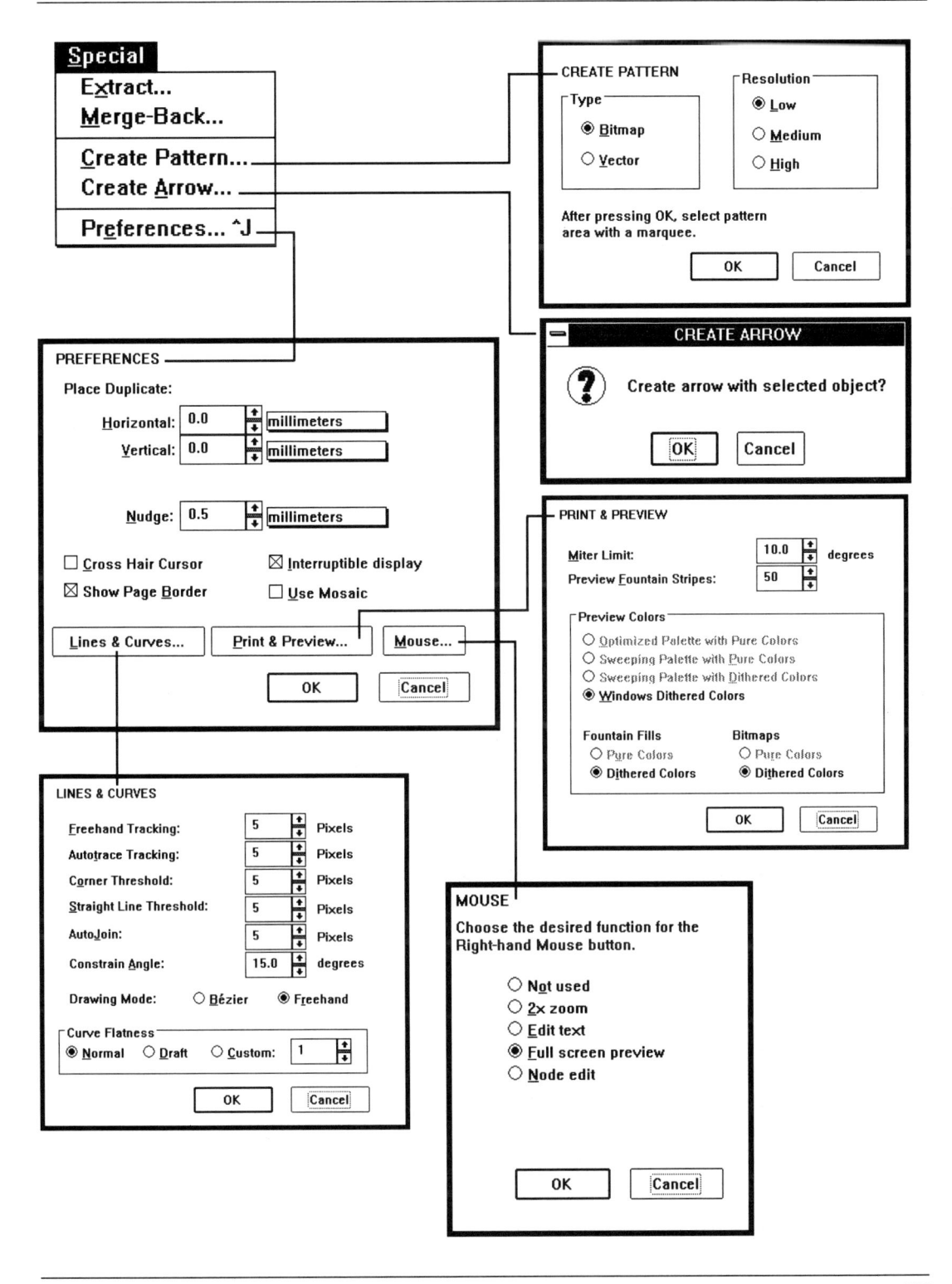

Appendix A: Dialog Boxes

Special
- E_x_tract...
- _M_erge-Back...
- _C_reate Pattern...
- Create _A_rrow...
- Pr_e_ferences... ^J

CREATE PATTERN

Type:
- ◉ _B_itmap
- ○ _V_ector

Resolution:
- ◉ _L_ow
- ○ _M_edium
- ○ _H_igh

After pressing OK, select pattern area with a marquee.

[OK] [Cancel]

CREATE ARROW

(?) Create arrow with selected object?

[OK] [Cancel]

PREFERENCES

Place Duplicate:
- _H_orizontal: 0.0 millimeters
- _V_ertical: 0.0 millimeters

_N_udge: 0.5 millimeters

- ☐ _C_ross Hair Cursor
- ☒ _I_nterruptible display
- ☒ Show Page _B_order
- ☐ _U_se Mosaic

[Lines & Curves...] [Print & Preview...] [Mouse...]

[OK] [Cancel]

PRINT & PREVIEW

Miter Limit: 10.0 degrees
Preview _F_ountain Stripes: 50

Preview Colors:
- ○ _O_ptimized Palette with Pure Colors
- ○ Sweeping Palette with P_u_re Colors
- ○ Sweeping Palette with _D_ithered Colors
- ◉ _W_indows Dithered Colors

Fountain Fills:
- ○ P_u_re Colors
- ◉ _D_ithered Colors

Bitmaps:
- ○ Pu_r_e Colors
- ◉ Di_t_hered Colors

[OK] [Cancel]

LINES & CURVES

- _F_reehand Tracking: 5 Pixels
- Auto_t_race Tracking: 5 Pixels
- _C_orner Threshold: 5 Pixels
- _S_traight Line Threshold: 5 Pixels
- Auto_J_oin: 5 Pixels
- Constrain _A_ngle: 15.0 degrees

Drawing Mode: ○ _B_ézier   ◉ F_r_eehand

Curve Flatness:
◉ _N_ormal ○ _D_raft ○ _C_ustom: 1

[OK] [Cancel]

MOUSE

Choose the desired function for the Right-hand Mouse button.

- ○ _N_ot used
- ○ _2_x zoom
- ○ _E_dit text
- ◉ _F_ull screen preview
- ○ _N_ode edit

[OK] [Cancel]

APPENDIX A: DIALOG BOXES

THE TEXT TOOL

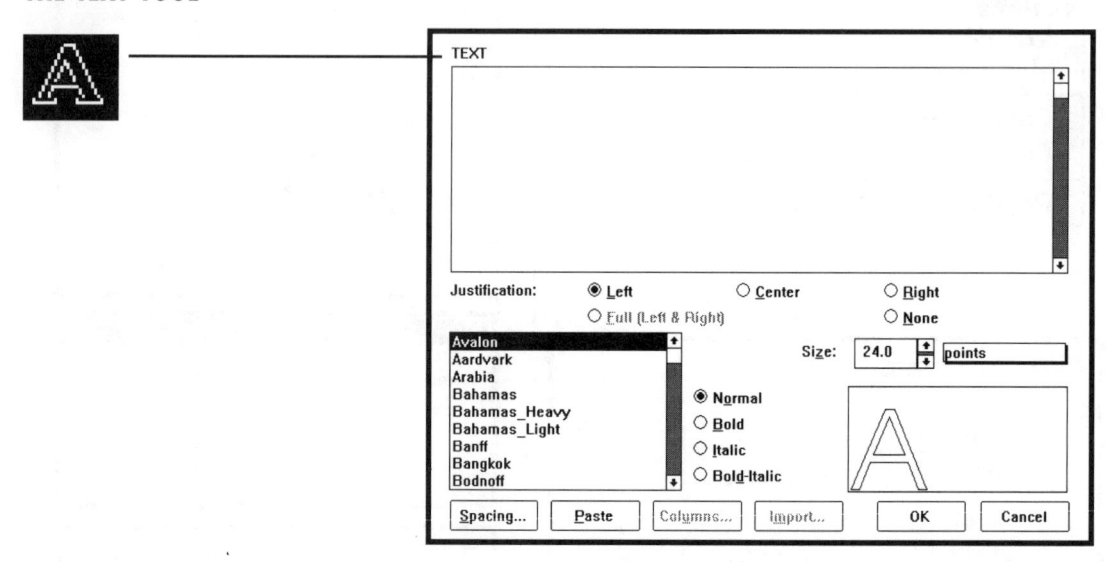

THE OUTLINE TOOL FLY-OUT

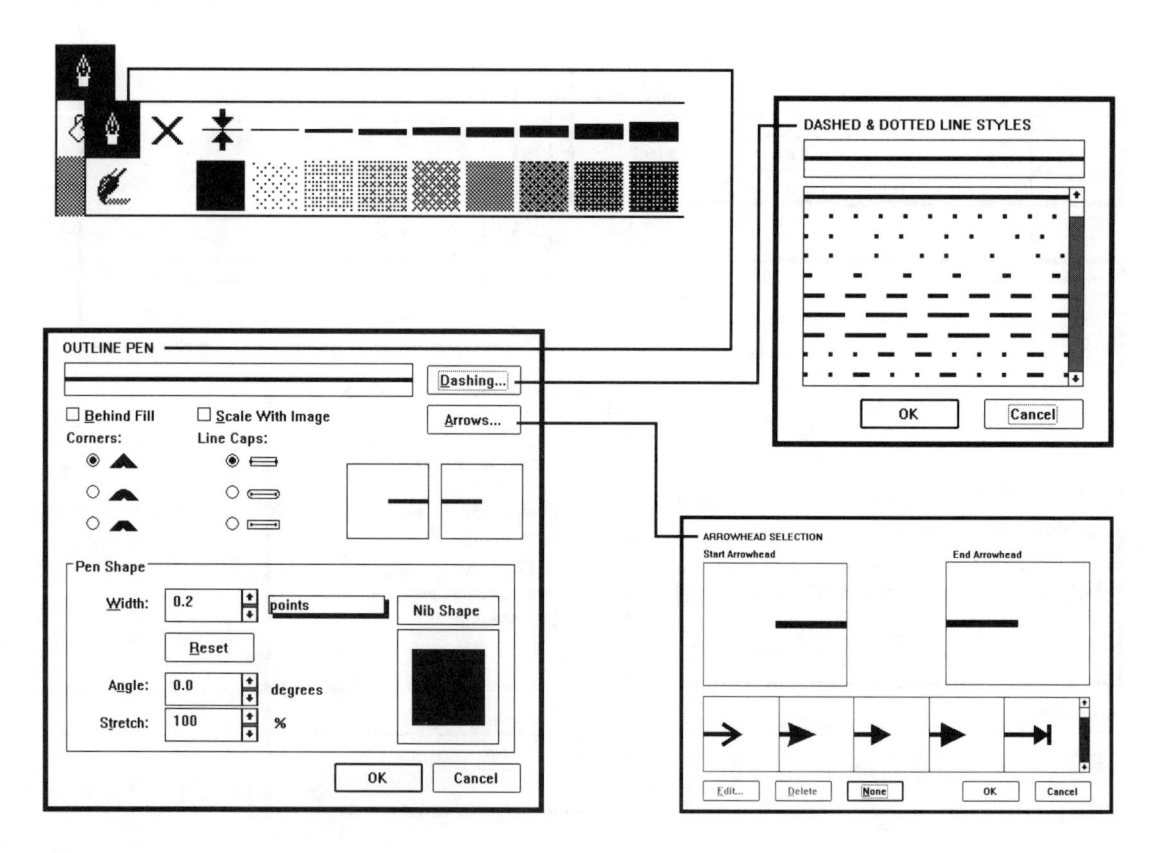

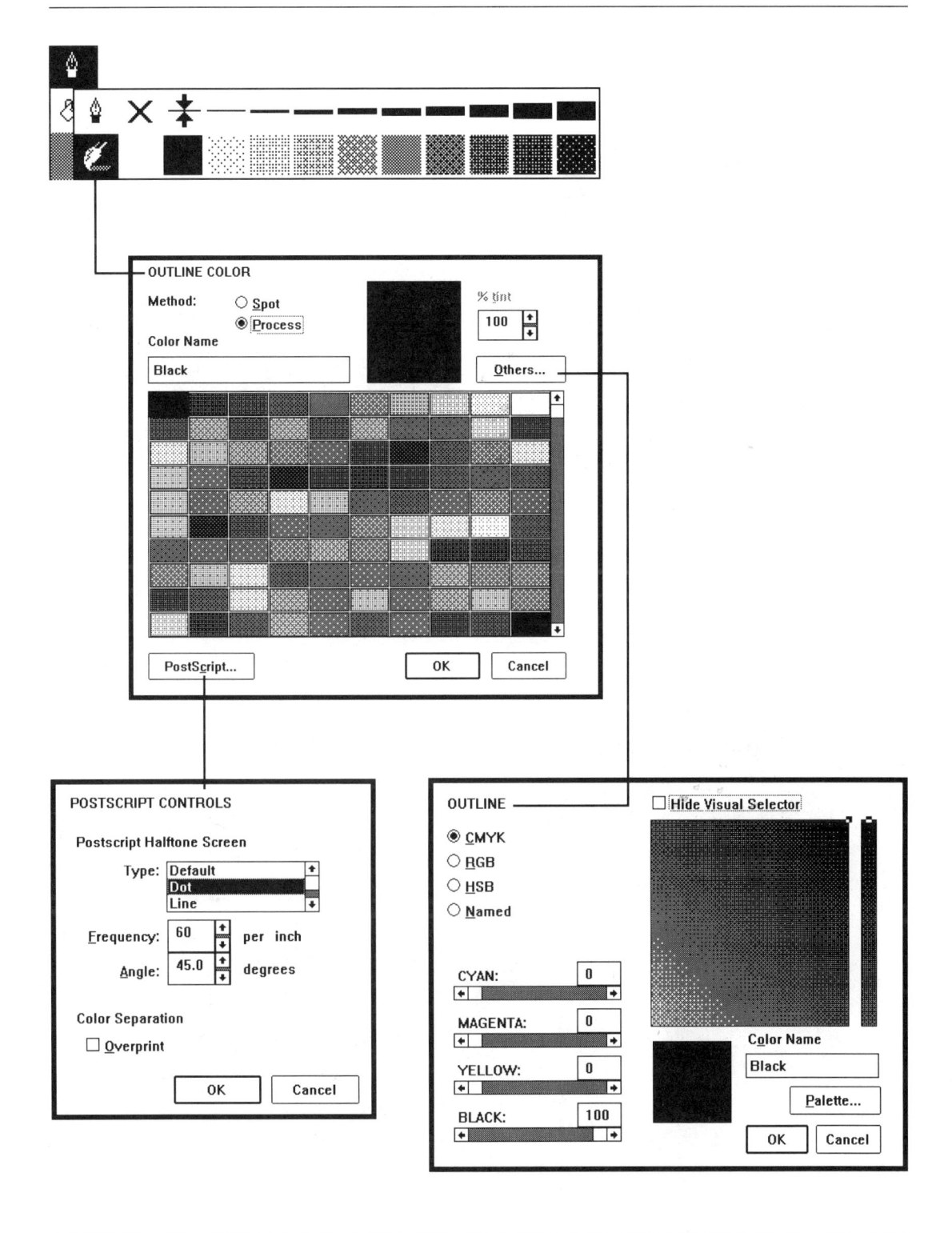

APPENDIX A: DIALOG BOXES

OUTLINE COLOR

Method: ○ Spot
         ● Process

Color Name: Black

% tint: 100

Others...

PostScript...   OK   Cancel

POSTSCRIPT CONTROLS

Postscript Halftone Screen

Type: Default / Dot / Line

Frequency: 60 per inch
Angle: 45.0 degrees

Color Separation
☐ Overprint

OK   Cancel

OUTLINE   ☐ Hide Visual Selector

● CMYK
○ RGB
○ HSB
○ Named

CYAN: 0
MAGENTA: 0
YELLOW: 0
BLACK: 100

Color Name: Black

Palette...

OK   Cancel

Appendix A: Dialog Boxes

THE FILL TOOL FLY-OUT

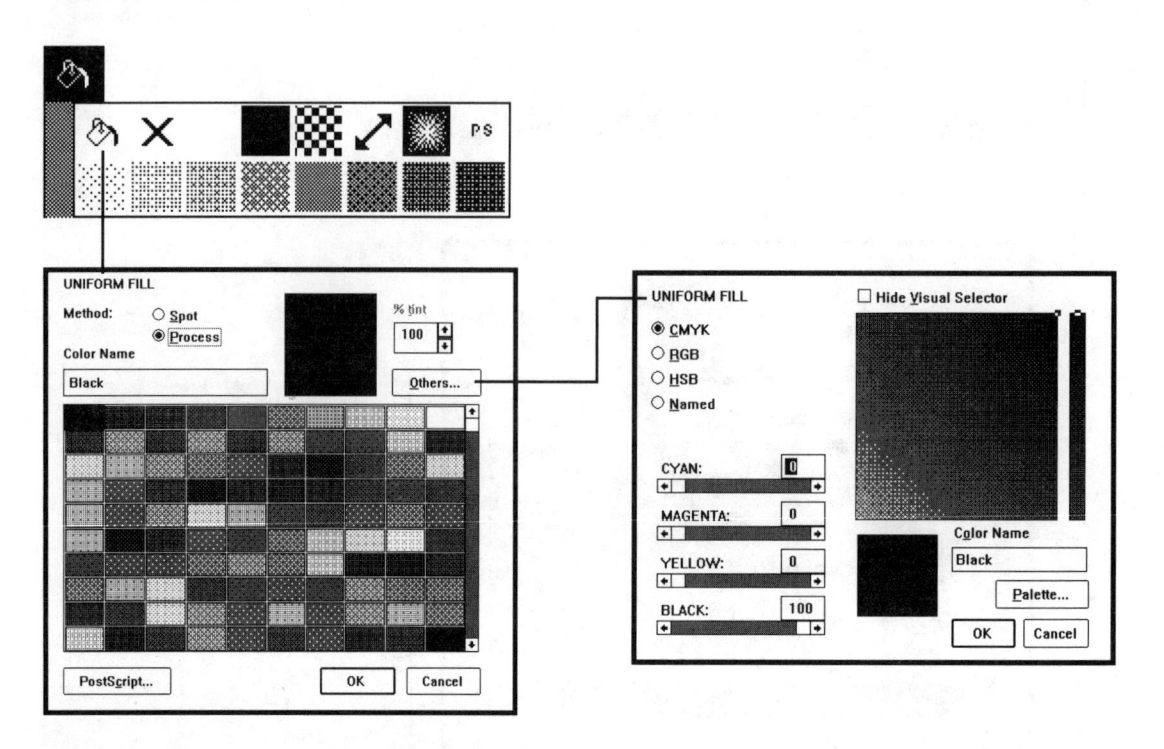

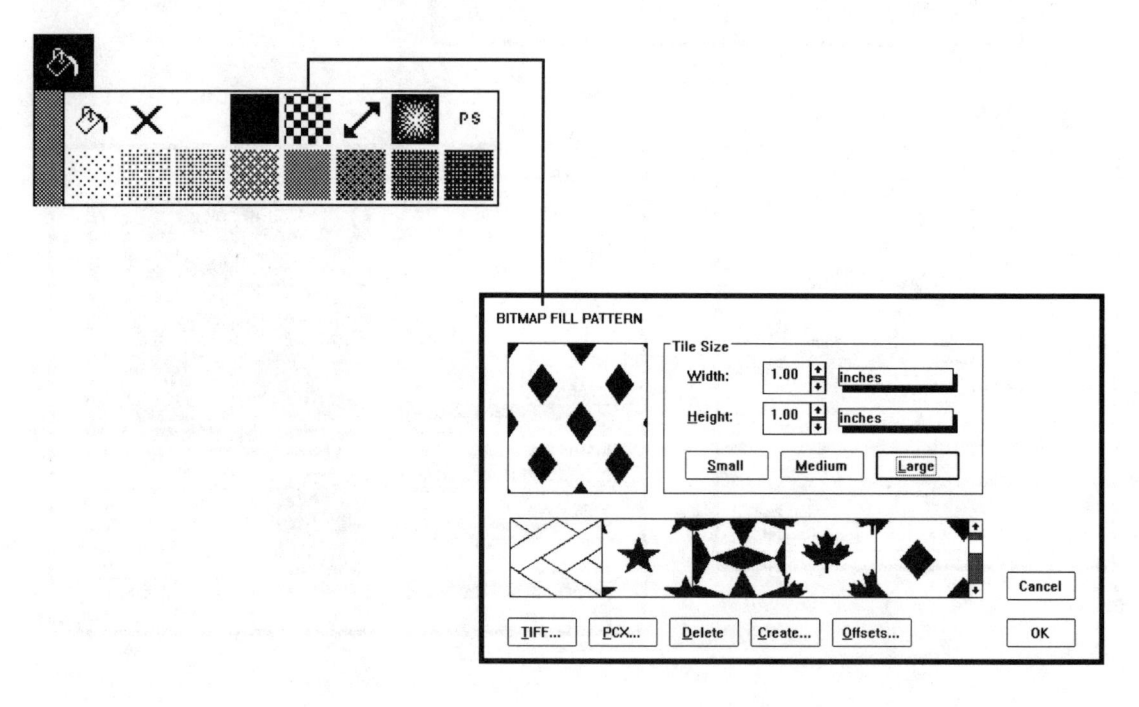

UNIFORM FILL

Method: ○ Spot ● Process
Color Name: Black
% tint: 100

PostScript... OK Cancel

UNIFORM FILL

● CMYK
○ RGB
○ HSB
○ Named

☐ Hide Visual Selector

CYAN: 0
MAGENTA: 0
YELLOW: 0
BLACK: 100

Color Name: Black

Palette...
OK Cancel

BITMAP FILL PATTERN

Tile Size
Width: 1.00 inches
Height: 1.00 inches

Small Medium Large

TIFF... PCX... Delete Create... Offsets... OK Cancel

136

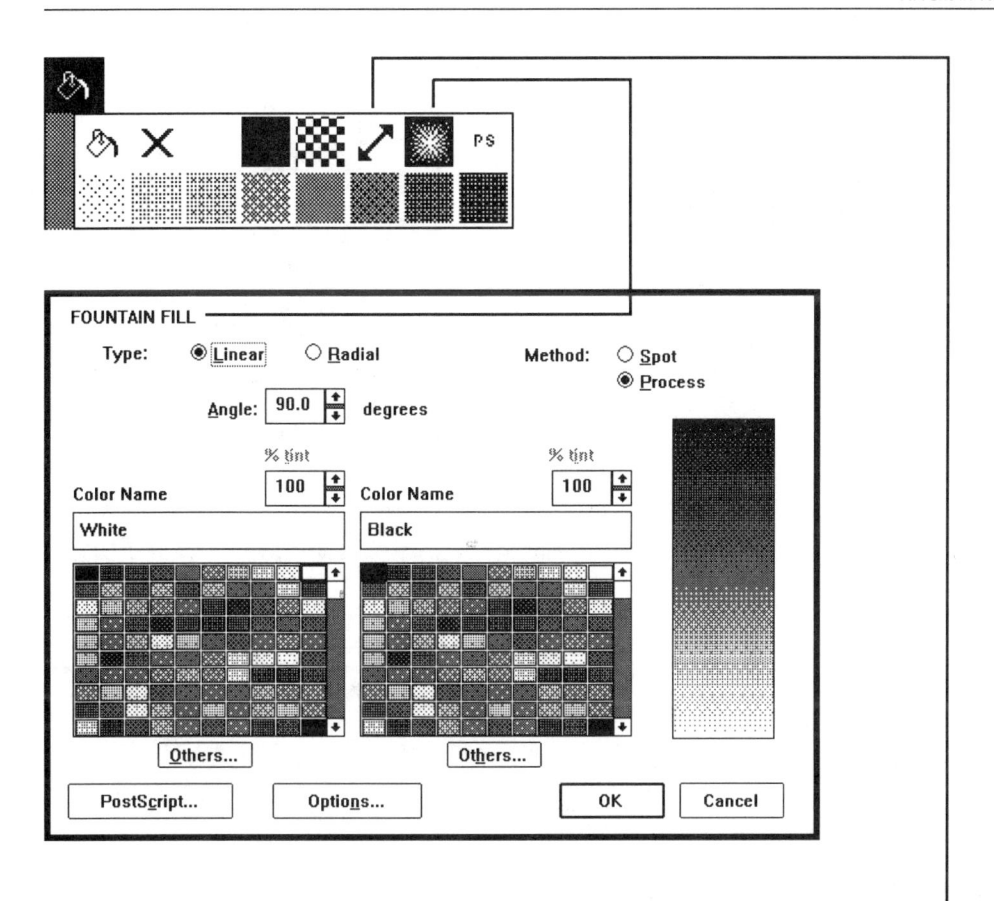

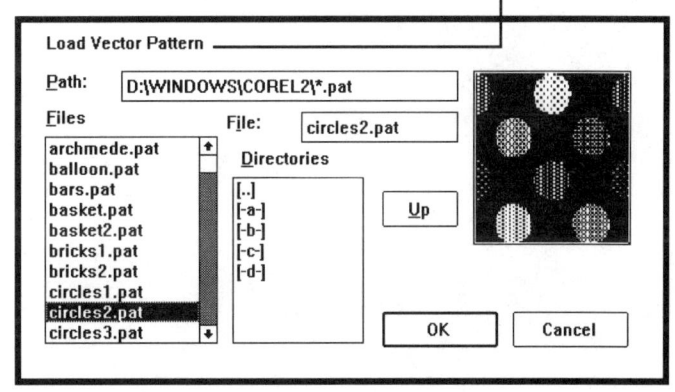

APPENDIX A: DIALOG BOXES

FOUNTAIN FILL

Type: ● Linear ○ Radial

Method: ○ Spot ● Process

Angle: 90.0 degrees

% tint: 100
Color Name: White

% tint: 100
Color Name: Black

Others...   Others...

PostScript...   Options...   OK   Cancel

Load Vector Pattern

Path: D:\WINDOWS\COREL2*.pat

Files:
- archmede.pat
- balloon.pat
- bars.pat
- basket.pat
- basket2.pat
- bricks1.pat
- bricks2.pat
- circles1.pat
- **circles2.pat**
- circles3.pat

File: circles2.pat

Directories:
- [..]
- [-a-]
- [-b-]
- [-c-]
- [-d-]

Up   OK   Cancel

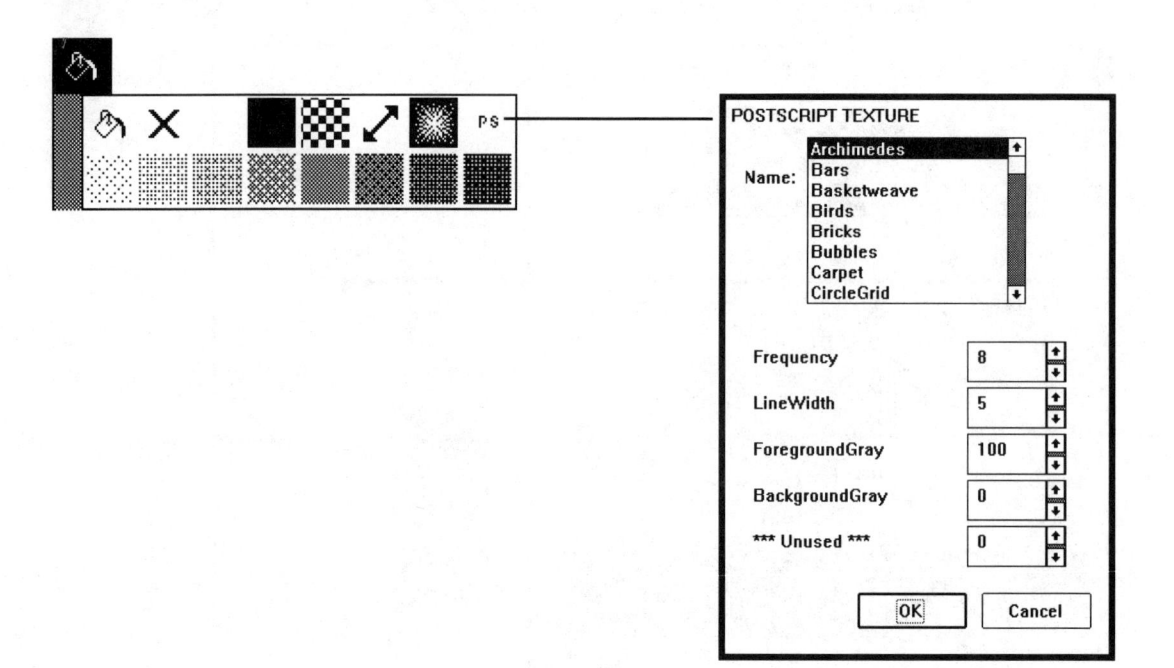

Appendix A: Dialog Boxes

POSTSCRIPT TEXTURE

Name: Archimedes
Bars
Basketweave
Birds
Bricks
Bubbles
Carpet
CircleGrid

Frequency: 8
LineWidth: 5
ForegroundGray: 100
BackgroundGray: 0
*** Unused ***: 0

OK   Cancel

Index

A
Add New Envelope command   71
Add New Perspective command   73
Align command   86
Align To Baseline command   88
Arrange menu   79, 131
Auto Update command   97

B
Back One command   80
Bitmap Fill Pattern   43
Blend command   74
Break Apart command   84

C
Character Attributes command   19, 63
Clear command   11, 61
Clear Envelope command   70
Clear Perspective command   72
Color   36
   CMYK   39
   color dialog boxes   37
   Converting Spot to Process   41
   default color settings   49
   HSB   40
   Named   40
   Pantone   37, 41
   PostScript Controls dialog box   42
   Process color   38
   RGB   39
   Spot color   37
color palette   4, 8
coloring bitmaps   36
Combine command   15, 82
Control Panel   58
Control points   16
Convert To Curves command   12, 85
Copy command   60
Copy Envelope From command   71
Copy Perspective from command   73
Copy Style From command   62
CorelTRACE   109
   CorelDraw menu   123
   Import menu   122
   Importing CorelTRACE images into CorelDRAW   116
   Open menu   122
   output options   110
   Preferences menu   113, 124
   Tracing Options menu   111
   Using CorelTRACE   109
   View Image menu   112
Create Arrow command   101
Create Pattern command   100
Cut command   60

D
Display menu   91, 131
Duplicate command   61

E
Edit Envelope command   69
Edit menu   11, 59, 128
Edit Perspective command   72
Edit Text command   62
Effects menu   69, 130
Ellipse Tool   7, 9, 27
   drawing circles   27
   resizing   27
Exit command   58
Export command   54
Extract command   99
Extrude command   76

F

File Manager 2
File menu 3, 51, 127
Fill Indicator 50
Fill Tool 7, 9, 42, 136
    Bitmap Fill Pattern dialog box 43
    Fountain Fills 47
    Load Vector Pattern dialog box 46
    PostScript Fill 49
    Uniform Fill dialog box 43
Fit Text To Path command 87
Forward One command 80
Fountain Fills 47
    Linear Fill 48
    Radial Fill 48
Full Screen Preview command 95

G

Grid Setup command 92
Group command 81
Guidelines Setup command 93

I

Import command 53
Installation 1
    summary of installation steps 1

L

Lines & Curves dialog box 23, 104
Load Vector Pattern dialog box 46

M

maximize button 4, 5
menu bar 4, 5
Merge Back command 100
minimize button 4, 5
MOSAIC 117
    File menu 119
    Using MOSAIC 117
mouse cursor 4, 6
Mouse dialog box 107
MS-DOS Executive 2

N

Node Edit dialog box 13, 14
    Add 14
    Align 17
    Break 14
    Cusp 16
    Delete 14
    Join 15
    Smooth 16
    Symmet 17
    toCurve 16
    toLine 15
Nodes 11, 13

O

Open command 3, 52
Outline Pen dialog box 33
    Arrows 34
    Behind Fill 35
    Corners 35
    Dashing 34
    Line Caps 35
    Pen Shape 36
    Scale With Image 35
Outline Tool 7, 9, 33, 134

P

Page Setup command 57
Paragraph Text dialog box 28, 30
    columns 28, 30
    importing text 30
    justification 28
    Paste command 31
Paste command 61
pasteboard area 4, 6
Pencil Tool 7, 9, 23
    autotrace 25
    bezier mode 25
    freehand mode 24
Pick Tool 7, 9, 10
    deleting objects 11
    marquee selection 11

moving objects   10
multiple selection   11
rotating and skewing objects   10
selecting objects   10
Preferences command   23, 102
Preview Selected Only command   97
Print & Preview dialog box   105
Print command   55
Print Merge command   57
Program Manager   2

R

Rectangle Tool   7, 9, 26
   drawing squares   26
   resizing   26
Redo command   59
Refresh Wire Screen command   98
Repeat command   60
Reverse Order command   80
rulers   4, 6

S

Save As command   53
Save command   52
screen components   5
scroll bars   4, 7
Select All command   63
selection handles   10
Shape Tool   7, 9, 11
   changing character attributes   19
   changing node properties   13
   cropping bitmaps   19
   kerning   18
   leading   18
   modifying ellipses   12
   modifying rectangles   12
   moving individual letters   18
   moving nodes   13
   selecting multiple nodes   13
Show Bitmaps command   98
Show Color Palette command   95
Show Preview command   95
Show Preview Toolbox command   96

Show Rulers command   94
Show Status Line command   94
Snap To Grid command   91
Snap To Guidelines command   93
Special menu   23, 99, 132
starting CorelDRAW   2
Status Line   6, 26, 27
Straighten Text command   89

T

Text dialog box   28
   Paste command   31
Text Spacing dialog box   29
Text Tool   7, 9, 27, 134
   changing size   29
   changing type style   29
   placing text   28
   Symbols   31
   text alignment   29
title bar   4, 5
To Back command   80
To Front command   79
Toolbox   7, 9
Tools   4, 9
Transform menu   129

U

Undo command   59
Ungroup command   82
using the tools   9

W

Windows   2
Windows Program Manager   109, 117
Windows system menu   4, 5
working page   4, 6

Z

Zoom Tool   7, 9, 20